G000273931

## How to access your on-line resources

Kaplan Financial students will have a MyKaplan account and these extra resources will be available to you online. You do not need to register again, as this process was completed when you enrolled. If you are having problems accessing online materials, please ask your course administrator.

If you are not studying with Kaplan and did not purchase your book via a Kaplan website, to unlock your extra online resources please go to www.en-gage.co.uk (even if you have set up an account and registered books previously). You will then need to enter the ISBN number (on the title page and back cover) and the unique pass key number contained in the scratch panel below to gain access.

You will also be required to enter additional information during this process to set up or confirm your account details.

If you purchased via the Kaplan Publishing website you will automatically receive an e-mail invitation to register your details and gain access to your content. If you do not receive the e-mail or book content, please contact Kaplan Publishing.

## Your code and information

This code can only be used once for the registration of one book online. This registration and your online content will expire when the final sittings for the examinations covered by this book have taken place. Please allow one hour from the time you submit your book details for us to process your request.

Please scratch the film to access your unique code.

Please be aware that this code is case-sensitive and you will need to include the dashes within the passcode, but not when entering the ISBN.

# CIMA

# Subject F1

# Financial Reporting

# Study Text

Published by: Kaplan Publishing UK

Unit 2 The Business Centre, Molly Millars Lane, Wokingham, Berkshire. RG41 2QZ

### Notice

The text in this material and any others made available by any Kaplan Group company does not amount to advice on a particular matter and should not be taken as such. No reliance should be placed on the content as the basis for any investment or other decision or in connection with any advice given to third parties. Please consult your appropriate professional adviser as necessary. Kaplan Publishing Limited, all other Kaplan group companies, the International Accounting Standards Board, and the IFRS Foundation expressly disclaim all liability to any person in respect of any losses or other claims, whether direct, indirect, incidental, consequential or otherwise arising in relation to the use of such materials. Printed and bound in Great Britain.

Kaplan is not responsible for the content of external websites. The inclusion of a link to a third party website in the text should be ne taken as an endorsement.

### Acknowledgements

Questions from past live assessments have been included by kind permission of CIMA.

We are grateful to the CIMA for permission to reproduce past examination questions. The answers to CIMA Exams have been prepared by Kaplan Publishing, except in the case of the CIMA November 2010 and subsequent CIMA Exam answers where the official CIMA answers have been reproduced. Questions from past live assessments have been included by kind permission of CIMA

This Product includes propriety content of the International Accounting Standards Board which is overseen by the IFRS Foundation, and is used with the express permission of the IFRS Foundation under licence. All rights reserved. No part of this publication may be reproduced, stored in a retrieval system, or transmitted in any form or by any means, electronic, mechanical, photocopying, recording, or otherwise, without prior written permission of Kaplan Publishing and the IFRS Foundation.

The IFRS Foundation logo, the IASB logo, the IFRS for SMEs logo, the "Hexagon Device", "IFRS Foundation", "eIFRS", "IAS", "IASB", "IFRS for SMEs", "IFRS", "IASs", "IFRSs", "International Accounting Standards" and "International Financial Reporting Standards", "IFRIC" and "IFRS Taxonomy" are Trade Marks of the IFRS Foundation.

### Trade Marks

The IFRS Foundation logo, the IASB logo, the IFRS for SMEs logo, the "Hexagon Device", "IFRS Foundation", "eIFRS", "IAS", "IASB", "IFRS for SMEs", "NIIF" IASs" "IFRS", "IFRSs", "International Accounting Standards", "International Financial Reporting Standards", "IFRIC", "SIC" and "IFRS Taxonomy".

Further details of the Trade Marks including details of countries where the Trade Marks are registered or applied for are available from the Foundation on request.

This product contains material that is ©Financial Reporting Council Ltd (FRC). Adapted and reproduced with the kind permission of the Financial Reporting Council. All rights reserved. For further information, please visit www.frc.org.uk or call +44 (0)20 7492 2300.

**British Library Cataloguing-in-Publication Data**

A catalogue record for this book is available from the British Library. ISBN: 978-1-78740-199-0

Printed and bound in Great Britain

# Contents

# Introduction

This document references IFRS® Standards and IAS® Standards, which are authored by the International Accounting Standards Board (the Board), and published in the 2016 IFRS Standards Red Book.

# How to use the Materials

These official CIMA learning materials have been carefully designed to make your learning experience as easy as possible and to give you the best chances of success in your objective tests.

The product range contains a number of features to help you in the study process. They include:

- a detailed explanation of all syllabus areas

- extensive 'practical' materials

- generous question practice, together with full solutions.

This Study Text has been designed with the needs of home study and distance learning candidates in mind. Such students require very full coverage of the syllabus topics, and also the facility to undertake extensive question practice. However, the Study Text is also ideal for fully taught courses.

The main body of the text is divided into a number of chapters, each of which is organised on the following pattern:

- **Detailed learning outcomes.** These describe the knowledge expected after your studies of the chapter are complete. You should assimilate these before beginning detailed work on the chapter, so that you can appreciate where your studies are leading.

- **Step-by-step topic coverage.** This is the heart of each chapter, containing detailed explanatory text supported where appropriate by worked examples and exercises. You should work carefully through this section, ensuring that you understand the material being explained and can tackle the examples and exercises successfully. Remember that in many cases knowledge is cumulative: if you fail to digest earlier material thoroughly, you may struggle to understand later chapters.

- **Activities.** Some chapters are illustrated by more practical elements, such as comments and questions designed to stimulate discussion.

- **Question practice.** The text contains three styles of question:
    - Exam-style objective test questions (OTQs).
    - 'Integration' questions – these test your ability to understand topics within a wider context. This is particularly important with calculations where OTQs may focus on just one element but an integration question tackles the full calculation, just as you would be expected to do in the workplace.

- 'Case' style questions – these test your ability to analyse and discuss issues in greater depth, particularly focusing on scenarios that are less clear cut than in the objective tests, and thus provide excellent practice for developing the skills needed for success in the Management Level Case Study Examination.

- **Solutions.** Avoid the temptation merely to 'audit' the solutions provided. It is an illusion to think that this provides the same benefits as you would gain from a serious attempt of your own. However, if you are struggling to get started on a question you should read the introductory guidance provided at the beginning of the solution, where provided, and then make your own attempt before referring back to the full solution.

If you work conscientiously through this Official CIMA Study Text according to the guidelines above you will be giving yourself an excellent chance of success in your objective tests. Good luck with your studies!

Quality and accuracy are of the utmost importance to us so if you spot an error in any of our products, please send an email to mykaplanreporting@kaplan.com with full details, or follow the link to the feedback form in MyKaplan.

Our Quality Co-ordinator will work with our technical team to verify the error and take action to ensure it is corrected in future editions.

## Icon explanations

 **Definition** – These sections explain important areas of knowledge which must be understood and reproduced in an assessment environment.

 **Key point** – Identifies topics which are key to success and are often examined.

 **Supplementary reading** – These sections will help to provide a deeper understanding of core areas. The supplementary reading is **NOT** optional reading. It is vital to provide you with the breadth of knowledge you will need to address the wide range of topics within your syllabus that could feature in an assessment question. **Reference to this text is vital when self-studying.**

 **Test your understanding** – Following key points and definitions are exercises which give the opportunity to assess the understanding of these core areas.

 **Illustration** – To help develop an understanding of particular topics. The illustrative examples are useful in preparing for the Test your understanding exercises.

**New** – Identifies topics that are brand new in subjects that build on, and therefore also contain, learning covered in earlier subjects.

 **Tutorial note** – Included to explain some of the technical points in more detail.

### Study technique

Passing exams is partly a matter of intellectual ability, but however accomplished you are in that respect you can improve your chances significantly by the use of appropriate study and revision techniques. In this section we briefly outline some tips for effective study during the earlier stages of your approach to the objective tests. We also mention some techniques that you will find useful at the revision stage.

### Planning

To begin with, formal planning is essential to get the best return from the time you spend studying. Estimate how much time in total you are going to need for each subject you are studying. Remember that you need to allow time for revision as well as for initial study of the material.

With your study material before you, decide which chapters you are going to study in each week, and which weeks you will devote to revision and final question practice.

Prepare a written schedule summarising the above and stick to it!

It is essential to know your syllabus. As your studies progress you will become more familiar with how long it takes to cover topics in sufficient depth. Your timetable may need to be adapted to allocate enough time for the whole syllabus.

Students are advised to refer to the examination blueprints (see page P.13 for further information) and the CIMA website, www.cimaglobal.com, to ensure they are up-to-date.

The amount of space allocated to a topic in the Study Text is not a very good guide as to how long it will take you. The syllabus weighting is the better guide as to how long you should spend on a syllabus topic.

**Tips for effective studying**

(1) Aim to find a quiet and undisturbed location for your study, and plan as far as possible to use the same period of time each day. Getting into a routine helps to avoid wasting time. Make sure that you have all the materials you need before you begin so as to minimise interruptions.

(2) Store all your materials in one place, so that you do not waste time searching for items every time you want to begin studying. If you have to pack everything away after each study period, keep your study materials in a box, or even a suitcase, which will not be disturbed until the next time.

(3) Limit distractions. To make the most effective use of your study periods you should be able to apply total concentration, so turn off all entertainment equipment, set your phones to message mode, and put up your 'do not disturb' sign.

(4) Your timetable will tell you which topic to study. However, before diving in and becoming engrossed in the finer points, make sure you have an overall picture of all the areas that need to be covered by the end of that session. After an hour, allow yourself a short break and move away from your Study Text. With experience, you will learn to assess the pace you need to work at. Each study session should focus on component learning outcomes – the basis for all questions.

(5) Work carefully through a chapter, making notes as you go. When you have covered a suitable amount of material, vary the pattern by attempting a practice question. When you have finished your attempt, make notes of any mistakes you made, or any areas that you failed to cover or covered more briefly. Be aware that all component learning outcomes will be tested in each examination.

(6) Make notes as you study, and discover the techniques that work best for you. Your notes may be in the form of lists, bullet points, diagrams, summaries, 'mind maps', or the written word, but remember that you will need to refer back to them at a later date, so they must be intelligible. If you are on a taught course, make sure you highlight any issues you would like to follow up with your lecturer.

(7) Organise your notes. Make sure that all your notes, calculations etc. can be effectively filed and easily retrieved later.

## Progression

There are two elements of progression that we can measure: how quickly students move through individual topics within a subject; and how quickly they move from one course to the next. We know that there is an optimum for both, but it can vary from subject to subject and from student to student. However, using data and our experience of student performance over many years, we can make some generalisations.

A fixed period of study set out at the start of a course with key milestones is important. This can be within a subject, for example 'I will finish this topic by 30 June', or for overall achievement, such as 'I want to be qualified by the end of next year'.

Your qualification is cumulative, as earlier papers provide a foundation for your subsequent studies, so do not allow there to be too big a gap between one subject and another. For example, F1 *Financial reporting* builds on your knowledge of financial accounting from BA3 *Fundamentals of financial accounting* and lays the foundations for F2 *Advanced financial reporting*.

We know that exams encourage techniques that lead to some degree of short term retention, the result being that you will simply forget much of what you have already learned unless it is refreshed (look up Ebbinghaus Forgetting Curve for more details on this). This makes it more difficult as you move from one subject to another: not only will you have to learn the new subject, you will also have to relearn all the underpinning knowledge as well. This is very inefficient and slows down your overall progression which makes it more likely you may not succeed at all.

In addition, delaying your studies slows your path to qualification which can have negative impacts on your career, postponing the opportunity to apply for higher level positions and therefore higher pay.

You can use the following diagram showing the whole structure of your qualification to help you keep track of your progress. Make sure you carefully review the 2019 CIMA syllabus transition rules and seek appropriate advice if you are unsure about your progression through the qualification.

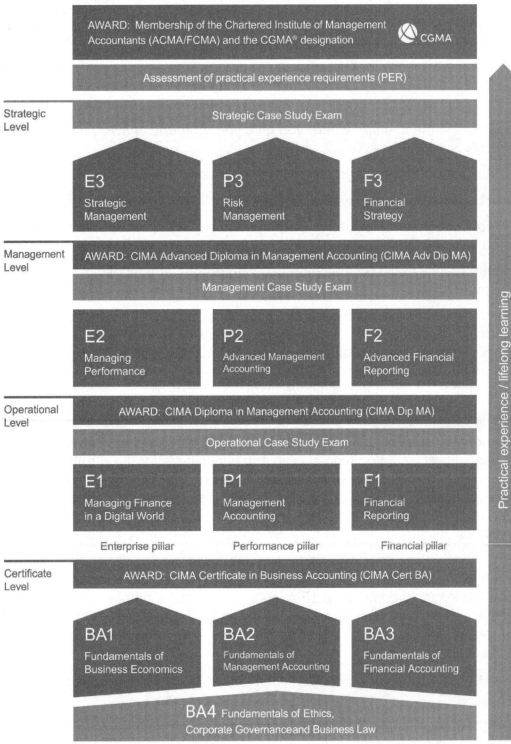

Reproduced with permission from CIMA

## Objective test

Objective test questions require you to choose or provide a response to a question whose correct answer is predetermined.

The most common types of objective test question you will see are:

- Multiple choice, where you have to choose the correct answer(s) from a list of possible answers. This could either be numbers or text.

- Multiple choice with more choices and answers, for example, choosing two correct answers from a list of eight possible answers. This could either be numbers or text.

- Single numeric entry, where you give your numeric answer, for example, profit is $10,000.

- Multiple entry, where you give several numeric answers.

- True/false questions, where you state whether a statement is true or false.

- Matching pairs of text, for example, matching a technical term with the correct definition.

- Other types could be matching text with graphs and labelling graphs/diagrams.

In every chapter of this Study Text we have introduced these types of questions, but obviously we have had to label answers A, B, C etc. rather than using click boxes. For convenience, we have retained quite a few questions where an initial scenario leads to a number of sub-questions. There will be no questions of this type in the objective tests.

### Guidance re CIMA on-screen calculator

As part of the CIMA objective test software, candidates are now provided with a calculator. This calculator is on-screen and is available for the duration of the assessment. The calculator is available in each of the objective tests and is accessed by clicking the calculator button in the top left hand corner of the screen at any time during the assessment. Candidates are permitted to utilise personal calculators as long as they are an approved CIMA model. Authorised CIMA models are listed here: https://www.cimaglobal.com/Studying/study-and-resources/.

All candidates must complete a 15-minute exam tutorial before the assessment begins and will have the opportunity to familiarise themselves with the calculator and practise using it. The exam tutorial is also available online via the CIMA website.

Candidates may practise using the calculator by accessing the online exam tutorial.

### Fundamentals of objective tests

The objective tests are 90-minute assessments comprising 60 compulsory questions, with one or more parts. There will be no choice and all questions should be attempted. All elements of a question must be answered correctly for the question to be marked correctly. All questions are equally weighted.

## CIMA syllabus 2019 – Structure of subjects and learning outcomes

Details regarding the content of the new CIMA syllabus can be located within the CIMA 2019 professional syllabus document.

Each subject within the syllabus is divided into a number of broad syllabus topics. The topics contain one or more lead learning outcomes, related component learning outcomes and indicative knowledge content.

A learning outcome has two main purposes:

(a)  To define the skill or ability that a well prepared candidate should be able to exhibit in the examination.

(b)  To demonstrate the approach likely to be taken in examination questions.

The learning outcomes are part of a hierarchy of learning objectives. The verbs used at the beginning of each learning outcome relate to a specific learning objective, e.g.

**Calculate** the break-even point, profit target, margin of safety and profit/volume ratio for a single product or service.

The verb '**calculate**' indicates a level three learning objective. The following tables list the verbs that appear in the syllabus learning outcomes and examination questions.

## The examination blueprints and representative task statements

CIMA have also published examination blueprints giving learners clear expectations regarding what is expected of them.

The blueprint is structured as follows:

*   Exam content sections (reflecting the syllabus document)

*   Lead and component outcomes (reflecting the syllabus document)

*   Representative task statements.

A representative task statement is a plain English description of what a CIMA finance professional should know and be able to do.

The content and skill level determine the language and verbs used in the representative task.

CIMA will test up to the level of the task statement in the objective tests (an objective test question on a particular topic could be set at a lower level than the task statement in the blueprint).

The format of the objective test blueprints follows that of the published syllabus for the 2019 CIMA Professional Qualification.

Weightings for content sections are also included in the individual subject blueprints.

# CIMA VERB HIERARCHY

CIMA place great importance on the definition of verbs in structuring objective tests. It is therefore crucial that you understand the verbs in order to appreciate the depth and breadth of a topic and the level of skill required. The objective tests will focus on levels one, two and three of the CIMA hierarchy of verbs. However, they will also test levels four and five, especially at the management and strategic levels.

| Skill level | Verbs used | Definition |
|---|---|---|
| **Level 5**<br>**Evaluation**<br><br>How you are expected to use your learning to evaluate, make decisions or recommendations | Advise | Counsel, inform or notify |
| | Assess | Evaluate or estimate the nature, ability or quality of |
| | Evaluate | Appraise or assess the value of |
| | Recommend | Propose a course of action |
| | Review | Assess and evaluate in order, to change if necessary |
| **Level 4**<br>**Analysis**<br><br>How you are expected to analyse the detail of what you have learned | Align | Arrange in an orderly way |
| | Analyse | Examine in detail the structure of |
| | Communicate | Share or exchange information |
| | Compare and contrast | Show the similarities and/or differences between |
| | Develop | Grow and expand a concept |
| | Discuss | Examine in detail by argument |
| | Examine | Inspect thoroughly |
| | Interpret | Translate into intelligible or familiar terms |
| | Monitor | Observe and check the progress of |
| | Prioritise | Place in order of priority or sequence for action |
| | Produce | Create or bring into existence |
| **Level 3**<br>**Application**<br><br>How you are expected to apply your knowledge | Apply | Put to practical use |
| | Calculate | Ascertain or reckon mathematically |
| | Conduct | Organise and carry out |
| | Demonstrate | Prove with certainty or exhibit by practical means |
| | Prepare | Make or get ready for use |
| | Reconcile | Make or prove consistent/compatible |

| Skill level | Verbs used | Definition |
|---|---|---|
| **Level 2**<br>**Comprehension**<br><br>What you are expected to understand | Describe | Communicate the key features of |
| | Distinguish | Highlight the differences between |
| | Explain | Make clear or intelligible/state the meaning or purpose of |
| | Identify | Recognise, establish or select after consideration |
| | Illustrate | Use an example to describe or explain something |
| **Level 1**<br>**Knowledge**<br><br>What you are expected to know | List | Make a list of |
| | State | Express, fully or clearly, the details/facts of |
| | Define | Give the exact meaning of |
| | Outline | Give a summary of |

Information concerning formulae and tables will be provided via the CIMA website, www.cimaglobal.com.

# SYLLABUS GRIDS

## F1: Financial Reporting

**What the finance function does and its implications**

**Content weighting**

| Content area | | Weighting |
|---|---|---|
| A | Regulatory environment of financial reporting | 10% |
| B | Financial statements | 45% |
| C | Principles of taxation | 20% |
| D | Managing cash and working capital | 25% |
| | | **100%** |

# F1A: Regulatory environment of financial reporting

The preparation of financial statements is regulated by laws, standards, generally accepted accounting principles and by codes. The regulations ensure that financial statements of different entities are comparable and that they present a reasonably accurate picture of the performance, position and prospects of the organisation to their users. This section covers who the regulators are, what they do and why and how the regulations are applied. The objective is to provide candidates with a strong foundation for preparing and interpreting financial statements.

| Lead outcome | Component outcome | Topics to be covered | Explanatory notes |
|---|---|---|---|
| 1  Identify regulators and describe their role. | a. Identify the major regulators.<br>b. Describe what they do.<br>c. Explain why they regulate financial reporting. | • National regulators<br>• IFRS foundation<br>• IASB<br>• International Organisation for Securities Commissions (IOSCO)<br>• Standard setting process<br>• Differences between rules-based and principles-based regulations<br>• Others such as International Integrated Reporting Council (IIRC) | Who are the regulators who determine how financial statements are prepared? What do they do? What value do they contribute to the production of financial statements? Coverage will include national and international regulators, stock exchange regulators and various accounting and financial reporting standards boards and major influential bodies like the IIRC. |
| 2.  Apply corporate governance principles to financial reporting. | a. Describe the role of the board in corporate governance.<br>b. Apply corporate governance and financial stewardship principles to financial reporting. | • Need and scope for corporate governance regulations<br>• Different approaches to corporate governance regulations | Boards have overall responsibility for ensuring that executives of organisations create value for their stakeholders and safeguard their assets. The role of boards is incorporated in various corporate governance codes. What are the main principles as they apply to financial reporting and the oversight of boards? |

# F1B: Financial statements

One of the roles of finance is to narrate how organisations create and preserve value. The financial statements are the means by which narration is done to particular audiences. This section enables candidates to prepare basic financial statements using financial reporting standards. It covers the main elements of the financial statements, what they intend to convey, the key financial reporting standards and how they are applied to prepare financial statements.

| Lead outcome | Component outcome | Topics to be covered | Explanatory notes |
|---|---|---|---|
| 1. Identify the main elements of financial statements. | a. Identify the main elements of financial statements contained in the IFRS conceptual framework. | • Objectives and overall purpose of financial reporting<br>• Qualitative characteristics of financial information<br>• Reporting entity and its boundaries<br>• Recognition (and derecognition)<br>• Measurement bases<br>• Presentation and disclosure<br>• Concept of capital maintenance | This sets the main principles that underpin the preparation of financial statements. The focus is on the main principles. No detailed treatments are expected. |
| 2. Explain specific financial reporting standards. | Explain the specific financial reporting standards related to:<br>a. Non-current assets<br>b. Leases<br>c. Impairment<br>d. Inventory<br>e. Events after the period | • IAS 16 – Property, Plant & Equipment<br>• IFRS 5 – Non-current Assets Held for Sale or Discontinued Operations<br>• IFRS 16 – Leases<br>• IAS 36 – Impairment of Assets<br>• IAS 2 – Inventories<br>• IAS 10 – Events After the Reporting Period | Examine the requirements for how major items of the financial statements are to be recognised, measured and disclosed. This covers the main areas and not specialist topics. |
| 3. Apply financial reporting standards to prepare basic financial statements. | Apply financial reporting standards to prepare:<br>a. Statement of financial position<br>b. Statement of comprehensive income<br>c. Statement of changes in equity<br>d. Statement of cash flows | IAS 1 – Presentation of Financial Statements<br><br>IAS 7 – Statement of Cash Flows | Give hands-on experience of preparing basic financial statements by bringing in all the elements. |

# F1C: Principles of taxation

One of the implications of value creation is how that value is distributed to different stakeholders. Taxation is part of this distribution. This section helps candidates distinguish between types of taxes and to calculate corporate taxes. In a digital world where revenue is earned through online trading that spans national boundaries, candidates are introduced to the issues relating to taxation across international borders and the ethics of taxation.

| Lead outcome | Component outcome | Topics to be covered | Explanatory notes |
|---|---|---|---|
| 1. Distinguish between different types of taxes. | Distinguish between<br>a. Direct versus indirect<br>b. Corporate versus personal | • Features of direct and indirect taxes<br>• Features of corporate and personal taxes | Gives a broad overview of the different types of taxes, who they affect and why they are used. |
| 2. Calculate tax for corporates. | a. Explain the basis of taxation<br>b. Explain the difference between accounting profit and taxable profit<br>c. Calculate corporate tax | • Exempt income<br>• Income taxed under different rules<br>• Allowable expenditure<br>• Capital allowances<br>• Reliefs<br>• Tax on sale of asset | The focus shifts here to corporate taxation. The main area covered is the difference between accounting profit and profit for taxation purposes. No national law is applied here. The main thing here is coverage and application of principles. |
| 3. Explain some relevant issues that affect taxation. | Explain:<br>a. Taxation across international borders<br>b. Ethics of taxation | • Corporate residence<br>• Types of overseas operations (e.g., subsidiary or branch)<br>• Double taxation<br>• Transfer pricing<br>• Tax avoidance<br>• Tax evasion | Given the increase of cross-border trading and revenue generation in the digital world what are the key issues affecting international taxation? What are the ethical issues that arise in the computation and payment of taxes? |

## F1D: Managing cash and working capital

Cash is the life blood of any organisation. The ability to provide cash, at the appropriate cost when it is needed is one of the key contributions that finance makes to organisations. It fulfils finance's role of enabling organisations to create and preserve value. This section provides candidates with the tools to ensure that the organisation has enough cash to ensure its continuing operations.

| Lead outcome | Component outcome | Topics to be covered | Explanatory notes |
|---|---|---|---|
| 1. Distinguish between the types and sources of short-term finance. | Distinguish between<br><br>a. Types of short-term finance<br><br>b. Financial institutions | • Trade payables<br>• Overdrafts<br>• Short-term loans<br>• Debt factoring<br>• Trade terms<br>• Trade partners<br>• Banks | What are the main types of funds needed for the short term? Where can those funds be accessed? How does one determine which type or source of finance is appropriate? |
| 2. Explain and calculate operating and cash cycles. | Explain and calculate<br><br>a. Operating cycle<br><br>b. Cash flow cycle | • Inventory days<br>• Trade receivable days<br>• Trade payable days | The operating and cash cycle is one of the main means of putting together various elements of cash and near-cash items in a coherent manner to explain the cash needs of the organisation. What are these elements? How do they affect the availability and adequacy of cash for short-term operations? |
| 3. Apply different techniques used to manage working capital. | a. Apply policies relating to elements of operating and cash cycle<br><br>b. Prepare forecasts<br><br>c. Explain risks relating to working capital | • Receivables management<br>• Payables management<br>• Inventory management<br>• Risk of overtrading<br>• Short-term cash flow forecasting<br>• Investing short-term cash | What are the policies that organisations should put in place to manage working capital? How is the appropriate level determined, forecasted and accessed? What are the risks associated with accessing such funds? |

# Features of Taxation and the Regulatory Environment

## Chapter learning objectives

| Lead | Component outcome |
| --- | --- |
| C1 Distinguish between different types of taxes | Distinguish between<br><br>a. Direct versus indirect<br><br>b. Corporate vs personal |
| C2 Calculate tax for corporates | a. Explain the basis of taxation |
| C3 Explain some relevant issues that affect taxation. | Explain<br><br>b. Ethics of taxation |

## 1    Session content

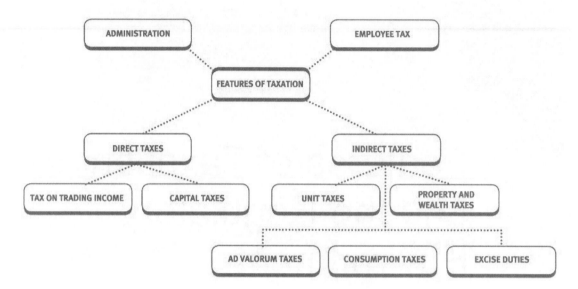

## 2    Introduction

Governments need tax revenues to finance expenditure on public services such as hospitals, schools, policing, retirement pensions, social benefits and to finance government borrowing. Governments can use tax to stimulate one sector of the economy and control another. For example, allowances on capital expenditure may develop the manufacturing sector, while high taxes on tobacco and alcohol may discourage sales.

In **Wealth of Nations**, Adam Smith proposed that a good tax should have the following characteristics:

- fair (reflect person's ability to pay)
- absolute (certain not arbitrary)
- convenient (easy to pay)
- efficient (low collection costs)

The 3 major principles of good tax policy are as follows:

- equity – A good tax should be fairly levied between one taxpayer and another.
- efficiency – A good tax should be cheap and easy to collect, i.e. UK tax system uses the PAYE (pay-as-you-earn) to collect tax at source on salaries and wages.
- economic effects – A good tax should consider the way in which a tax should be collected.

**What is a good tax?**

The American Institution of Certified Public Accountants lists the following principles that a good tax policy should have:

- equity and fairness

- transparency and visibility

- certainty

- economy in collection

- convenience of payment

- simplicity

- appropriate government revenues (determining the amount of tax revenues and date of collection)

- minimum tax gap (the difference between actual collection and amount due)

- neutrality

- economic growth and efficiency

It is not always possible to incorporate all ten into a tax system

 **Definition of terms**

A tax is either a direct or an indirect tax.

**Direct taxes**

These are imposed directly on the person or enterprise required to pay the tax, i.e. tax on personal income such as salaries, tax on business profits or tax on disposals of chargeable assets. The person or enterprise must pay the tax directly to the tax authorities on their income. Examples in the UK of direct taxes would be income tax, capital gains tax or corporation tax.

**Indirect taxes**

This tax is imposed on one part of the economy with the intention that the tax burden is passed on to another. The tax is imposed on the final consumer of the goods or services. The more the consumer consumes the greater the tax paid. An example would be sales tax such as Value Added Tax (VAT) in the UK.

### Tax bases

A tax base is something that is liable for tax. Taxes can be classified by tax base, that is, by what is being taxed. Taxes may be based on the following:

- Income: For example, income taxes and taxes on an entity's profits.

- Capital or wealth: For example, taxes on capital gains and taxes on inherited wealth.

- Consumption: For example, excise duties and sales taxes/value-added tax (VAT).

For example, in the US, the Federal government taxes income as its main source of revenue. State governments use taxes on income and consumption, while local governments rely almost entirely on taxing property and wealth.

### Incidence

The incidence of a tax is the distribution of the tax burden, i.e. who is paying the tax.

 **What is incidence?**

**Incidence**

This can be split into two elements:

1   **Formal incidence:** this is the person who has direct contact with the tax authorities, i.e. who is legally obliged to pay the tax.

2   **Actual incidence:** this is the person who actually ends up bearing the cost of the tax, i.e. who actually bears the burden of tax.

If we consider VAT – the formal incidence would be the entity making the sale because they will be responsible for making the payment to the relevant tax authorities. The actual incidence would be the consumer who bears the cost of the tax when they make a purchase from the entity.

### Taxable person

The person accountable for the tax payment, e.g. individual or entity.

### Competent jurisdiction

A taxable person normally pays tax in the country of origin. Competent jurisdiction is the tax authority that has the legal power to assess and collect the taxes. This is usually the combined responsibility of the central government and local authorities within a country. The tax law is enforceable by sanction (fines or imprisonment).

### Hypothecation

This means that certain taxes are devoted entirely to certain types of expenditure, e.g. road tax is used entirely on maintaining roads e.g. the London congestion charge is used to pay for transport for the area.

## Tax gap

This is the gap between the tax theoretically collectable and the amount actually collected. The tax authorities will aim to minimise this gap.

## Tax rate structure

There are three types of taxes:

(1) **Progressive taxes**: These take an increasing proportion of income as income rises. (E.g. UK Income tax – 20%, 40%, 50%).

(2) **Proportional taxes**: These take the same proportion of income as income rises.

(3) **Regressive taxes**: These take a decreasing proportion of income as income rises. (E.g. UK National Insurance contributions – 11% then 1%).

 **Tax rate structure**

Progressive tax means the proportion of tax increases as income increases, i.e. salary $10,000 pays tax of $1,000 = 10% but a salary of $20,000 pays tax of $3,000 = 15%.

Proportionate tax means the proportion of tax remains the same, regardless of the level of income, i.e. salary $10,000 pays tax of $1,000 = 10% and a salary of $20,000 pays tax of $2,000 = 10%.

Regressive tax means the proportion of tax reduces as income increases, i.e. salary $10,000 pays tax of $1,000 = 10% but a salary of $20,000 pays tax of $1,800 = 9%.

## Source of tax rules

The sources of tax rules are as follows:

- Legislation produced by a national government of the country, e.g. Finance Acts in the UK.

- Precedents based on previous legislation. Tax authorities also issue interpretations, e.g. Tax bulletins in the UK.

- Directives from international bodies such as European Union guidelines on VAT.

- Agreements between different countries such as double tax treaties, e.g. UK/US Double tax treaties.

 **Income can be taxed twice**

Foreign income is often taxed twice, once in the country of origin and once in the country of residency (see chapter 3 for corporate residency). In order to avoid this "double taxation", countries enter into tax treaties, (see chapter 2 for types of double taxation relief).

## 3    Direct taxes

There are two types of direct tax you need to consider:

- Tax on trading income
- Capital taxes

### Tax on trading income

Trading income relates to income from the main business activity.

The tax base should be profits.

The accounting profit needs to be adjusted for tax purposes as in many countries there are differences between what the accounting standards allow you to show as an income/expense and what the tax system deems to be the income/expense. These adjusted profits will enable you to calculate the taxable profit.

The standard pro-forma is as follows:

|  | $ |
|---|---|
| Accounting profit | X |
| Less income exempt from tax or taxed under other rules | (X) |
| Add: disallowable expenses | X |
| Add: accounting depreciation | X |
| Less: tax depreciation | (X) |
| Taxable profit | X |

The taxable profit will then be charged at the appropriate tax rate for that accounting period.

The rules for allowed and disallowed items will vary according to the tax regime of the country in question. This will always be given in the assessment question.

The calculation of tax on trading income will be looked at in further detail in the next chapter of this publication.

### Capital taxes

Capital tax gains are gains made on the disposal of investments and other non-current assets. The most common assets taxed are listed stocks and shares.

At a simple level, the gain is calculated as proceeds from sale less cost of the asset.

In most countries, the computation is based on cost but in a few countries an allowance is made for inflation. In the UK, the cost can be indexed, in certain cases, using the Retail Price Index. Indexation will be calculated on all allowable costs from the date of purchase to the disposal date of the asset. This indexation allowance will **reduce** the gain.

The standard pro-forma is as follows:

|  | $ |
|---|---|
| Proceeds | X |
| Less: costs to sell | (X) |
|  | |
| Net proceeds | X |
| Less: cost of original asset | (X) |
| Less: costs to buy | (X) |
| Less: enhancement costs | (X) |
| Less: indexation allowance | (X) |
|  | |
| Chargeable gain | X |

The chargeable gain will then be charged at the appropriate tax rate for that accounting period.

The calculation of capital taxes will be looked at in further detail in the next chapter of this publication.

## 4 Indirect taxes

### Types of indirect taxes

Indirect taxes will either be:

(1) **Unit taxes**

This is a tax based on the number or weight of items, e.g. excise duties.

(2) **Ad valorem taxes**

This is a tax based on the value of items, e.g. sales tax.

### Examples of indirect taxes

(1) **Excise duties**

This is a type of unit tax and it is on certain products such as alcoholic drinks, tobacco, mineral oils and motor vehicles. It is based on the weight or size of the tax base. These duties are imposed to:

- discourage over consumption of harmful products;

- to pay for extra costs, such as increased healthcare or road infrastructure;

- to tax luxuries (in the USA, this would include fishing equipment, firearms and air tickets).

The characteristics of commodities that make them most suitable for excise duties are:

- few large producers

- inelastic demand with no close substitutes

- large sales volumes

- easy to define products covered by the duty

## (2) Property taxes

Many countries impose tax on property based on either the capital value or the annual rental value. Most countries tax land and buildings although in the USA, certain states also impose a tax on cars, livestock and boats.

## (3) Wealth taxes

Some countries also impose a wealth tax on an individual's or enterprise's total wealth. The wealth can include pension funds, insurance policies and works of art.

## (4) Consumption taxes

These are taxes imposed on the consumption of goods and added to the purchase price. There are two types of consumption tax.

- **Single stage taxes**

   Single stage taxes apply to one level of production only, for example at either the manufacturing, wholesale or retail level. The USA is a country which uses a retail sales tax although the tax rate is determined at the local state government level instead of at the central government or federal level.

- **Multi-stage sales tax**

   This is a tax charged each time a component or product is sold. There are two types of multi-stage sales tax:

   Cascade tax, and

   Valued added tax (VAT).

## (5) Cascade tax

This is where tax is taken at each stage of production and is a business cost because no refunds are provided by local government.

Students will not be required to answer calculation style questions on cascade tax in their examination.

## (6)    Value added tax (VAT)

VAT is charged each time a component or product is sold but the government allows businesses to claim back all the tax they have paid (input tax). The entire tax burden is passed to the final consumer. The VAT system is used by almost all countries in the world.

**VAT payable = output tax – input tax**

Output tax – VAT charged on sales to customers

Input tax – VAT paid on purchases

VAT aims to tax most business transactions which are referred to as taxable supplies.

Therefore, supplies could be:

Standard Rated    – Taxed at the standard rate of VAT

Higher Rated       – Taxed at a higher rate

Zero Rated          – Taxed at a rate of 0% (Basic food, e.g. bread)

Exempt               – Not subject to VAT

In the UK, supplies such as food, children's clothing and exports are zero rated for the purpose of VAT. Businesses who sell zero rated sales are allowed to claim back input VAT on purchases.

Alternatively, in the UK, supplies such as finance and insurance are exempt for the purpose of VAT. Businesses who make exempt sales cannot claim back input VAT on purchases.

You will not be required to know the types of goods and services that are zero rated or exempt for the exam; the examiner will make this clear in the question.

 It is important to identify the type of supply in order to claim back input tax. Input tax can only be claimed back on taxable supplies, i.e. zero and standard rated goods and services.  Exempt supplies are outside the VAT system and VAT cannot be charged to customers but neither can the input tax on purchases be claimed back.

Taxable supplies, therefore, have a selling price exclusive of VAT (net price) and a selling price inclusive of VAT (gross price).

If the exclusive price is given, VAT is calculated by:

**exclusive price × tax rate**

If the inclusive price is given VAT is calculated by:

$$\frac{\textbf{inclusive price}}{\textbf{100 + tax rate}} \times \textbf{tax rate}$$

## VAT registration

VAT registration is required by a taxable person making a taxable supply.

A taxable person can be an individual or a company.

A taxable supply can zero, standard or higher rated sales.

They will be required to register for VAT when their taxable turnover (zero, standard or higher rated sales) reach a certain limit (this will vary from tax year to tax year).

When registered they must:

- Issue VAT invoices

- Keep appropriate VAT records

- Charge VAT on taxable supplies to customers

- Be able to claim back VAT from purchases that are used for taxable supplies

- Complete a quarterly VAT return and make payments

For example, in the UK VAT **cannot** be recovered on:

- Cars (unless for resale, i.e. by a car dealer)

- Entertaining (unless for staff entertaining)

## 5 Impact of employee taxation

Employees are taxed on their earnings under income tax. Earnings can include salaries, bonuses, commissions and benefits in kind.

Benefits in kind are non-cash benefits in lieu of further cash payments such as:

- company cars

- living accommodation

- loans

- private medical insurance

The basis of assessment is based on the individual country:

- France – amount earned in previous year

- Switzerland – average of previous two years' earnings

- UK – amount actually received in the current tax year

Employees can deduct certain expenses which are wholly, exclusively and necessary for employment, such as business travel, contributions to pension plans, donations to charity through a payroll deduction scheme and professional subscriptions.

Both employees and companies have to pay social security taxes based on salaries paid to employees. In the UK, this tax is used to fund benefits such as the public health service and retirement benefits and is called national insurance.

Most governments expect enterprises to withhold tax on employees' salaries and report earnings to the tax authorities. In the UK, this tax system is referred to as Pay-As-You-Earn (PAYE).

The benefits of having a PAYE system are:

- Tax is collected at source, hence taxpayers are less likely to default payment.

- Tax authorities receive regular payments from employers – helps to budget cash flows for the government.

- The tax authority only has to deal with the employer, rather than a number of individuals.

- Most of the administration costs are borne by the employer, instead of the government.

Certain countries, such as the USA, require banks to collect property taxes with the mortgage payments. In addition to this, in the USA there is a separate Unemployment Compensation Tax.

 You will not be assessed on the calculation of employment taxation but you should have a general appreciation of how an entity deals with taxation with regard to employees.

The standard pro-forma for calculating employee tax would be as follows:

|  | $ |
| --- | --- |
| Salary | X |
| Plus: bonus, commission, benefits | X |
| Less: subscriptions | (X) |
| Less: pension contributions | (X) |
| Less: charity donations | (X) |
| Less: personal allowances | (X) |
| Taxable income | X |

The taxable income will then be charged at the appropriate tax rate for the tax year.

This will normally be done by the entity using the PAYE system.

## 6　Administration

### Record-keeping

Enterprises need to keep records to satisfy tax requirements for the following taxes.

### Corporate income tax

All records required to support their financial statements and also the additional documents required to support the adjustments made to those statements when completing their tax returns.

### Sales tax

Adequate records should be maintained of all the sales and purchases records such as:

- Orders and delivery notes
- Purchase and sales invoices
- Credit and debit notes
- Purchase and sales books
- Import and export documents
- Bank Statements
- Cashbooks and receipts
- VAT account

### Overseas subsidiaries

Tax authorities would require documentation about the transfer pricing policy between the subsidiary and the parent. These are the prices charged for goods or services provided by one to the other. Most tax authorities require the price to be the same as it would be if charged to a third party.

Overseas subsidiaries will be looked at in more detail in the following chapters.

### Employee tax

Employers have to keep detailed records of employee tax and social security contributions. They will also be required to prepare a number of year end returns to show the total deductions they have made from employees' wages, the employer's contributions and an analysis of any other amounts deducted. The employer is also required to provide details to the employee.

Tax authorities set deadlines for the payment of tax and the submission of the tax return. The enterprise will either be required to pay tax following an assessment from the tax authorities or will pay tax via self-assessment. In the UK and the USA, tax is paid via self-assessment. The tax authorities will then check the tax return to confirm whether the correct tax has been paid.

## Minimum retention of records

There will be a minimum length of time for the retention of records; in the UK this is six years for all records relating to earnings and capital gains. The purpose of this is to enable the tax authorities to question or challenge records up to several years later.

## Payment of tax

This will depend on the rules of the tax authority and will depend on the type of tax that is due. The tax is not always paid when the return is filed, it may happen earlier or later. Interest will be charged on late payments of tax.

## Power of tax authorities

The revenue authorities have various powers to impose penalties and interest on late payment of tax. In addition, they have the power to:

- Review and query filed returns.
- Request special reports if they believe inaccurate information has been submitted.
- Examine records of previous years (in the US, tax authorities can go back 20 years).
- Enter and search the entity's premises and seize documents.
- Pass on information to foreign tax authorities.

## Tax avoidance and tax evasion

**Tax avoidance** is tax planning to arrange affairs, within the scope of the Law, to minimise the tax liability. This could be setting up a subsidiary overseas in a low tax economy.

There have been a number of large entities that have been accused of tax avoidance in recent times. The public perception would be that the entities are not paying their fair share of tax and these entities have been criticised in the press for setting up their tax affairs so that they pay very little tax.

This has led to these entities receiving very negative publicity and often had an adverse effect on the overall business.

**Tax evasion** is the illegal manipulation of the tax system to avoid paying tax. Evasion is the intentional disregard of the law to escape tax and can include claiming a tax deduction for expenses that are not tax deductible, under declaring income and claiming fictitious expenses.

The tax authorities use various methods to prevent both tax avoidance and tax evasion:

1 Reducing opportunity, e.g. by deduction of tax at source and the use of third party reporting.

2 Simplifying tax structure by minimising the relief, allowances and exemptions.

3    Increasing detection through auditing tax returns and payments.

4    Developing good communication between tax authorities and enterprises.

5    Changing social attitudes towards evasion and avoidance by maintaining an honest and customer friendly tax system. The government should create a fair tax system and should encourage an increasing commitment.

6    Reducing lost revenue by reviewing the penalty structure.

**Test your understanding 1 – Practice questions**

1    **Which of the following is not usually a source of tax rules in a country:**

   A    Local legislation

   B    Double tax treaties

   C    Statements of practice of tax authorities

   D    International law

2    **What does 'competent jurisdiction' mean in the context of an enterprise being subject to a tax liability?**

   A    Country where enterprise has an office

   B    Country which has enforcement laws that apply to an enterprise

   C    Country where enterprise has business operations

   D    Country where enterprise has employees

3    BM has a taxable profit of $30,000 and receives a tax assessment of $3,000.

   BV has a taxable profit of $60,000 and receives a tax assessment of $7,500.

   BM and BV are resident in the same tax jurisdiction.

   **This tax could be said to be:**

   A    a progressive tax

   B    a regressive tax

   C    a direct tax

   D    a proportional tax

4   Country IDT has a duty that is levied on all drinks of an alcoholic nature where the alcohol is above 20% by volume. This levy is $2 per 1 litre bottle. This duty could be said to be:

A   Ad valorem tax

B   Unit tax

C   Direct tax

D   VAT

5   Which ONE of the following powers is a tax authority least likely to have granted to them?

A   Power of arrest

B   Power to examine records

C   Power of entry and search

D   Power to give information to other countries' tax authorities

6   List THREE possible reasons why governments set deadlines for filing returns and/or paying taxes.

## 7  Summary diagram

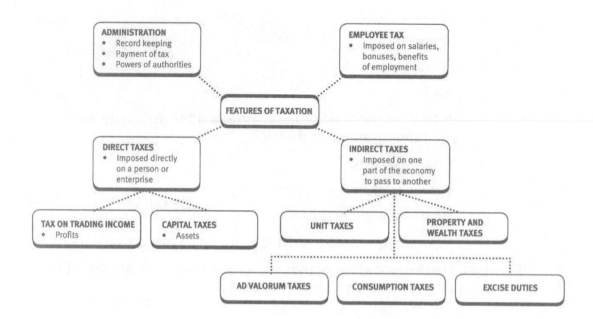

## Test your understanding answers

**Test your understanding 1 – Practice questions**

1    D – International Law.

2    B – Country that has enforceable laws that apply to an enterprise.

3    A – $3,000 tax on $30,000 = 10% and $7,500 tax on $60,000 = 12.5%. The tax rates increase as the income rises, hence a progressive tax.

4    B – Unit tax. This is a tax based on the number or weight of items, e.g. excise duties.

5    A – Power of arrest.

6    Answers could be:

Entities will know when payment is required;

It enables the tax authorities to forecast their cash flows more accurately;

Provides a reference for late payment – useful for applying penalties for not paying;

To prevent entities spending tax money deducted from employees. If tax is deducted from employees at source and not paid to the tax authorities fairly quickly, there is more chance of an entity spending the amount deducted, instead of paying it to the tax authorities.

# Corporate Income Tax and Capital Tax Computations

## Chapter learning objectives

| Lead | Component outcome |
|---|---|
| C2. Calculate tax for corporates | b. Explain the difference between accounting profit and taxable profit |
| | c. Calculate corporate tax |

## 1    Session content

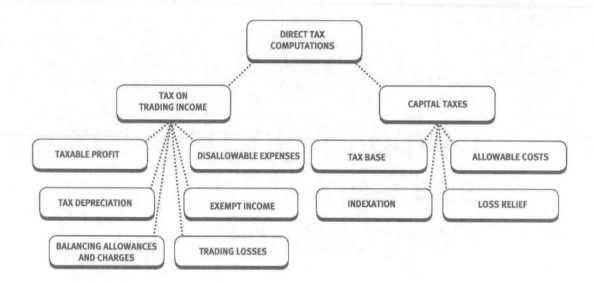

## 2    Tax on trading income

A reminder of the standard pro-forma (covered in the previous chapter) to calculate corporate income tax is as follows:

|                                                        | $   |
|--------------------------------------------------------|-----|
| Accounting profit                                      | X   |
| Less: income exempt from tax or taxed under other rules | (X) |
|                                                        |     |
| Add: disallowable expenses                             | X   |
| Add: accounting depreciation                           | X   |
| Less: tax depreciation                                 | (X) |
|                                                        |     |
| Taxable profit                                         | X   |

The taxable profit will then be charged at the appropriate tax rate for that accounting period.

Remember that the rules for allowed and disallowed items will vary according to the tax regime of the country in question. This will always be given in the assessment question, so ensure that you read the question carefully.

The **accounting profit** is the profit before tax shown in the statement of profit or loss in the annual financial statements.

**Income exempt from tax or taxed under other rules** is any income included in the accounting profit which does **not** relate to the main trading activity, i.e. rental income, dividend income, interest receivable, that maybe taxed under other rules or income exempt from taxation under that particular country's rules.

**Disallowable expenses** are expenses that have been deducted from the accounting profit, i.e. they are allowable under the accounting standards, but for tax purposes can't be claimed. These expenses will differ from country to country and the examiner will always tell you the rules for that particular country in the question. Examples of disallowable expenses in the UK are entertaining customers, gift aid payments and political donations.

**Depreciation** is added back because it is an accounting entry that is not allowed for tax purposes because it is too subjective (i.e. you can choose the way to depreciate your assets). It is replaced with tax depreciation.

**Tax depreciation** may be called capital allowances in the exam. The rules will be given in the exam to tell you what can be claimed. It is a replacement for depreciation. They are often given on a reducing balance basis. Allowances are given if the asset is owned at the accounting date, i.e. no time apportionment for mid-year acquisitions.

As an incentive to encourage new investment, certain jurisdictions offer 100% first year capital allowances. The entire tax value of the asset is allowed as capital allowances in the first year of acquisition.

---

**Test your understanding 1 – Trading income**

In year ending 31/03/20X2, an entity George made an accounting profit of $80,000. Profit included $5,500 of entertaining costs which are disallowable for tax purposes and $8,000 of income exempt from taxation.

George has no capital items.

Tax is charged at 25%.

**Calculate the tax payable for the year ended 31/03/X2.**

---

**Illustration 1 – Trading income**

In year ending 31/12/20X1, an entity Zippy made an accounting profit of $50,000. Profit included $3,500 of entertaining expenses which are disallowable for tax purposes and $5,000 of income exempt from taxation.

Zippy has $70,000 of non-current assets which were acquired on 01/01/20X0 and are depreciated at 10% on cost. Tax depreciation rates are 20% reducing balance.

**Calculate the accounting depreciation for the year ended 31/12/X1.**

### Solution

The accounting depreciation is $70,000 × 10% = $7,000

### Illustration 2 – Trading income

**Using the information from illustration 1 calculate the tax depreciation for the year ended 31/12/X1.**

### Solution

**Tax depreciation**

| | | |
|---|---|---|
| WDV at start of year | $56,000 | ($70,000 × 80%) |
| Tax depreciation at 20% | $11,200 | |

The asset had been purchased in the previous accounting period, therefore tax depreciation has already been claimed for y/e 31 /12/X0. This year's tax depreciation must be calculated on the tax WDV at the beginning of the year, i.e. $56,000.

WDV means written down value. This represents the cost of the asset less accumulated tax depreciation.

### Illustration 3 – Trading income

**Using the information from illustrations 1 and 2 calculate the taxable profit for the year ended 31/12/X1.**

### Solution

| | $ |
|---|---|
| Accounting profit | 50,000 |
| Less: exempt income | (5,000) |
| Add back: disallowable expenses | 3,500 |
| Add back: depreciation (illustration 1) | 7,000 |
| Less: tax depreciation (illustration 2) | (11,200) |
| **Taxable profit** | **44,300** |

**Illustration 4 – Trading income**

Using the information from illustrations 1 to 3 calculate the tax payable for the year ended 31/12/X1. You should assume a tax rate of 30%.

 **Solution**

|  | $ |
|---|---|
| Accounting profit | 50,000 |
| Less: exempt income | (5,000) |
| Add back: disallowable expenses | 3,500 |
| Add back: depreciation (illustration 1) | 7,000 |
| Less: tax depreciation (illustration 2) | (11,200) |
|  |  |
| Taxable profit | 44,300 |
| **Tax at 30%** | **13,290** |

 **Test your understanding 2 – Trading income**

In year ending 31/03/20X2, an entity Bungle made an accounting profit of $60,000. Profit included $4,500 of political donations which are disallowable for tax purposes and $4,000 of income exempt from taxation.

Bungle has $10,000 of plant and machinery which was acquired on 01/04/20X0 and purchased a new machine costing $5,000 on 01/04/20X1. This new machine is entitled to FYAs (first year allowances) of 100% instead of the usual tax depreciation. All plant and machinery is depreciated in the accounts at 10% on cost. Tax depreciation rates on plant and machinery are 20% reducing balance.

Bungle also has a building that cost $100,000 on 01/04/20X0 and is depreciated in the accounts at 4% on a straight line basis. Tax depreciation is calculated at 3% on a straight line basis.

**Calculate the total accounting depreciation for the year ended 31/03/X2.**

 **Test your understanding 3 – Trading income**

Using the information from TYU 2 calculate the total tax depreciation for the year ended 31/03/X2.

## Test your understanding 4 – Trading income

**Using the information from TYU's 2 and 3 calculate the taxable profit for the year ended 31/03/X2.**

## Test your understanding 5 – Trading income

**Using the information from TYU's 2 to 4 calculate the tax payable for the year ended 31/03/X2. You should assume a tax rate of30%.**

In the previous illustrations and TYUs we have used a constant rate of tax to calculate the tax payable, e.g. 30%. However, sometimes the tax rate may change during the year and therefore taxable profits will need to be prorated. For tax purposes profits are assumed to be accrued evenly.

## Illustration 5 – Trading income

Using the illustrations 1 to 4, recalculate the tax if the rates were as follows:

01/04/X0 – 31/03/X1 = 28%

01/04/X1 – 31/03/X2 = 30%

## Solution

The taxable profit for Zippy was $44,300 for accounting period to 31/12/X1.

Tax would be:

($44,300 × 3/12 × 28%) + ($44,300 × 9/12 × 30%) = $13,068.50

The taxable profit is pro-rated based on the amount of months that fall into each of the tax rate periods, i.e.

01/01/X1 – 31/03/X1 = 3 months at the rate of 28%
01/04/X1 – 31/12/X1 = 9 months at the rate of 30%

## Test your understanding 6 – Trading income

An entity has an accounting period ending 30/06/X1 and a taxable profit of $800,000.

The rates of tax were as follows:

01/04/X0 – 31/03/X1 = 26%

01/04/X1 – 31/03/X2 = 28%

**Calculate the tax liability for the period ending 30/06/X1.**

## 3 Balancing allowances and charges

When an asset is sold any accounting profit or loss must be disallowed for tax purposes and replaced with the tax equivalent known as a balancing allowance or charge.

A balancing allowance (BA) = a tax loss on disposal

A balancing charge (BC) = a tax profit on disposal

The tax pro-forma could then be expanded to include the effect of the asset disposal as follows:

|  | $ |
|---|---|
| Accounting profit | X |
| Less: income exempt from tax or taxed under other rules | (X) |
| Add: disallowable expenses | X |
| Add: accounting depreciation | X |
| Add: accounting loss on disposal of an asset | X |
| Less: accounting profit on disposal of an asset | (X) |
| Less: tax depreciation | (X) |
| Add: tax profit on disposal of an asset (BC) | X |
| Less: tax loss on disposal of an asset (BA) | (X) |
| Taxable profit | X |

The taxable profit will then be charged at the appropriate tax rate for that accounting period.

 Always remember the tax amount should replace the accounting amount, i.e. reverse the accounting entry and pay tax on the tax profit or receive relief on the tax loss.

When an asset is disposed of, we will calculate, for accounting purposes, the accounting profit or loss on disposal. This will be calculated by:

|  | $ |
|---|---|
| Proceeds | X |
| Less: Carrying amount (SOFP) | (X) |
| Accounting profit/(loss) | X |

If the proceeds are greater than the carrying amount = profit

If the proceeds are less than the carrying amount = loss

An accounting profit or loss will be treated as disallowable for tax purposes. A profit will be deducted from the accounting profit (similar to non-trade income) and a loss will be added to the accounting profit (similar to depreciation).

This will then be replaced by either a balancing charge or allowance for tax purposes.

These are calculated in a similar way as the accounting profit or loss on disposal:

|  | $ |
|---|---|
| Proceeds | X |
| Less: tax written down value (TWDV) | (X) |
| Balancing charge/(allowance) | X |

If the proceeds are greater than the TWDV = balancing charge
If the proceeds are less than the TWDV = balancing allowance

A balancing charge will be added back to the accounting profit and a balancing allowance will be deducted from the accounting profit, when computing the taxable profit.

Capital allowances (tax depreciation) are not normally given in the year of disposal of the asset – these are replaced by balancing allowances or charges.

### Test your understanding 7 – Balancing allowances/charges

Bungle has $10,000 of plant and machinery which was acquired on 01/04/20X0 .

All plant and machinery is depreciated in the accounts at 10% on cost.

Tax depreciation rates on plant and machinery are 20% reducing balance.

All plant and machinery was sold for $6,000 on 01/04/X2.

**Calculate the accounting profit or loss on disposal for the year ended 31/03/X3.**

### Test your understanding 8 – Balancing allowances/charges

**Using the information from TYU 7 calculate the tax balancing allowance or charge on disposal for the year ended 31/03/X3.**

### Test your understanding 9 – Balancing allowances/charges

**Using the information from TYU's 7 and 8 calculate the tax payable for the year ended 31/03/X3 assuming the accounting profit is $50,000 and there are no other tax adjustments. Tax is payable at a rate of 25%.**

## Test your understanding 10 – Balancing allowances/charges

Re-calculate your answer to TYU 9 if the asset was sold for $9,000 instead of $6,000.

## Trading losses

When an entity makes a trading loss the assessment for that tax year will be nil.

The entity must now claim loss relief based on the rules of the country's tax regime. The assessment will tell you the rules of the country in the question.

Possible ways of relieving a loss are:

- Carry losses forwards against future profits of the **same** trade.
- Carry losses backwards against previous periods.
- Offset losses against group company profits.
- Offset losses against capital gains in the same period.

It is important to read the rules of the tax regime for the country. All countries are different as some allow losses to be carried backwards and forwards, others only allow losses to be carried forwards. Many countries do not allow trading losses to be offset against capital gains in any period.

## Illustration 6 – Trading income

In country X, trading losses in any year can be carried back and set off against trading profits in the previous year, and any unrelieved losses can be carried forward to set against the first available trade profits in future years.

Hall and Co had the following trading profits and losses in year 1 to 4.

| Year | Trading profit/(losses) |
|------|-------------------------|
| 1 | 25,000 |
| 2 | (45,000) |
| 3 | 15,000 |
| 4 | 35,000 |

**What are Hall and Co's taxable profits in each year?**

Corporate Income Tax and Capital Tax Computations

**Solution**

| Year | Trading profit/(loss) | Workings |
|------|-----------------------|----------|
| 1 | – | 25,000 – 25,000 |
| 2 | – | |
| 3 | – | 15,000 – 15,000 |
| 4 | 30,000 | 35,000 – 5,000 (balance of the loss) |

The trading loss is carried back first against the trading profit in year 1, this must be done to the maximum extent, i.e. you can't use part of the profit for relief if all of it is needed. The balance of the loss must then be carried forward against the **first available trading profit** in year 3, again to the maximum extent required until it has been relieved in full. There is usually no limit on how many years you are able to carry forward a trading loss.

**Test your understanding 11 – Trading losses**

In country A, trading losses in any year can be carried back and set off against profits in the previous year, and any unrelieved losses can be carried forward to set against profits in future years.

Looser had the following trading profits and losses in year 1 to 4.

| Year | Trading profit/(loss) |
|------|-----------------------|
| 1 | 20,000 |
| 2 | (45,000) |
| 3 | 19,000 |
| 4 | 25,000 |

**What are Looser's taxable profits in each year?**

### Trading losses on cessation of business

If an enterprise ceases to trade, most countries allow the entity to carry back the loss against profits of previous years to generate a tax refund. In the UK, this is called Terminal Loss Relief and enables the loss to be carried back three years. The assessment will tell you the terminal loss rules of that country.

## Test your understanding 12 – Cessation losses

In 20X3, Dunbadly closed its business having made a trading loss of $60,000. In Dunbadly's country of residence, trading losses may be carried back two years on a LIFO basis.

|  | 20X1 | 20X2 | 20X3 |
| --- | --- | --- | --- |
|  | $ | $ | $ |
| Trading profits/losses | 100,000 | 50,000 | (60,000) |

**What is the impact on taxable profits for each year?**

## 4 Capital taxes

Capital tax gains are gains made on the disposal of investments and other non-current assets. The most common assets taxed are listed stocks and shares. In the UK, the common capital tax is called Capital Gains Tax.

At a simple level, the gain is calculated as proceeds from sale less cost of the asset.

In most countries, the computation is based on cost but in a few countries an allowance is made for inflation. In the UK, the cost can be indexed, in certain cases, using the Retail Price Index. Indexation will be calculated on all allowable costs from the date of purchase to the disposal date of the asset. This indexation allowance will **reduce** the gain.

The standard pro-forma is as follows:

|  | $ |
| --- | --- |
| Proceeds | X |
| Less: costs to sell | (X) |
|  | — |
| Net proceeds | X |
| Less: cost of original asset | (X) |
| Less: costs to buy | (X) |
| Less: enhancement costs | (X) |
| Less: indexation allowance | (X) |
|  | — |
| Chargeable gain | X |

The chargeable gain will then be charged at the appropriate tax rate for that accounting period.

Costs that can be deducted from proceeds are:

- original cost of purchasing the asset
- costs to buy the assets, i.e. legal fees, estate agent fees
- costs to sell the assets, i.e. legal fees, estate agent fees
- enhancement/improvement costs, i.e. extensions to an existing asset
- indexation allowance – if this exists in the country of residency of the asset being disposed of

### Illustration 7 – Capital taxes

An entity bought an asset for $20,000 on 01/02/X0. The asset was sold for $50,000 on 21/11/X9.

Capital gains are taxed at 30%.

**What is the capital tax to be paid on the disposal?**

### Solution

|  | $ |
|---|---|
| Sale proceeds | 50,000 |
| Less: Cost | (20,000) |
| Chargeable gain | 30,000 |

**Capital tax = $30,000 × 30% = $9,000**

### Illustration 8 – Capital taxes

An entity bought an asset for $20,000 on 01 /02/X0. The asset was sold for $50,000 on 21/11/X9.

Indexation allowance can be claimed at 30% from February 20X0 to November 20X9.

Capital gains are taxed at 30%.

**What is the indexation allowance the entity can claim on disposal of the asset?**

### Solution

The indexation allowance can be claimed on the cost of the asset = $20,000 × 30% = $6,000

## Illustration 9 – Capital taxes

Using the information from illustration 8 calculate the capital tax to be paid on the disposal?

## Solution

|  | $ |
|---|---|
| Sale proceeds | 50,000 |
| Less: Cost | (20,000) |
|  | ———— |
|  | 30,000 |
| Less: Indexation allowance 20,000 × 30% (illustration 8) | (6,000) |
|  | ———— |
| Chargeable gain | 24,000 |
|  | ———— |

**Capital tax = $24,000 × 30% = $7,200**

## Test your understanding 13 – Capital taxes

An entity bought a building for $50,000 on 01/02/X0. They incurred costs at the date of purchase of $1,500 for legal fees.

The building was extended on 01/04/X2 at a cost of $12,000 and repairs to the roof were undertaken on 01/06/X3 after a violent storm, costing $5,000.

The building was sold for $150,000 on 21/11/Y1 and costs to sell were incurred of $2,000.

Calculate the chargeable gain on the disposal?

## Test your understanding 14 – Capital taxes

Using the information from TYU 13 calculate the indexation allowance for the asset assuming the following indexation factors were given:

February 20X0 to November 20Y1 was 30%

April 20X2 to November 20Y1 was 20%

June 20X3 to November 20Y1 was 10%

**Test your understanding 15 – Capital taxes**

**Using the information from TYU's 13 and 14 calculate the capital tax assuming a rate of 30%.**

**Items exempt from Capital Tax**

Usually, certain types of assets are exempt from Capital Tax. In the UK, under capital gains tax, exempt assets include:

- Qualifying Corporate Bonds

- private motor vehicles

- chattels sold for less than £6,000 (tangible movable property)

- wasting chattels, e.g. boats and animals.

Certain disposals are exempt from Capital Gains Tax and include:

- gifts to charities or certain assets such as works of art

- gifts to museums or government institutions

You will not be expected to remember these; the examiner will state in the question if any items are exempt.

### Capital losses

Most countries keep capital losses separate from trading activities.

Possible ways of relieving capital losses are:

- Carry forwards against future capital gains.

- Carry back against previous capital gains.

- Offset against trading income in the current period.

Most countries only allow capital losses to be carried forwards against future capital gains but the examiner will explain the rules of the country in the question.

## Illustration 10 – Capital losses

In country X, capital losses can be set off against capital gains in the same tax year, but unrelieved capital losses cannot be carried back. Unrelieved capital losses may be carried forward and set against capital gains in future years.

Hall and Co had the following taxable gains and losses in year 1 to 4.

| Year | Taxable gain/(loss) |
|------|---------------------|
| 1 | 3,000 |
| 2 | (4,000) |
| 3 | 2,500 |
| 4 | 3,000 |

**What are Hall and Co's taxable gains in each year?**

## Solution

| Year | Capital gain/(loss) | Workings |
|------|---------------------|----------|
| 1 | 3,000 | |
| 2 | – | |
| 3 | – | 2,500 – 2,500 |
| 4 | 1,500 | 3,000 – 1,500 (balance of the loss |

The capital loss **can't** be carried back against year 1, only carried forward against the **first available** capital gain. There is no limit to how many years it can be carried forward for.

## Test your understanding 16 – Loss relief

In country Y, capital losses can be set off against capital gains in the same tax year, but unrelieved capital losses cannot be carried back. Unrelieved capital losses may be carried forward and set against capital gains in future years.

Trading losses in any year can be carried back and set off against profits in the previous year, and any unrelieved losses can be carried forward to set against profits in future years. They cannot be relieved against capital gains.

Robbie and Co had the following trading profits/losses and capital gains/losses in years 1 to 3.

Calculate the taxable gains and profits for all years.

| Year | Capital gain/(loss) | Trading profit/(loss) |
|---|---|---|
| 1 | 4,000 | 27,000 |
| 2 | (6,000) | (30,000) |
| 3 | 9,000 | 16,000 |

 **Rollover relief**

In some countries, gains may be postponed using rollover relief. Rollover relief enables an entity to postpone paying tax on a gain if it reinvests the same proceeds in a replacement asset. The gain is effectively postponed until the replacement asset is sold at some time in the future. For example, an entity sells an asset for $100,000, creating a gain of $10,000. If the entity decides to re-invest the $100,000 proceeds into a replacement asset the $10,000 gain can be deferred in full until the replacement asset is sold.

Some countries may also have rules allowing partial deferral of the gain for partial re-investment. For example the entity sells an asset for $100,000, creating a gain of $10,000. If the entity decides to re-invest $95,000 of the proceeds into a replacement asset the country may have a rule stating the lower of the gain or the proceeds not re-invested should be chargeable immediately and the remainder of the gain to be deferred until the replacement asset is sold. In this scenario the entity has not re-invested $5,000 of the proceeds and has created a gain from the first sale of $10,000. This would mean the entity must pay tax immediately on the $5,000 not re-invested and therefore the remainder of the gain ($10,000 – $5,000) would be deferred until the replacement asset is sold.

Countries which operate this system of relief will have strict rules on the types of assets which will qualify for this type of relief and the time scales in which the replacement asset must be purchased. However, for examination purposes you should assume the gain can be deferred as long a replacement asset is acquired, as detailed rules are not examinable.

**5    Group issues**

A group exists when one entity controls another entity, commonly through acquisition of a certain amount of ordinary shares (>50%). The entity with control is now called the parent company and the entity under control is described as a subsidiary.

From a financial reporting perspective, this topic will be investigated further within the CIMA F2 syllabus. However, from an F1 viewpoint, groups present some taxation issues that must be considered.

When an entity is part of a group we must consider two issues for tax purposes:

1    Group loss relief and

2    appropriations of profit.

### Group loss relief

**Tax consolidation** enables a tax group to be recognised, allowing trading losses to be surrendered between different entities.

It is important to appreciate, each entity will still produce their own individual accounts and will be taxed individually. However, if they are part of a group for tax purposes it may enable them to transfer losses between group members to save tax for the group as a whole.

Some countries enable losses to be surrendered only between resident companies, whilst others allow overseas entities to be included based on profits within that country. Generally, tax groups are different from groups for accounting purposes. There are various restrictions on the transfer of losses – such as, in the UK, where only losses of the current accounting period can be surrendered.

**Capital losses** cannot usually be surrendered between group entities. In the UK, group entities can transfer ownership of an asset to a group entity at nil gain/nil loss. A capital gain or loss only arises when an asset is sold outside the group to a third party. In this way, the entire capital loss group is effectively treated as one entity by the authorities for capital gains tax.

 Group relief may be used to:

- Save tax (the surrendering entity may pay tax at a lower rate that the group entity receiving the loss).

- Enable relief to be gained earlier (the surrendering entity may only be able to carry losses forwards which result in the entity waiting for loss relief).

## Appropriations of profit

Appropriations of profit such as dividends cannot be deducted in arriving at an entity's taxable profits and are therefore taxable in the hands of the entity, i.e. tax relief is not given for the dividend.

The dividend is then distributed to the shareholders who may be taxed on the income as part of their personal tax.

As a result, the dividend is often taxed twice. There are four main systems to deal with this situation:

- Classical system

- Imputation system

- Partial imputation system

- Split rate system

### Corporate tax system V the personal tax system

#### Classical system

The shareholder is treated as independent from the entity. The dividend is taxed twice, firstly as part of the entity's taxable earnings and secondly when received by the shareholder as part of shareholder's personal income.

#### Imputation system

The shareholder receives a tax credit equal to the underlying corporate income tax paid by the entity. In this way, the entity is taxed on the taxable earnings which are used to pay the dividend, whilst the shareholder receives a full credit and hence pays no tax on the dividend income.

#### Partial imputation system

A tax credit is offered to the shareholder but only for part of the underlying corporate income tax paid by the entity on its taxable earnings used to pay the dividend.

#### Split rate system

These systems distinguish between distributed profits and retained profits and charge a lower rate of corporate income tax on distributed profits to avoid the double taxation of dividends.

#### Re-characterising debt

As a general rule interest is tax deductible and dividends are not. It is therefore advantageous from a tax perspective for group entities to transfer funds from one entity to another in the form of interest on inter-company loans rather than dividends.

Many countries have addressed this issue by limiting the amount of interest that is tax deductible. Interest in excess of this value will be classified as a dividend. The rules which govern the amount of interest that is eligible for tax relief in this situation are known as thin capitalisation rules.

## Test your understanding 17 – Practice questions

1 **Explain the meaning of indexation allowance.**

2 An entity has an accounting profit of $100,000 and includes entertaining costs of $10,000 and accounting depreciation of $15,000. The entity operates in a country where these expenses are disallowed for tax purposes but tax depreciation of $9,000 is allowable. **Calculate the taxable profit for the entity.**

3 An entity disposes of an asset for $40,000 which cost $15,000 to purchase plus purchase costs of $2,000. The entity operates in a country where indexation allowance can be claimed amounting to $5,000. **Calculate the chargeable gain on disposal.**

4 **Explain the meaning of chargeable gains and capital taxes.**

5 **Balancing charges increase taxable profits, true or false?**

## Test your understanding 18

ABC is an entity with tax residency in country Z. ABC has an accounting profit for the year ended 31 December 20X2 of $430,000, after charging the following disallowable expenses:

Depreciation $21,000

Amortisation $7,500

ABC are entitled to tax depreciation of $25,500 for the year ended 31 December 20X2.

Tax is charged at 25%

**ABC's tax payable for the year ended 31 December 20X2 is:**

A    $101,125

B    $103,250

C    $106,375

D    $108,250

## Test your understanding 19

Country A has the following tax regulations in force:

- The tax year is 1 May to 30 April

- All corporate profits are taxed at 20%

- Depreciation cannot be charged against taxable income, tax depreciation must be used as alternative.

- Tax depreciation is allowed at the following rates

  - on buildings 5% straight line

  - on all other non-current tangible assets are allowed at 25% reducing balance.

- No tax allowances granted on land or furniture or fittings.

FL commenced trading on 1 May 20X5 when it purchased all its non-current assets.

FL's non-current asset balances were:

| | Cost 1 May 20X5 | Carrying value 1 May 20X7 | Tax written down value 1 May 20X7 |
|---|---|---|---|
| | $ | $ | $ |
| Land | 40,000 | 40,000 | – |
| Buildings | 160,000 | 147,200 | 144,000 |
| Plant and equipment | 42,000 | 2,000 | 23,624 |
| Furniture and fittings | 30,000 | 10,000 | – |

There were no additions of non-current assets between 1 May 20X5 and 30 April 20X7 however on the 2 May 20X7, FL disposed of all its plant and equipment for $10,000 and purchased new plant and equipment for $60,000. The new plant and equipment qualified for a first year tax allowance of 50%.

FL's statement of profit or loss for the year ended 30 April 20X8

| | $ |
|---|---:|
| Gross profit | 420,000 |
| Administrative expenses | (228,000) |
| Gain on disposal of plant and equipment | 8,000 |
| Depreciation – furniture and fittings | (10,000) |
| Depreciation – buildings | (6,400) |
| Depreciation – plant and equipment | (12,000) |
| Distribution costs | (98,000) |
| | 73,600 |
| Finance cost | (14,000) |
| Profit before tax | 59,600 |

Calculate FL's corporate income tax due for the year ended 30 April 20X8.

$_____ (Your answer should be rounded down to the nearest $.)

**Test your understanding 20**

PMX purchased an asset for $300,000 on 1 September 20X4 on which it incurred additional purchase costs of $2,500.

PMX is based in country Z who allow indexation. The relevant index increased by 60% in the period from 1 September 20X4 to 31 August 20Y1.

PMX sold the asset on the 1st of September 20Y1 for $600,000 incurring selling costs of $4,500.

Tax is charged at 25%.

**Assuming all purchase and selling costs are tax allowable, how much tax was due from PMX on the disposal of this asset?**

A     $27,875

B     $28,250

C     $32,125

D     $73,250

### Test your understanding 21

LS, an entity operating in Country N, purchased land on 1 March 20X6 for $2,550,000 incurring purchase costs as follows:

• Surveyor fees $15,000

• Legal fees $24,000

LS spent a further $45,000 clearing the land to make it suitable for development.

Country N's tax regulations classified all of the expenditure as capital expenditure.

On 1 February 20X9 LS sold the land for $3,000,000, incurring tax allowable costs of $18,000. No indexation is allowable on the sale of land.

Tax is charged at a rate of 25%.

Calculate the capital tax payable by LS on the disposal of land.

$_____ (Your answer should be rounded down to the nearest $.)

### Test your understanding 22 – Practice questions

1    **Accounting depreciation is replaced by tax depreciation:**

   A    To reduce the amount of depreciation allowed for tax

   B    To increase the amount of depreciation allowed for tax

   C    To ensure that standard rates of depreciation are used by all organisations for tax purposes

   D    So that government can more easily manipulate the amount of tax organisations pay

2    **Rollover relief allows:**

   A    Deferral of the payment of corporate income tax on gains arising from the disposal of a business asset

   B    Stock values to be rolled over, replacing cost of purchases with current values

   C    Trading losses to be carried forward or rolled over to future periods

   D    Capital losses to be carried forwards or rolled over to future periods

3 **An imputation system of corporate income tax means:**

A    All the underlying corporate income tax on the dividend distribution is passed as a credit to the shareholders

B    The organisation pays corporate income tax on its profits and the shareholder pays income tax on the dividend received

C    Withholding tax paid on dividends is passed as a credit to shareholders

D    A percentage of the underlying tax is passed as credit to shareholders

## 6    Summary diagram

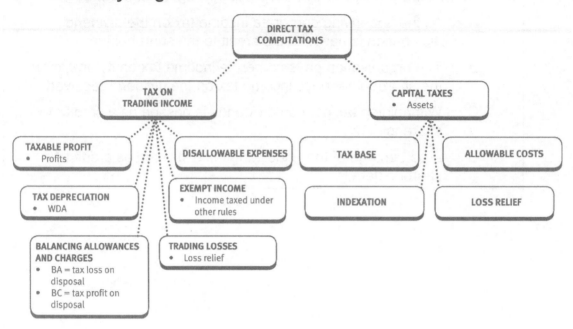

## Test your understanding answers

### Test your understanding 1 – Trading income

|  | $ |
| --- | --- |
| Accounting profit | 80,000 |
| Less: exempt income | (8,000) |
| Add back: disallowable expenses | 5,500 |
| Taxable profit | 77,500 |
| **Tax at 25%** | **19,375** |

### Test your understanding 2 – Trading income

**Plant and machinery**

Accounting depreciation    $1,500    ($10,000 + $5,000 × 10%)

**Building**

Accounting depreciation    $4,000    ($100,000 × 4%)

**Total accounting depreciation = ($1,500 + $4,000) = $5,500**

### Test your understanding 3 – Trading income

**Plant and machinery**

Tax depreciation

TWDV at start of year    $8,000    ($10,000 × 80%)

Tax depreciation at 20%    $1,600

The asset had been purchased in the previous accounting period, therefore tax depreciation has already been claimed for Ye. 31/03/X1. This year's tax depreciation must be calculated on the tax written down value at the beginning of the year, i.e. $8,000.

The new plant and machinery is given 100% FYA which means relief in given on the total cost in the year of purchase of $5,000.

The building tax depreciation of 3% is based on cost of $100,000 = $3,000

**Total tax depreciation = ($1,600 + $5,000 + $3,000) = $9,600**

**Test your understanding 4 – Trading income**

|  | $ |  |
| --- | --- | --- |
| Accounting profit | 60,000 |  |
| Less exempt income | (4,000) |  |
| Add back disallowable expenses | 4,500 |  |
| Add accounting depreciation | 5,500 | (TYU 2) |
| Less tax depreciation | (9,600) | (TYU 3) |
| **Taxable profit** | **56,400** |  |

**Test your understanding 5 – Trading income**

|  | $ |  |
| --- | --- | --- |
| Accounting profit | 60,000 |  |
| Less exempt income | (4,000) |  |
| Add back disallowable expenses | 4,500 |  |
| Add accounting depreciation | 5,500 | (TYU 2) |
| Less tax depreciation | (9,600) | (TYU 3) |
| Taxable profit | 56,400 |  |
| **Tax at 30%** | **16,920** |  |

**Test your understanding 6 – Trading income**

Tax payable is:

($800,000 × 9/12 × 26%) + ($800,000 × 3/12 × 28%) = $212,000

The accounting period runs from 01/07/X0 to 30/06/X1.

9 months of the accounting period profit (01/07/X0 – 31/03/X1) is charged at 26% and 3 months of the accounting period profit (01/04/X1 – 30/06/X1) is charged at 28%.

**Test your understanding 7 – Balancing allowances/charges**

Carrying amount at the date of sale = $10,000 – $2,000 = $8,000

Accounting depreciation ($10,000 × 10% × 2 years) = $2,000

**Total accounting loss = (proceeds $6,000 – CA $8,000) = $2,000**

## Test your understanding 8 – Balancing allowances/charges

Plant and machinery

| | | |
|---|---|---|
| Tax depreciation in year 1 | $2,000 | ($10,000 × 20%) |
| TWDV at start of year 2 | $8,000 | ($10,000 × 80%) |
| Tax depreciation at 20% | $1,600 | |

The total tax depreciation = $2,000 + $1,600 = $3,600.

Tax written down value at the date of sale = $10,000 – $3,600 = $6,400

**Total tax loss = (proceeds $6,000 – TWDV $6,400) = $400**

**This $400 would be classed as a balancing allowance**

## Test your understanding 9 – Balancing allowances/charges

| | $ | |
|---|---|---|
| Accounting profit | 50,000 | |
| Add accounting loss | 2,000 | (TYU 7) |
| Less tax loss (BA) | (400) | (TYU 8) |
| | | |
| Taxable profit | 51,600 | |
| **Tax at 25%** | **12,900** | |

## Test your understanding 10 – Balancing allowances/charges

| | $ | |
|---|---|---|
| Accounting profit | 50,000 | |
| Less accounting profit | (1,000) | (W1) |
| Add tax profit (BC) | 2,600 | (W2) |
| | | |
| Taxable profit | 51,600 | |
| **Tax at 25%** | **12,900** | |

(W1)

Carrying amount at the date of sale = $10,000 – $2,000 = $8,000

Accounting depreciation ($10,000 × 10% × 2 years) = $2,000

**Total accounting profit = (proceeds $9,000 – CA $8,000) = $1,000**

(W2)

| | | |
|---|---|---|
| Tax depreciation in year 1 | $2,000 | ($10,000 × 20%) |
| TWDV at start of year 2 | $8,000 | ($10,000 × 80%) |
| Tax depreciation at 20% | $1,600 | |

The total tax depreciation = $2,000 + $1,600 = $3,600.

Tax written down value at the date of sale = $10,000 − $3,600 = $6,400

**Total tax profit = (proceeds $9,000 − TWDV $6,400) = $2,600**

**This $2,600 would be classed as a balancing charge**

## Test your understanding 11 – Trading losses

| Year | Trading profit/(loss) | Workings |
|---|---|---|
| 1 | – | 20,000 – 20,000 |
| 2 | – | |
| 3 | – | 19,000 – 19,000 |
| 4 | 19,000 | 25,000 – 6,000 (balance of the loss) |

The trading loss is carried back first against the trading profit in year 1, this must be done to the maximum extent, i.e. you cannot use part of the profit for relief if all of it is needed. The balance of the loss must then be carried forward against the **first available trading profit** in year 3, again to the maximum extent and this means year 4 will be reduced by the remainder of the loss $6,000, i.e. ($45,000 − $20,000 − $19,000). Year 4 will therefore have trading profits of $19,000 ($25,000 − $6,000).

## Test your understanding 12 – Cessation losses

| | 20X1 | 20X2 | 20X3 |
|---|---|---|---|
| | $ | $ | $ |
| Trading profits | 100,000 | 50,000 | – |
| Loss relief | (10,000) | (50,000) | – |
| | | | |
| **Revised trading profits** | 90,000 | – | – |

On cessation, trading losses must be carried back on a LIFO basis, i.e. most recent trading profits are used first. When you carry back make sure you relieve the loss against the profit to the maximum possible extent in the year, you can't use part of it.

If the loss has been carried back as far as possible, (years dependent on the rule for that country), and still not fully relieved, then the remainder of the loss would be wasted.

### Test your understanding 13 – Capital taxes

|  |  | $ |
|---|---|---|
| Sale proceeds |  | 150,000 |
| Less: cost to sell |  | (2,000) |
|  |  | ———— |
| Net proceeds |  | 148,000 |
| Cost to purchase | 50,000 |  |
| Cost to buy | 1,500 |  |
| Enhancements | 12,000 | (63,500) |
|  | ———— | ———— |
| **Chargeable gain** |  | **84,500** |

NB: Roof repairs are not an allowable cost for deduction, i.e. they are not a "new" capital cost or a cost to buy/sell. They are a cost to replace an existing structure.

### Test your understanding 14 – Capital taxes

The indexation allowance would be as follows:

($50,000 + $1,500) × 30% = $15,450

12,000 × 20% = $2,400

**Total allowance = $15,450 + $2,400 = $17,850**

The allowance is given based on the movement in the RPI between the purchase date and the disposal date to give relief for inflation.

## Test your understanding 15 – Capital taxes

|  |  | $ |
|---|---:|---:|
| Sale proceeds |  | 150,000 |
| Less: cost to sell |  | (2,000) |
|  |  | ———— |
| Net proceeds |  | 148,000 |
| Cost to purchase | 50,000 |  |
| Cost to buy | 1,500 |  |
| Enhancements | 12,000 | (63,500) |
|  | ———— | ———— |
|  |  | 84,500 |
| Less: Indexation allowance |  |  |
| ($50,000 + $1,500) × 30% | (15,450) |  |
| 12,000 × 20% | (2,400) | (17,850) |
|  |  | ———— |
| Chargeable gain |  | 66,650 |

**Capital tax = $66,650 × 30% = $19,995**

## Test your understanding 16 – Loss relief

| Year | Capital gain/(loss) | Trading profit/(loss) |
|:---:|:---:|:---:|
| 1 | 4,000 | – |
| 2 | – | – |
| 3 | 3,000 | 13,000 |

The capital loss **cannot** be carried back against year 1, only carried forward against the **first available** capital gain. It will be used against the gain in year 3 to reduce it to $3,000 ($9,000 – $6,000).

The trading loss is carried back first against year 1 to reduce the profit to nil. The remainder of the loss of $3,000 ($30,000 – $27,000) is carried forward against year 3 to reduce the profit to $13,000 ($16,000 – $3,000).

**Test your understanding 17 – Practice questions**

1    Indexation allowance is a relief given on the disposal of capital assets. The relief is based on e.g. the movement in the Retail Price Iindex between the date costs were incurred on the asset and the disposal date and represents relief for inflation. The indexation allowance will reduce the amount of gain charged for tax purposes.

2    Taxable profit = $100,000 + $10,000 + $15,000 – $9,000 = $116,000

3    Chargeable gain = $40,000 – $15,000 – $2,000 – $5,000 = $18,000

4    Chargeable gains are created when assets are sold at a profit. They are calculated based on the difference between proceeds and allowable costs. Capital taxes represent the tax charged on the chargeable gains.

5    True. Balancing charges represent the tax profit on disposal of an asset for corporate tax purposes. They are calculated on the difference between proceeds and tax written down value. The balancing charge will increase the taxable profits.

 **Test your understanding 18**

**D**

|  | $ |
|---|---|
| Accounting profit | 430,000 |
| Add depreciation | 21,000 |
| Add amortisation | 7,500 |
|  | 458,500 |
| less tax depreciation | (25,500) |
|  | 433,000 |
| Taxable profit | 433,000 |
| Tax @ 25% | 108,250 |

## Test your understanding 19

The answer is $5,675

FL – Corporate income tax

| | $ |
|---|---:|
| Profit for the year | 59,600 |
| Add back: | |
| Depreciation – buildings | 6,400 |
| Depreciation – plant and equipment | 12,000 |
| Depreciation – furniture and fittings | 10,000 |
| Less: Accounting gain on disposal | (8,000) |
| | 80,000 |
| Less: Tax depreciation | |
| FYA – Plant and equipment ($60,000 × 50%) | (30,000) |
| Buildings ($160,000 × 5%) | (8,000) |
| Disposal balancing allowance | (13,624) |
| (Proceeds $10,000 – TWDV $23,624) | |
| | 28,376 |
| Tax at 20% | 5,675 |

## Test your understanding 20

**A**

| | $ |
|---|---:|
| Disposal proceeds | 600,000 |
| Selling costs | (4,500) |
| Net proceeds | 595,500 |
| Cost | (300,000) |
| Additional costs | (2,500) |
| | 293,000 |
| Indexation ($302,500 × 60%) | (181,500) |
| Taxable gain | 111,500 |
| Tax @ 25% | 27,875 |

**Test your understanding 21**

**The answer is $87,000**

|  | $ | $ |
|---|---|---|
| Disposal proceeds |  | 3,000,000 |
| Less: Costs of disposal |  | (18,000) |
|  |  | 2,982,000 |
| Acquisition costs: |  |  |
| Purchase cost | 2,550,000 |  |
| Costs arising on purchase ($15,000 + $24,000) | 39,000 |  |
| Clearing land costs | 45,000 |  |
|  |  | (2,634,000) |
| Taxable gain |  | 348,000 |
| Tax @ 25% |  | 87,000 |

**Test your understanding 22 – Practice questions**

1  C – To ensure that standard rates of depreciation are used by all organisations for tax purposes.

2  A – Deferral of the payment of corporate income tax on gains arising from the disposal of a business asset.

3  A – All the underlying corporate income tax on the dividend distribution is passed as a credit to the shareholders.

# International Taxation

## Chapter learning objectives

**Lead**

C3. Explain some relevant issues that affect taxation

**Component outcome**

Explain:

a. Taxes across international borders

b. Ethics of taxation

# 1    Session content

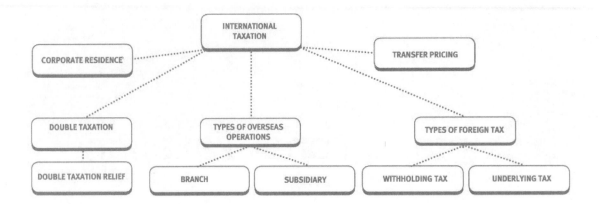

# 2    International taxation

### Tax in a digital world

Business are transforming as a result of the developments created by technological innovation. Retailers allow customers to place orders online, logistics companies can track parcels across the globe, education companies offer on-line courses enabling students to attend courses simultaneously despite being located within different continents, music and entertainment companies offer streaming services via monthly subscriptions.

As businesses utilise these new found opportunities offered by the digital economy, new tax issues and problems arise. Examples include:

–    which tax jurisdiction should entities pay tax in?

–    what happens when these companies are taxed in multiple countries?

Similar tax problems have always existed for multi-national companies, but the use of technology has increased the regularity of occurrence of these issues – it is no longer solely an issue for large companies.

Tax regulators are having to consider new ways of ensuring tax is fairly charged on the income earned by companies within the digital economy.

### Corporate residence

Entities normally pay taxation on their worldwide income in the country they are deemed to be resident in.

An enterprise is deemed to be resident for tax purposes either in the place of incorporation or place of control/central management.

Generally an entity will be treated as being resident in the country of control, i.e. place where the head office is located or board meetings held.

The generation of revenues from online activity increases the complication of determining the corporate residence of an entity. If income is generated online from various countries, is it correct to have a corporate residence based on the location of an entity's head office?

This can create ethical issues for directors operating within the digital economy. Should they establish residence in the areas where they earn most of their profits or should they seek residency in low tax rate tax havens simply to avoid taxes?

## Double taxation

An entity may end up being taxed in more than one country, this is called double taxation.

For example, an entity may earn income in country X, despite being located in country Y.

Double taxation may arise if that income is taxed in the country where it was earned (X) as well as the country where the entity is resident (Y). Double taxation relief is often available in this situation.

## Double taxation relief

There are three main methods of giving double taxation relief:

1   Exemption – The countries agree on certain types of income which will be exempt or partially exempt in one country or the other.

2   Tax credit – Tax paid in one country may be allowed as a tax credit in another country. Relief is normally restricted to the lower of the foreign or country of residency tax.

3   Deduction – Tax relief is gained by deducting the foreign tax from the foreign income so that only the "net" amount will be subject to tax in the country of residency.

## Types of overseas operations

An overseas operation can be run as a branch or a subsidiary.

### Subsidiary (see chapter 2 section 4)

The features of operating as a subsidiary are:

- The overseas subsidiary is a separate entity for tax purposes. The holding company will only pay tax on any dividends received from the subsidiary.

- Loss relief is not available for the group because the overseas subsidiary will be paying tax under a different tax regime.

- The overseas subsidiary cannot claim the same tax depreciation as the parent on any assets, although may receive an alternative type of tax depreciation or the equivalent in the overseas country. Assets transferred from the parent may also result in a capital gains tax liability.

### Branch

The features of operating as a branch are:

- The branch is treated as an extension of the activity and all profits from it will be subject to local taxation.

- Loss relief is available for the group.

- Assets can be transferred between the branch and holding company at no gain/no loss.

- The branch can claim tax depreciation on all assets.

## Types of foreign tax

### Withholding tax

Some countries will deduct tax at source on items such as interest, royalties, rent, dividends and capital gains. The net income (gross payment less tax) is then received by the beneficiary in the foreign country.

### Underlying tax

When an entity pays out a dividend, it is done so out of post-tax profits. Therefore, the amount of profit distributed as a dividend will have already suffered tax on profits.

If an entity receives a dividend from an overseas subsidiary, the dividend will have been taxed once in the overseas country as part of normal tax on profits, and then again in the country of receipt, as income on dividends. This tax is known as underlying tax.

This is calculated as follows:

$$\frac{\text{Tax on profits}}{\text{Profit after tax}} \times \text{Gross dividend}$$

Both withholding and underlying tax may be reduced by various methods of double tax relief. Methods of double tax relief include exemption, tax credits for foreign tax suffered, and deduction of foreign tax from tax due in the home country.

 You will not be assessed on the calculation of foreign taxation but you should have a general appreciation what it represents.

The following examples are shown for illustrative purposes only and the student will not be required to answer this type of question in their assessment.

## Illustration 1 – International taxation

Homely is a UK entity and owns 100% of the shares in a foreign entity called Faraway.

During the year Faraway earned the following income:

| | |
|---|---|
| Profit before tax | $200,000 |
| Income tax | $(40,000) |
| Profit after tax | $160,000 |

Faraway pays a dividend of $80,000 out of profit after tax to Homely. This dividend is subject to 15% withholding tax.

**What is the total foreign tax suffered on the dividend?**

## Solution

| | $ |
|---|---|
| Withholding tax | |
| $80,000 × 15% | 12,000 |
| Underlying tax | |
| ($40,000/$160,000) × $80,000 | 20,000 |
| | ──── |
| **Total foreign tax** | **32,000** |

This means:

The dividend distributed by Faraway was $80,000.

The foreign country deducted withholding tax of $12,000 and, therefore, the shareholder would only receive $68,000 in cash.

The profits in Faraway were taxed before the $80,000 was distributed. Therefore, the underlying tax is the amount of tax the dividend has already suffered prior to distribution when it was taxed as a profit.

## Illustration 2 – Double tax relief

Use the information from the previous illustration:

**A tax treaty exists between the two countries using the tax credit method, calculate the tax payable in the UK (Homely's country of residence) assuming a tax rate of 40%.**

## Solution

| | $ |
|---|---:|
| Net dividend received | 68,000 |
| Add back WHT | 12,000 |
| | |
| | 80,000 |
| Add back UT | 20,000 |
| | |
| **Gross dividend** | 100,000 |
| **Total foreign tax** ($100,000 – $68,000) | **32,000** |
| **Tax in UK** | |
| Tax at 40% | 40,000 |
| Less DTR (lower of foreign and UK tax) | (32,000) |
| | |
| Tax paid in UK | 8,000 |

## Test your understanding 1 – International taxation

Britas is a UK entity and owns 80% of the shares in a foreign entity called Cheers.

During the year, Cheers earned the following income:

| | |
|---|---:|
| Profit before tax | $372,000 |
| Income tax | $(62,000) |
| | |
| Profit after tax | $310,000 |

Cheers pays a total dividend of $100,000 out of profit after tax to its shareholders. This dividend is subject to 5% withholding tax.

**Calculate the total foreign tax suffered on the dividend and show how double tax relief would apply in the UK using the tax credit method, assuming a rate of 40% tax is charge.**

## OECD model tax convention

The OECD model addresses the issues of double residency.

This model states that business profits of an enterprise will only be taxable in a state if an enterprise has a permanent establishment in that country. A permanent establishment could include the following:

1    A factory

2    A workshop

3    An office

4    A branch

5    A place of management

6    A mine, an oil or gas well, or a place of extraction of natural resources

7    A construction project or building site if it lasts more than 12 months

If an entity has a permanent establishment in a country, it can be taxed in that country, causing a possible problem of double taxation.

 Where an entity is deemed to have residency in several countries, the OECD model suggests that the entity is resident in the country of its effective management.

## Transfer pricing

Transfer pricing applies to group situations when either goods are sold inter-company at a favourable price or loans are made on favourable terms. Therefore, this results in transactions not taking place at "arm's length" and profits of the group are distorted.

These transactions may arise as an attempt to avoid tax. An overseas entity may be attempting to move profits to another country at a lower tax rate.

This could damage public perception of the group. Entities may be criticised for not paying their fair share of tax.

The rules for transfer pricing are as follows:

1    Goods and services – An adjustment will be made in the corporate tax computation for the entity gaining the tax advantage to reflect profit that would have been achieved if the transaction had been arms-length.

2    Provision of loan finance – If the amount of loan finance provided to a connected company exceeds the amount a third party would be willing to provide, the loan is not at arms-length (it is not at normal commercial terms). This is referred to as thin capitalisation.

Any interest charged on this excess is not allowable for tax purposes and will therefore be disallowed.

### Test your understanding 2

Aston sells to Marvin, a group entity, 5,000 units at $1.50 each. The market value was $3 per each.

**Explain the effect of the transfer pricing legislation on this transaction.**

### Test your understanding 3

1   **Which of the following could NOT be used to indicate an enterprise is resident in a country?**

    A    Country in which directors' meetings are held

    B    Country of incorporation

    C    Country in which control and management is exercised

    D    Country in which goods are sold.

2   **In no more than 30 words, define the meaning of an overseas subsidiary.**

3   **Which of the following would not be subject to a withholding tax?**

    A    Profits of the enterprise

    B    Rental profits

    C    Equity dividends

    D    Interest received from finance companies

4   A double taxation treaty between two countries usually allows relief of foreign tax through a number of methods.

    **Which one of the following is not a method of relieving foreign tax?**

    A    Deduction based on lower tax

    B    Exemption from corporate tax in one country

    C    Tax Credits (deduction from tax liability)

    D    Loss relief

5   Permanent establishment is defined under the OECD model in several ways.

**Which of the following would not be classed as a 'permanent establishment'?**

A   An office

B   An agent with authority to enter into contracts

C   A workshop

D   A warehouse used for storage

---

### Test your understanding 4 – Practice questions

1   **The following details relate to EA:**

- Incorporated in Country A

- Carries out its main business activities in Country B

- Its senior management operate from Country C and effective control is exercised from Country C

- Assume countries A, B and C have all signed double tax treaties with each other, based on the OECD model tax convention.

**Which country will EA be deemed to be resident in for tax purposes?**

A   Country A

B   Country B

C   Country C

D   Both countries B and C

2   **Explain the meaning of withholding and underlying tax.**

## 3 Summary diagram

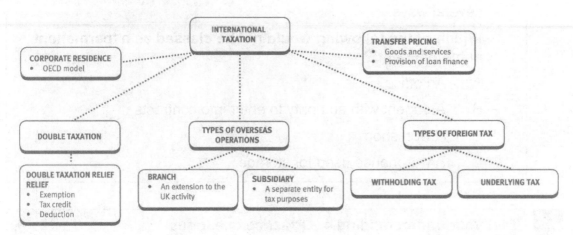

# Test your understanding answers

## Test your understanding 1 – International taxation

|  | $ |
|---|---|
| Net dividend received | 76,000 |
| WHT 5% | 4,000 |
|  | ——— |
| ($100,000 × 80%) | 80,000 |
| UT – $80,000 × (62/310) | 16,000 |
|  | ——— |
| **Gross dividend** | 96,000 |
| **Total foreign tax ($96,000 – $76,000)** | **20,000** |
| **Tax in UK** |  |
| Tax at 40% on gross dividend $96,000 | 38,400 |
| Less DTR (lower of foreign and UK tax) | (20,000) |
|  | ——— |
| Tax paid in UK | 18,400 |

## Test your understanding 2

Aston must increase its taxable profits by $7,500 ($1.50 × 5,000 units).

The taxable profits must reflect the sale at market value, i.e. arm's length price of $3 per unit.

## Test your understanding 3

1   D – The correct answer is country in which goods are sold.

2   An overseas subsidiary is an enterprise resident for tax purposes in a foreign country whose share capital is owned by an entity resident in another country.

3   A – Profits of the enterprise.

4   D – Loss relief.

5   D – A warehouse used for storage.

## Test your understanding 4 – Practice questions

1   C – Country C. An entity is considered to be resident in the country of effective management.

2   Withholding tax is a tax deducted at source from a payment before it is made to the recipient. Underlying tax is the tax on the profits out of which a dividend is paid.

# 4

# The Regulatory Environment

## Chapter learning objectives

| Lead | Component outcome |
|------|-------------------|
| A1. Identify regulators and describe their role | a. Identify the major regulators |
| | b. Describe what they do |
| | c. Explain why they regulate financial reporting |

# 1　Session content

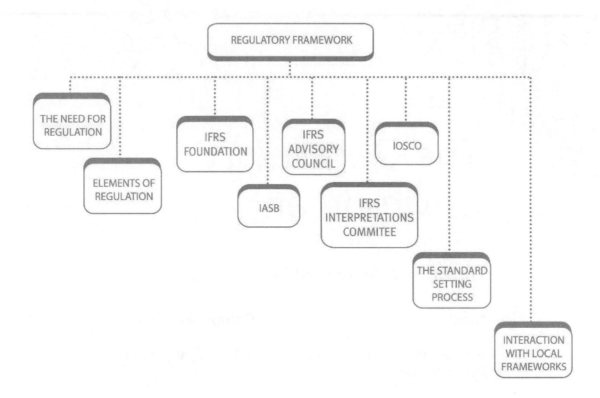

# 2　The regulatory environment

## Need for regulation

Financial statements will be used by shareholders and many other types of users to make decisions. In order that they can be relied upon by users, published financial statements should be subject to regulation.

Regulation can also promote consistency and comparability, so assisting users when interpreting financial statements.

Different countries will be subject to a variety of economic, social and political factors. As a result, the way in which published financial statements are regulated will vary from country to country.

**The need for regulation**

Financial statements and reports for shareholders and other users are prepared using principles and rules that can be interpreted in different ways. To provide guidance and try and ensure that they are interpreted in the same way each time, some form of regulation is required.

We have identified that taxable profits are based on accounting profit and that the number and type of adjustments required to compute taxable profits varies from country to country. Part of this variation was due to the differences in the tax regulations, but part of it was also due to the different approaches to the calculation of accounting profit. We have identified that in some countries taxable income is closely linked to the accounting profit and that accounting rules are largely driven by taxation laws. These countries are usually known as code law countries, countries where the legal system originated in Roman law. These countries tend to have detailed laws relating to trading entities and accounting standards are usually embodied within the law. Accounting regulation in these countries is usually in the hands of the government and financial reporting is a matter of complying with a set of legal rules.

In other countries the common law system is used, common law is based on case law and tends to have less detailed regulations. In countries with common law systems, the accounting regulation within the legal system is usually kept to a minimum, with detailed accounting regulations produced by professional organisations or other private sector accounting standard-setting bodies.

Whichever system is adopted, there is a need for every country to have a system for regulating the preparation of financial statements and reports.

## 3 Elements of a regulatory environment

A regulatory environment may consist of any of the following elements:

- local law;
- local accounting standards;
- international accounting standards;
- conceptual frameworks e.g. Statement of Principles in the UK;
- requirements of international bodies e.g. EU, IOSCO.

GAAP (Generally accepted accounting practice) encompasses the conventions, the rules and procedures necessary to define accepted accounting practice at a particular time. It includes not only broad guidelines of general application but also detailed practices and procedures. It includes local legislation requirements, accounting standards and any other local regulations. This will therefore vary from country to country as different countries have different regulations, i.e. UK GAAP, US GAAP

## The regulatory environment

The regulatory environment for accounting in individual countries will be affected by a number of legislative and quasi-legislative influences:

- national company law

- EU directives or other trading body directives

- security exchange rules.

### Why is regulation necessary

Regulation of accounting information is aimed at ensuring that users of financial statements receive a minimum amount of information that will enable them to make meaningful decisions regarding their interest in a reporting entity. A regulation is required to ensure that relevant and reliable financial reporting is achieved to meet the needs of shareholders and other users.

Accounting standards on their own would not provide complete regulation. In order to fully regulate the preparation of financial statements and the obligations of companies and directors, legal and market regulations are also required.

### Principles-based and rules-based approaches for accounting standards

Principles-based approach:

- based upon a conceptual framework such as the IASB's Framework®

- accounting standards are set on the basis of the conceptual framework.

Rules-based approach:

- 'Cookbook' approach

- accounting standards are a set of rules which companies must follow.

In the UK there is a principles-based approach in terms of the Statement of Principles and accounting standards and a rules-based approach in terms of the Companies Acts, EU directives and stock exchange rulings.

## Variation from country to country

Accounting and information disclosure practices around the world are influenced by a variety of economic, social and political factors. In addition to the legal system and tax legislation, a range of other factors that contribute to variations between the accounting regulations of countries are discussed below. The wide range of factors influencing the development of accounting regulations have resulted in a wide range of different systems, which has made it difficult and time-consuming to try and harmonise accounting practices around the world. With the growth in international investing, there is a growing need for harmonisation of financial statements between countries.

### Sources of finance and capital markets

There is more demand for financial information and disclosure where a higher proportion of capital is raised from external shareholders, rather than from banks or family members. Stock markets rely on published financial information by entities. Banks and family members are usually in a position to demand information directly from the entity, whereas shareholders have to rely on publicly available information.

### The political system

The nature of regulation and control exerted on accounting will reflect political philosophies and objectives of the ruling party, for example, environmental concerns.

### Entity ownership

The need for public accountability and disclosure will be greater where there is a broad ownership of shares as opposed to family ownership or government ownership.

### Cultural differences

The culture within a country can influence societal and national values which can influence accounting regulations.

### Harmonisation versus standardisation

Harmonisation tends to mean the process of increasing the compatibility of accounting practices by setting bounds to their degree of variation.

Standardisation tends to imply the imposition of a rigid and narrower set of rules. Standardisation also implies that one technically correct method can be identified for every aspect of accounting and then this can be imposed on all preparers of accounts.

Due to the variations between countries discussed above, full standardisation of accounting practices is unlikely. Harmonisation is more likely, as the agreement of a common conceptual framework of accounting may enable a closer harmonisation of accounting practices.

**The need for harmonisation of accounting standards**

Each country has its own accounting regulation, financial statements and reports prepared for shareholders and other uses are based on principles and rules that can vary widely from country to country. Multinational entities may have to prepare reports on activities on several bases for use in different countries, and this can cause unnecessary financial costs. Furthermore, preparation of financial statements based on different principles makes it difficult for investors and analysts to interpret and compare financial information. This lack of comparability in financial reporting can affect the credibility of the entity's reporting and the analysts' reports and can have a detrimental effect on financial investment. As a result, the number of companies using IFRS's is multiplying rapidly. The ability to use the same accounting rules removes the many of the problems caused by a lack of comparability between entities.

The increasing levels of cross-border financing transactions, securities trading and direct foreign investment has resulted in the need for a single set of rules by which assets, liabilities, expenses and income are recognised and measured.

The number of foreign listings on major exchanges around the world is continually increasing and many worldwide entities may find that they are preparing accounts using a number of different rules and regulations in order to be listed on various markets.

## 4 International financial reporting standards

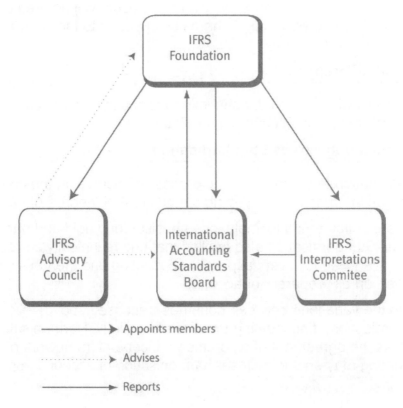

## IFRS Foundation

The IFRS Foundation was established in March 2001, after it was decided to restructure the IASC into two main bodies: the Trustees and the IASB (see below). The IFRS Foundation is a non-profit making body with a number of trustees'. The trustees are responsible for:

- appointing the members of the IASB, the International Financial Reporting Interpretations Committee and IFRS Advisory Council;

- reviewing annually the strategy of the IASB and its effectiveness;

- approving annually the budget and determining the funding of the IASB;

- reviewing broad strategic issues affecting accounting standards;

- promoting the IASB and its work and the rigorous application of IASs;

- establishing and amending operating procedures for the IASB, IFRS Interpretations Committee and IFRS Advisory Council.

## International Accounting Standards Board (IASB)

The IASB consists of a number of members and is responsible for developing international accounting standards, now referred to as International Financial Reporting Standards (IFRS Standards).

All members are appointed for a term of 5 years, renewable once.

The IASB has complete responsibility for all IASB technical matters, including the preparation and publication of IFRS Standards, Exposure Drafts, withdrawal of IFRS Standards and final interpretations by the IFRS Interpretations Committee.

The IASB have also adopted all IASs that were previously issued by the IASC.

## IFRS Advisory Council

The IFRS Advisory Council has approximately 30 members and provides a forum for organisations and individuals to participate in the standard setting process. The members are appointed by the trustees from various backgrounds, for a renewable term of 3 years and meet three times a year.

The objectives of the IFRS Advisory Council are:

- to give advice to the IASB on agenda decisions and priorities in its work;

- to inform the IASB of the views of organisations and individuals on the Council on major standard setting projects;

- to give other advice to the Board or to the Trustees.

## IFRS Interpretations Committee

The IFRS Interpretations Committee (formally known as IFRIC), assists the IASB by reviewing accounting issues that are likely to receive divergent or unacceptable treatment in the absence of authoritative guidance, with a view to reaching an appropriate accounting treatment. It was established in 2002 by the IFRS Foundation to replace the Standing Interpretations Committee (SIC)®. Previously SIC Interpretations were issued, now IFRS Interpretation Committee Interpretations are issued.

The IFRS Interpretations Committee has two main responsibilities:

- Review, on a timely basis, new financial reporting issues not specifically addressed in IFRSs.

- Clarify issues where unsatisfactory or conflicting interpretations have developed, with a view to reaching a consensus on the most appropriate treatment.

## International Organisation of Securities Commissions (IOSCO)

IOSCO is the representative body of the world's securities markets regulators.

Financial information is vital to the operation of markets and differences in the financial information from entities in different countries can reduce the efficiency of markets.

IOSCO has been working with the IASB since 1987 in promoting the improvement of International Standards. Since the mid-1990s IOSCO and IASB have been working on a programme of 'core standards' which could be used by listed companies who offer securities abroad. This project was completed in 1999.

In May 2000, IOSCO issued a report to its members recommending that they use International Financial Reporting Standards when preparing their financial statements.

IOSCO representatives also sit as observers on the IFRS Interpretations Committee.

## The international integrated reporting council (IIRC)

The IIRC is a coalition behind the introduction of Integrated Reports <IR>. Integrated reporting promotes reporting on an entity's ability to create value. It considers the needs of a variety of stakeholders and enables an entity to disclose details regarding all aspects of value creation, e.g. staff skills sets, staff morale, intellectual property and reputation. <IR> do not include merely financial information and results (like the financial statements).

The Integrated report and the IIRC are considered in greater depth within the CIMA F2 syllabus.

## 5 Standard-setting process

There is no strict procedure for the development of an IFRS standard. However, the process may involve the following steps:

- Establishment of an advisory committee to give advice on the issues arising on the project. The IASB will consult with this committee and IFRS Advisory Committee throughout the process.

- On major projects, the IASB develops and publishes a Discussion Paper for public comment. This will give an overview of the issue, possible approaches to address the issue, views of the authors or the IASB and an invitation to comment.

- Following the receipt and review of comments, an Exposure Draft is produced for public comment. The Exposure Draft is based upon the earlier Discussion Paper, together with the IASB review of feedback received from the public – i.e. mainly firms of accountants and companies who are likely to be affected by the introduction of a new or changed reporting standard.

    The Exposure Draft is therefore the draft reporting standard made available for final review, which can still be amended before final approval as a reporting standard.

- Following the receipt and review of comments, the approved IFRS will be published, including a date from which it will become effective.

 **The role of national standard setters**

- The harmonisation process has gathered pace in the last few years. From 2005 all European listed entities were required to adopt IFRS in their group financial statements. Many other countries including Australia, Canada and New Zealand decided to follow a similar process. National standard setters are committed to a framework of accounting standards based on IFRS.

- Additionally, the US are committed to harmonise with IFRS and the US's Financial Accounting Standard Board (FASB) and the IASB are aiming for convergence over the next few years.

- The overall impact of the above is that the trend towards closer international harmonisation of accounting practices is now set. It will become increasingly difficult for domestic standard setters to justify domestic standards at odds with IFRSs.

**The role of accounting standard setters and the IASB**

- In February 2005, the IASB issued a memorandum setting out the responsibilities of the IASB and national standard setters. It is most relevant to those who have adopted or converged with IFRSs'. It deals with the responsibilities of national standard setters to facilitate adoption or convergence with IFRS.

- It includes the responsibilities of the IASB to ensure that it makes information available on a timely basis so that national standard setters can be informed of the IASB's plans. Sufficient time should be allowed in relation to consultative documents so that national standard setters have adequate time to prepare the information in their own context and to receive comments from their own users.

- The national standard setters should deal with domestic barriers to adopting or converging with IFRS. They should avoid amending an IFRS when adopting it in their own jurisdiction, so that the issue of noncompliance with the IFRS does not arise. They should encourage their own constituents to communicate their technical views to the IASB and they themselves should respond with comments on a timely basis. They should also make known any differences of opinion that they have with a project as early as possible in the process.

## 6 Interaction with local frameworks

The IASB invites comments from national standard-setters on Exposure Drafts. This enables local standard-setters to contribute to the development of IFRS, as well as encouraging application of IFRSs by companies within these localities. If IFRSs are similar to national standards, this will make it easier for entities to adopt them.

The IFRS advisory council also consults national standard-setters and co-ordinate the agendas and priorities of the IASB and national standard-setters.

Some countries will adopt IFRS Standards as their local accounting standards, or will be heavily influenced by IFRS Standards when preparing local standards. This may particularly be the case in countries without a strong and independent accountancy profession.

A country choosing to adopt international standards can apply them in a number of ways:

- Adoption of international standards as local GAAP – This is usually in countries where the accounting profession isn't well developed and they adopt the international standards with little or no amendments. This is quick to implement but does not take into account any specific requirements of that country.

- International standards used as a model to create local GAAP – This involves countries taking the international standards and then amending them to reflect that countries' needs.

- International standards used as persuasive influence in preparing local GAAP – This is where a country already has its own standards but they may differ to the IFRS standards. They will use the IFRS Standards to update their local standards to ensure that they comply with IFRS Standards in all material aspects.

Alternatively a country may choose to prepare local GAAP with no reference to international standards!

### Test your understanding 1 – Setting standards

Yozz is a small developing country which currently has no accounting standards and in which a new professional accounting body was recently created.

Yozz's government has asked the new professional accounting body to prepare a report setting out the country's options for developing and implementing a set of high quality financial reporting standards.

**Required:**

As an advisor to the professional accounting body, outline THREE options open to Yozz for the development of financial reporting standards. Identify any advantages or disadvantages for each option.

### Test your understanding 2 – Roles

The existing procedures for setting international accounting standards are now well established.

**Required:**

Explain the roles of the following in relation to the regulatory environment to develop and publish IFRS Standards:

- The IFRS Foundation;

- The International Accounting Standards Board (IASB);

- The IFRS Interpretations Committee.

### Test your understanding 3 – The development of a standard

Explain how the standard-setting authority approaches the task of producing a new financial reporting standard, with particular reference to the ways in which comment or feedback from interested parties is obtained.

## Test your understanding 4

1    **Under the current structure of regulatory bodies, which of the bodies listed below acts as the overall supervisory body?**

A    IFRS Interpretations Committee

B    International Accounting Standards Board

C    IFRS Advisory Council

D    IFRS Foundation

2    **Which of the bodies listed below is responsible for reviewing IFRS Standards and issuing guidance on their application?**

A    IFRS Interpretations Committee

B    International Accounting Standards Board

C    IFRS Advisory Council

D    IFRS Foundation

3    **Which of the bodies listed below is responsible for issuing IFRS Standards?**

A    IFRS Interpretations Committee

B    International Accounting Standards Board

C    IFRS Advisory Council

D    IFRS Foundation

4    **Which of the bodies listed below is responsible for the approval of IFRS Interpretations?**

A    IFRS Interpretations Committee

B    International Accounting Standards Board

C    IFRS Advisory Council

D    IFRS Foundation

5    **Which of the following best describes the role of the IFRS Advisory Council?**

A    To prepare interpretations of International Accounting Standards

B    To provide the IASB with the views of its' members on standard setting projects

C    To promote the use of International Accounting Standards amongst its members

D    To select the members of the IASB

# 7    Summary diagram

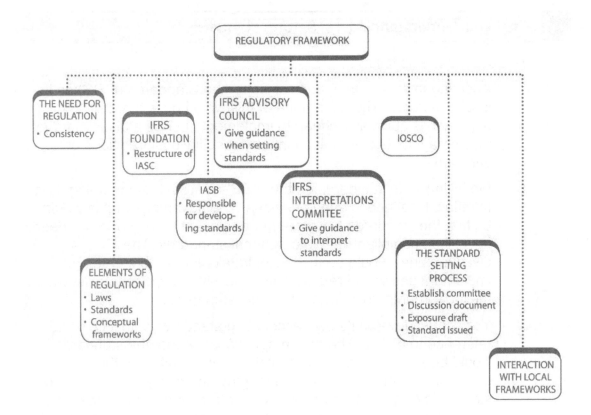

## Test your understanding answers

**Test your understanding 1 – Setting standards**

The options are as follows:

1    Adopting International Financial Reporting Standards (IFRS) as its local standards. The advantage of this would be is that this approach is quick and cheap to implement but has a disadvantage that it may not take into account any specific local traditions or variations.

2    Modelling local standards on the IASB's IFRSs, but amending them to reflect local needs and conditions. The advantage of this would be that the standards would be more relevant to the country's needs but still be compliant with international standards. The disadvantages would be that it would take longer to create and implement and would require someone with expertise to exist within the local country to help create these standards.

3    Yozz could develop its own accounting standards with little or no reference to IFRSs. The advantage would be that the standards would be specific to the needs of the country but have the disadvantage that they could be lengthy and costly to create. The standards may not be compliant with international standards and also require a person in Yozz with the appropriate expertise to help create these standards.

## Test your understanding 2 – Roles

### The IFRS Foundation

The IFRS Foundation is an independent organisation made up of 22 Trustees. The Trustees hold the responsibility for governance and fundraising and will publish an annual report on IASB's activities, including audited financial statements and priorities for the coming year. They will review annually the strategy of the IASB and its effectiveness and approve the annual budget and determine the basis of funding.

The Trustees also appoint the members of the IASB, the IFRS Advisory Council and the IFRS Interpretations Committee. Although the Trustees will decide on the operating procedures of the committees in the IASB family, they will be excluded from involvement in technical matters relating to accounting standards.

### The IASB

The Board has complete responsibility for all IASB technical matters, including the preparation and issuing of International Financial Reporting Standards and Exposure Drafts, and final approval of Interpretations by the International Financial Reporting Interpretations Committee. Some of the full-time members of staff are responsible for liaising with national standard-setters in order to promote the convergence of accounting standards.

IASB publishes its standards in a series of pronouncements called International Financial Reporting Standards (IFRSs). It has also adopted the standards issued by the board of its predecessor, the International Accounting Standards Committee.

The Board may form advisory committees or other specialist technical groups to advise on major projects and outsource detailed research or other work to national standard-setters.

### IFRS Interpretations Committee

The IFRS Interpretations Committee provides timely guidance on the application and interpretation of IFRSs, normally dealing with complex accounting issues that could, in the absence of guidance, produce wide-ranging or unacceptable accounting treatments.

**Test your understanding 3 – The development of a standard**

The process for the development of a standard involves the following steps:

- During the early stages of a project, the IASB may establish an Advisory Committee to advise on the issues arising in the project. Consultation with this committee and the IFRS Advisory Council occurs throughout the project.

- The IASB may develop and publish Discussion Papers for public comment.

- Following receipt and review of comments, the IASB develops and publishes an Exposure Draft for public comment.

- Following the receipt and review of comments, the IASB issues a final International Financial Reporting Standard.

When the IASB publishes a standard, it also publishes a Basis of Conclusions to explain publicly how it reached its conclusions and to provide background information that may help users apply the standard in practice.

Each IASB member has one vote on technical matters and the publication of a Standard, Exposure Draft, or final IFRS Interpretation requires approval by eight of the Board's 15 members. Other decisions including agenda decisions and the issue of a Discussion Paper, require a simple majority of the Board members present at a meeting, provided that the meeting is attended by at least 50 per cent of the members.

Meetings of the IASB, IFRS Advisory Council and IFRS Interpretations Committee are open to public observation. Where the IASB issues Exposure Drafts, Discussion Papers and other documents for public comment, the usual comment period is 90 days. Draft IFRS Interpretations Committee Interpretations are exposed for a 60-day comment period.

**Test your understanding 4 – Practice questions**

1   D

2   A

3   B

4   B – IFRS Interpretations are subject to IASB approval.

5   B

# Code of Ethics

## Chapter learning objectives

| Lead | Component outcome |
|------|-------------------|
| A1. Identify regulators and describe their role | c. Explain why they regulate financial reporting |

# 1 Session content

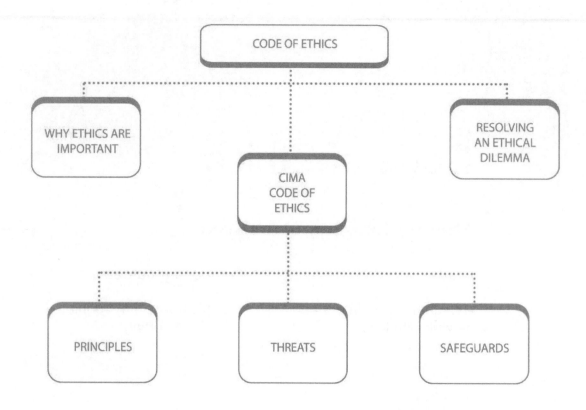

# 2 Introduction

Chartered Management Accountants (and registered students) have a duty to observe the highest standards of conduct and integrity and, to uphold the good standing and reputation of the profession. They must also refrain from any conduct which might discredit the profession. Members and registered students must have regard for these guidelines irrespective of their field of activity, of their contract of employment, or of any other professional memberships they may hold.

In January 2015, CIMA and the AICPA launched the Code of Ethics for CGMAs (Chartered Global Management Accountants). The CGMA code is aligned with the requirements contained in the 2015 CIMA code of ethics (Part C) and the AICPA code of professional conduct. Accordingly, CIMA members who hold the CGMA designation and are compliant with the CIMA code will also be in compliance with the CGMA code.

CIMA upholds the aims and principles of equal opportunities and fundamental human rights worldwide, including the handling of personal information. CIMA promotes the highest ethical and business standards, and encourages members to be responsible professionals.

Good ethical behaviour may be above that required by the law. In a highly competitive, complex business world, it is essential that CIMA members sustain their integrity and remember the trust and confidence which is placed in them by whoever relies on their objectivity and professionalism. Members must avoid actions or situations which are inconsistent with their professional obligations.

They should also be guided not merely by the terms but by the spirit of this code.

CIMA members should conduct themselves with courtesy and consideration towards all with whom they have professional dealings and should not behave in a manner which could be considered offensive or discriminatory.

To ensure that CIMA members protect the good standing and reputation of the profession, members must inform the institute if they are convicted or disqualified from acting as an officer of an entity, or if they are subject to any sanction resulting from disciplinary action taken by another professional body.

The CGMA designation is designed to elevate management accounting and further emphasize its importance for businesses worldwide. Part C of the code is designed to provide guidance to all CIMA members around the world who are members in business and professional accountants in business and, those who hold the CGMA credential. When a CGMA is also a member in public practice the CGMA should also comply with the applicable guidance of the CIMA code of ethics and apply the most restrictive provisions.

Part C of the 2015 CIMA Code of Ethics (effective from 1 January 2015) is consistent with the Code of Ethics for CGMA designation holders and any future substantive revisions to the CIMA code will be incorporated into the Code of Ethics for CGMA designation holders. Accordingly, CIMA members who are in compliance with the CIMA code are also in compliance with the CGMA code.

If a member cannot resolve an ethical issue by following this code or by consulting the ethics support information on CIMA's website, he or she should seek legal advice as to both his or her legal rights and any obligations he or she may have. The CIMA charter, bylaws and regulations should also be referred to for definitive rules on many matters. For further information see www.cimaglobal.com/ethics.

**NB:** All references to 'professional accountants' in this code should be taken to refer, as appropriate, to CIMA members or registered students.

 ## 3　Why are ethics important?

Ethics relate to fairness, honesty and responsibility. Ethics are a set of moral principles to guide behaviour.

They are important because:

Accountants should perform their work properly. Ethics describe "how" an entity does its business not what it does. If an accountant carried out work in bad faith this can affect the accountant (who may be disciplined by CIMA), it may have an effect on the business, e.g. financial viability, and in the public sector tax payers' money could be wasted.

## 4    CIMA's code at a glance

### Principles

Whether you are employed in business or the public sector or work in practice, CIMA's code of ethics can help you to identify and deal with situations where your professional integrity may be at risk. The code describes the high ethical standards every CIMA member and student must demonstrate, and gives guidance on how to uphold these.

Five fundamental principles form the basis of the code: integrity, objectivity, professional competence and due care, confidentiality and professional behaviour. These are summarised below, but a full explanation, along with guidance on applying the principles, is available in the complete code of ethics.

- **Objectivity** means not allowing bias, conflict of interest, or the influence of other people to override your professional judgement. To protect your objectivity, you should avoid relationships that could bias or overly influence your professional opinion.

- **Professional competence and due care** is an ongoing commitment to maintain your level of professional knowledge and skill so that your client or employer receives a competent professional service. This should be based on current developments in practice, legislation and techniques, and you must also make sure that those working under your authority have the appropriate training and supervision. Work should be completed carefully, thoroughly and diligently, in accordance with relevant technical and professional standards, e.g. accountants will use judgement and estimation when preparing financial statements such as identifying accruals/prepayments, making provisions, counting and valuing inventory, and choosing depreciation methods.

- **Professional behaviour** requires you to comply with relevant laws and regulations. You must also avoid any action that could negatively affect the reputation of the profession.

- **Integrity** means being straightforward, honest and truthful in all professional and business relationships. You should not be associated with any information that you believe contains a materially false or misleading statement, or which is misleading because it omits or obscures the facts.

- **Confidentiality** means respecting the confidential nature of information you acquire through professional relationships such as past or current employment. You should not disclose such information unless you have specific permission or a legal or professional duty to do so. You should also never use confidential information for your or another person's advantage.

The code itself contains further explanation of these principles, and examples of how they can be applied for both Professional Accountants in Business (Part C) and Professional Accountants in Practice (Part B). It is impossible to define every situation that could create a threat to the principles, and it is equally impossible to set out specific safeguards for each case, so instead the code sets out common examples of when these principles might be threatened and guidance as to what action should be taken to reduce or remove the threats.

A principles-based code such as CIMA's is widely considered to be more effective than a set of rules. Whereas there can be a tendency to try and circumvent rules, principles are more flexible and can be applied in a wider variety of situations. Principles also encourage users to think about the underlying intent of the code rather than simply adopting a check-box approach to compliance with rules.

## Threats

To apply the fundamental principles of the code (integrity, objectivity, professional competence and due care, confidentiality, and professional behaviour), you first need to be able to identify and evaluate existing or potential threats to them. If a threat exists that is anything other than trivial, you will need to take action to remove the threat or reduce it to an acceptable level.

Although it is impossible to define all the situations that could create a threat to the fundamental principles, the code does identify five categories of common threat:

- **Self-interest threats** can occur as a result of your own or your close family's interests – financial or otherwise. These threats often result in what is commonly called a 'conflict of interest' situation. Working in business, a self-interest threat could result from concern over job security, or from incentive remuneration arrangements. For those in practice it might be the possibility of losing a client or holding a financial interest in a client.

- **Self-review threats** occur when you are required to re-evaluate your own previous judgement, for example if you have been asked to review and justify a business decision you made, or if you are reporting on the operation of financial systems that you were involved in designing or implementing.

- **Familiarity threats** can be present when you become so sympathetic to the interests of others as a result of a close relationship that your professional judgement becomes compromised. Sometimes this can result from long association with business contacts who influence business decisions, long association with colleagues, or from accepting gifts or preferential treatment from a client.

- **Intimidation threats** occur when you are deterred from acting objectively by actual or perceived threats. It could be the threat of dismissal over a disagreement about applying an accounting principle or reporting financial information, or it could be a dominant personality attempting to influence the decision making process.

- **Advocacy threats** can be a problem when you are promoting a position or opinion to the point that your subsequent objectivity is compromised. It could include acting as an advocate on behalf of an assurance client in litigation or disputes with third parties. In general, promoting the legitimate goals of your employer does not create an advocacy threat, provided that any statements you make are not misleading.

Whilst it is important that candidates can define ethical issues, they must also be able to apply them to a specific scenario and explain their implications. This would be more relevant for the operational case study where detailed written responses are commonplace. Candidates are likely to be given a scenario and will be required to explain the principles and/or threats that may result in the code not being adhered to.

## Safeguards

So what should you do if there is a threat (or potential threat), to the principles of the code?

CIMA's code of ethics has a 'threats and safeguards' approach to resolving ethical issues. This means that if you are in a situation where there might be a threat to any of the code's fundamental principles you should first **assess whether the threat is significant**. If it is, you should to take action to remove or mitigate it.

**Safeguards** are actions that will reduce or prevent an ethical issues arising. Safeguards can be found in employing organisations, such as whistle blowing or grievance procedures, or can be embedded within the profession in the form of standards or legislation. Safeguards are also the actions that a professional accountant takes to resolve an ethical conflict or dilemma.

If a colleague, employer or client has done something that you think is unethical, if you are under pressure to do something you think goes against the principles of the code of ethics or if you are facing a conflict of interest, then you will need to think about what safeguards or actions to take to resolve it. These safeguards could take a number of forms. The code does not describe all the safeguards that could be implemented, but instead gives general guidance for handling ethical issues, both for accountants working in business and for those in practice.

## 5 Resolving an ethical dilemma?

What should you do if you think you might be facing an ethical dilemma? How can you decide whether to take action?

All CIMA students should be able to identify, explain, resolve or address ethical problems.

If you think something might be unethical, you will need to think about the relevant facts, the ethical issues involved, the fundamental principles of CIMA's code of ethics that apply and internal company procedures. You can then identify and weigh up alternative courses of action, thinking about the consequences for those affected. What would be the outcome of going down a particular route? How would this compare with the alternatives?

An ethical dilemma exists when one or more principles of the code are threatened. You may have discovered something unethical, illegal or fraudulent going on where you work, or perhaps you feel that you have been asked to do something that compromises your professional integrity. Maybe someone is putting pressure on you to mislead, or to report in a way that is inconsistent, or goes against accepted accounting standards.

Conflicts of interest and confidentiality issues are also ethical problems. In general, ethical issues should be dealt with by taking actions (called safeguards) to reduce them to a level where they are no longer significant or of any consequence.

If you are not sure whether something is significant, it can help to think about what a reasonable third party might think if they had the facts of the situation. How would you feel if someone you know discovered how you had acted? Would you feel proud or embarrassed by your actions?

Whether you work in business, the public sector, or in practice, the following is a process for addressing situations where you have discovered possible fraud or malpractice or where you feel your professional integrity is at risk. If, having read this guidance, you are still unsure what to do or would like to talk the matter through, contact CIMA's ethics helpline for more help.

1   Start by gathering all the relevant information so you can be sure of the facts and decide whether there really is an ethical problem.

2   Raise your concern internally. Your manager could be an appropriate person to approach, or you could speak to a trusted colleague. If these are not options, consider escalating the issue, such as to your manager's boss, to the Board, or perhaps to a non-executive director. There might also be an internal grievance or whistle blowing procedure you can follow. If you are in practice, you could raise your concern with the client, unless you suspect money laundering.

3   If you have raised the issue within the entity, your concerns have not been addressed, and you feel that it is a significant or persistent problem, you should think about reporting it externally. You could speak to your entity's auditors (if you have them) or contact the relevant trade, industry or regulatory authority. Remember that confidentiality still applies, and get legal advice to be sure of your obligations and rights.

4       Finally, if you have exhausted these avenues and you are still unable to
        resolve the ethical conflict, you should consider how you could remove
        yourself from the situation. Sometimes it might be enough to stop working
        with a particular team or client or to refuse to be associated with a
        misleading report. In the most extreme cases of significant unethical
        behaviour, however, where this is likely to continue despite your best
        efforts to resolve it, you may need to consider resigning. Again, legal
        advice will help to clarify your rights and obligations and should be sought
        before you take the step of resigning.

Throughout the process, document the steps you take to resolve the issue. For
example, raise your concern in writing and keep copies of relevant
correspondence. This will allow you to demonstrate how you dealt with the
problem should you ever need to do so.

## Examples of ethical issues

Managers face ethical issues all of the time. Examples include:

- dealing with direct and indirect demands for bribes and attempts at
  extortion;

- dealing with attempts at unfair competition;

- expectations of social responsibility in relation to society and the
  environment;

- demand for safety and compliance with legislative standards in
  relation to products and production;

- honesty in advertising jobs and products;

- management of closures and redundancies;

- non-exploitation of countries and people;

- effects on customer of consuming products;

- dealing with oppressive governments;

- fairness in settling pay and work conditions.

## Illustration 1 – Ethical dilemma

You work for a large entity as the assistant financial controller. One of
your duties is to reconcile the sales ledger each month. Every month it
does not agree and you feel sure it is associated with irrecoverable debts
being written off in the individual customer accounts but not included in
the nominal ledger. You consider the differences to be material and have
bought this to the attention of the financial controller but he seems
unwilling to act.

**Required:**

What action would you take in this situation?

## Solution

The main ethical issue is integrity. It would not be appropriate for an accountant to assist someone with a potentially fraudulent act, or to allow misleading information to be presented to others.

There is also a potential issue of objectivity if you are placed under pressure by the financial controller, as this would mean you have a conflict of interest between your personal prospects and the requirement to behave with integrity.

The possible actions could be:

- informing the financial controller of your concern and also formally asking the financial controller to address it

- informing the financial controller that you are going to bring the matter to the attention of the financial director or the audit committee

It would not be advisable to report externally until legal advice has been taken. Hopefully, this situation can be resolved with one of the above actions.

## Test your understanding 1 – Ethical dilemma

You manage a number of trainee accountants whom the entity sponsors through training at their first attempt at each paper. In June 20X1 you employed a final level student who told you during her interview that she did not sit her final exams in May 20X1 but was going to sit them for the first time in November of that year. She had actually sat them in May 20X1 but worried that she would fail, tarnishing her record with the entity, and also she would not get financial support for her re-sit. She passed her exams in May 20X1.

### Required:

What action would you take in this matter?

**Test your understanding 2 – Practice questions**

1    **Which of the following is not a fundamental ethical principle identified by CIMA?**

   A     Integrity

   B     Objectivity

   C     Confidentiality

   D     Independence

2    **CGMA's code of ethics requires members to comply with five fundamental principles. Which of the following options include fundamental principles only?**

   A     Integrity, objectivity, honesty

   B     Professional competence and due care, professional behaviour, confidentiality

   C     Social responsibility, independence, scepticism

   D     Courtesy, reliability, responsibility

3    **In which of the following situations would the entity be viewed as having behaved unethically?**

   A     Delaying payments to its suppliers despite repeated requests to pay

   B     Printing warning signs on its potentially dangerous plastic packaging

   C     Informing investors that the profits forecasted may not actually materialise

   D     Stating that it will aim to recruit more people from ethnic minority groups

4    **Mumta thinks it is acceptable to take a "sickie" when she wants a day off. Which of the fundamental principles is she flouting?**

   A     Integrity

   B     Professional competence and due care

   C     Objectivity

   D     Confidentiality

5    You have an ethical dilemma.

   **What should you do first?**

   A     Inform the auditors

   B     Inform senior management

   C     Inform the appropriate professional body

   D     Speak to your immediate supervisor

6    Monica owns shares in the company she works for. Monica receives confidential information that could negatively affect the share price of her employer.

**What should she do?**

A    Talk to her manager and get some advice.

B    Sell her shares immediately before she makes a loss.

C    Do nothing.

D    Report her findings to the newspaper.

7    Rajesh is being pressured by his employer to change figures in his report as it will affect his manager's bonus.

**What threat is Rajesh facing?**

A    Self-review

B    Intimidation

C    Advocacy

D    Confidentiality

8    **Which of the following is not a reason to disclose confidential information?**

A    Disclosure permitted by law

B    Disclosure as part of required professional duties regarding a loan application by the entity to a bank

C    Disclosure to prevent a friend making a financial loss

D    Disclosure as part of professional duties regarding a legal case the entity is dealing with

## 6 Summary diagram

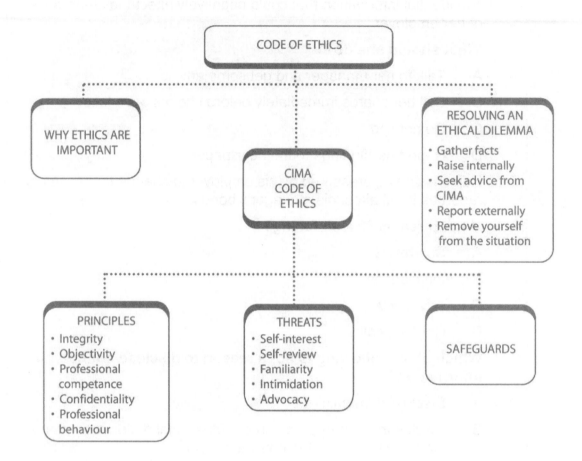

## Test your understanding answers

### Test your understanding 1 – Ethical dilemma

The main ethical issue is integrity.

The new employee has not behaved with integrity by lying, and doing so with the deliberate attempt to further her career, and to defraud the entity of her examination and tuition fees. This must be taken seriously as it could suggest that she may not behave with integrity in other situations.

Possible actions could be:

- the employee should be disciplined through the formal corporate disciplinary channels, such as a formal written warning;

- depending on how serious this is viewed, the entity could consider dismissal and possible reporting to CIMA.

### Test your understanding 2 – Practice questions

1   D

2   B

3   A – In situations B and C it is rectifying the results of previous doubtful actions. Option D is an example of an entity's ethical aspirations.

4   A – Mumta is not being honest and truthful

5   D – your first step should be to report internally to your immediate supervisor. If they do not act on your information you would take further steps to report higher internally and then externally to the auditors/professional body.

6   A – Monica should report her findings to her manager.

7   B

8   C

# Corporate Governance

## Chapter learning objectives

| Lead | Component outcome |
|---|---|
| A2. Apply corporate governance principles and financial reporting | a. Describe the role of the board in corporate governance |
| | b. Apply corporate governance and financial stewardship principles in financial reporting |

# 1 Session Content

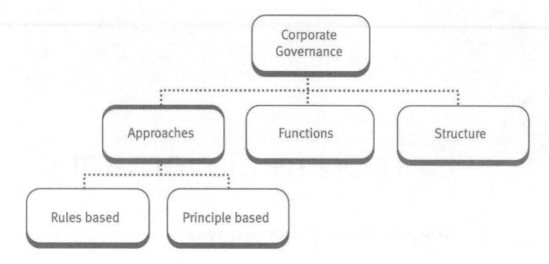

# 2 Introduction

Corporate governance has been around for many years, however in response to major accounting scandals (e.g. Enron), regulators sought to change the rules surrounding the governance of entities, particularly publicly owned ones.

The purpose was to protect shareholders by giving them more information about the entity.

The US was greatly affected by the "Enron" scandal and decided to use a rules based approach driven by the need to be compliant with legislation, whilst other countries, like the UK, decided to use a principle based approach, enabling more flexibility to corporate governance. The UK has seen wide ranging economic impacts caused by the over trading and subsequent liquidation of Carillion, with many awarded public sector contracts unable to be completed

In the US the Sarbanes Oxley Act (2002) introduced a set of rigorous corporate governance laws and at the same time the UK Corporate Governance Code (previously the Combined Code) introduced a set of best practice corporate governance initiatives into the UK.

### What is corporate governance?

 **Corporate governance** is the means by which a company is **directed** and **controlled**.

The aim of corporate governance initiatives is to ensure that entities are run well in the interests of their shareholders and the wider community. It concerns such matters as:

- the responsibilities of directors
- the appropriate composition of the board of directors
- the necessity for good internal control
- the necessity for an audit committee
- relationships with the external auditors.

It is particularly important for publicly traded entities because large amounts of money are invested in them, either by 'small' shareholders, or from pension schemes and other financial institutions. The wealth of these entities significantly affects the health of the economies where their shares are traded.

**Enron**

In the year 2000, Enron, a US based energy company, employed 22,000 people and reported revenues of $101 billion. In late 2001 they filed for bankruptcy protection. After a lengthy investigation it was revealed that Enron's financial statements were sustained substantially by systematic, and creatively planned, accounting fraud.

Iin the wake of the fraud case the shares of Enron fell from over $90 each to just a few cents each, a number of directors were prosecuted and jailed and their auditors, Arthur Andersen, were accused of obstruction of justice and forced to stop auditing public companies. This ruling against Arthur Andersen was overturned at a later date but the damage was done and the firm ceased trading soon after.

This was just one of a number of high profile frauds to occur at the turn of the millennium.

The Enron scandal is an example of the abuse of the trust placed in the management of publicly traded companies by investors. This abuse of trust usually takes one of two forms:

- the direct extraction from the company of excessive benefits by management, e.g. large salaries, pension entitlements, share options, use of company assets (jets, apartments etc.)

- manipulation of the share price by misrepresenting the company's profitability, usually so that shares in the company can be sold or options 'cashed in'.

In response regulators sought to change the rules surrounding the governance of companies, particularly publicly owned ones. In the US the Sarbanes Oxley Act (2002) introduced a set of rigorous corporate governance laws and at the same time the Combined Code introduced a set of best practice corporate governance initiatives into the UK.

**The history of corporate governance**

### The United States

The collapses of Enron and WorldCom in the United States gave renewed impetus to governments to take action in order to restore public confidence in the corporate sector.

Enron's problems came about because of unsustainable growth which had to be financed through increased borrowing. Following an investigation by the Securities and Exchange Commission, it became clear that, in order to hide its excessive borrowing and thus maintain confidence in its stock, Enron effectively created a number of subsidiaries, each a legal entity in its own right, for the purpose of keeping Enron's borrowing off its balance sheet and thus maintaining its creditworthiness.

In December 2001, Enron filed for protection under Chapter 11 of the United States Bankruptcy Code with debts of approximately $3 billion. The investigation also revealed that the persons primarily responsible for Enron's fraud and subsequent collapse were the directors, chief executives and the company's auditors.

To date there have been guilty pleas in relation to fraud, money laundering and insider dealing by Enron executives and a plea of guilty to obstructing justice by destroying Enron-related documents by Arthur Andersen, Enron's lead auditor. As may be imagined, the collapse of such a large corporation as Enron and the criminal activities revealed led to attention being given to the effectiveness of corporate governance measures.

The Sarbanes-Oxley Act was passed in July 2002 seeking to protect investors by improving the accuracy of corporate disclosure and reporting procedures and increasing corporate openness.

In addition, it had become clear that in many cases the relationship between corporations and their auditors was far too close. Auditors are required to carry out their work independently of the interests of the company's board or senior executives and to provide a check for the benefit of the shareholders. However, the auditors of Enron had conspired with the company in attempts to remove excessive debt from the Enron accounts. In practice, the independence of the auditors was compromised by the fact that they also received fees from the company for acting as financial consultants.

As a result, the Sarbanes-Oxley Act created the Public Company Accounting Oversight Board which is charged with the task of policing the auditing of public companies in the United States. All auditors of public companies must be registered with the board which is required to set up quality assurance procedures, ethics and independent standards to which auditors are required to adhere. The Act also prohibits auditors from providing certain non-audit services to the companies for which they act.

In addition, the Act requires the separate disclosure of the fees received by auditors for audit and all other fees. It follows that the independence of the scrutinisers is now also subject to scrutiny!

## The United Kingdom

In the United Kingdom, there were a number of scandals involving the likes of Guinness and Robert Maxwell and these highlighted the continuing ability of directors to involve public entities in mismanagement. These scandals and high-profile entity frauds made it clear that effective control of the directors of public companies was not being carried out by the shareholders, with the result that governments and regulators have had to look to other means for effective control mechanisms. More recently further high profile cases which question the effectiveness of principle-based approaches to corporate governance regulation have occurred (e.g. the BHS pension scandal).

Corporate governance of public listed entities was the subject of numerous reports prepared in the 1990s, including Cadbury and Greenbury, which culminated in the issue of the Combined Code. This was later developed into the first draft of the UK Corporate Governance Code in 1998.

## Europe

In 2003, the European Commission announced that it did not believe it necessary to formulate a separate code of European corporate governance. Rather such matters could safely be left to individual member states. However, it did see the need for a common approach to be taken in regard to fundamental governance issues throughout the European Union. These are to be developed over time through the issue of Directives. Thus such matters as the greater involvement in management of independent non-executive directors, more information regarding directors' remuneration and greater disclosure of and access to other financial information should form the basis of the corporate governance of all EU member states. It remains to be seen how this will be affected by the implications of Brexit, both in Europe and in the UK.

## 3 Approaches to corporate governance

There are different approaches to corporate governance.

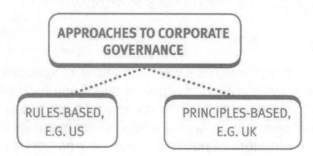

- A rules-based approach instils the code into law with appropriate penalties for transgression.

- A principles-based approach requires the entity to adhere to the spirit rather than the letter of the code. The entity must either comply with the code or explain why it has not through reports to the appropriate body and its shareholders.

The UK model is a principles-based one, although since adherence is part of stock exchange listing requirements it cannot be considered to be voluntary for large entities.

The US model is enshrined into law by virtue of Sarbanes Oxley Act (SOX). It is, therefore, a rules-based approach.

### Choice of governance regime

The decision as to which approach to use for a country can be governed by many factors:

- dominant ownership structure (bank, family or multiple shareholder)
- legal system and its power/ability
- government structure and policies
- state of the economy
- culture and history
- levels of capital inflow or investment coming into the country
- global economic and political climate.

### Comply or explain

A principles-based code requires the entity to state that it has complied with the requirements of the code or to explain why it could not do so in its annual report. This will leave shareholders to draw their own conclusions regarding the governance of the entity.

## 4 Rules-based approach to corporate governance

A rules-based approach instils the code into law with appropriate penalties for transgression. An example is the Sarbanes-Oxley regulations applicable in the US.

### Sarbanes-Oxley (SOX)

In 2002, following a number of corporate governance scandals such as Enron and WorldCom, tough new corporate governance regulations were introduced in the US by SOX.

- SOX is a rules-based approach to governance.

- SOX is extremely detailed and carries the full force of the law.

- SOX includes requirements for the Securities and Exchange Commission (SEC) to issue certain rules on corporate governance.

- It is relevant to US companies, directors of subsidiaries of US-listed businesses and auditors who are working on US-listed businesses.

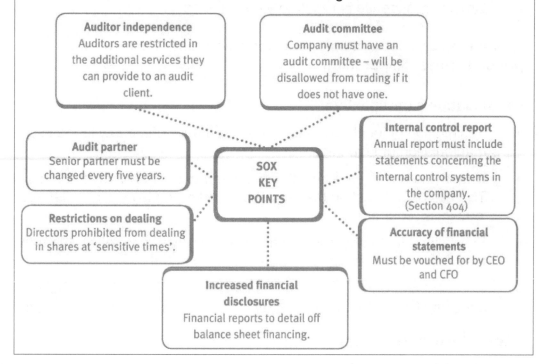

**Arguments in favour of a rules-based approach (and against a principles-based approach)**

### Organisation's perspective:

- Clarity in terms of what the entity must do – the rules are a legal requirement, clarity should exist and hence no interpretation is required.

- Standardisation for all companies – there is no choice as to complying or explaining and this creates a standardised and fairer approach for all businesses.

- Binding requirements – non-compliance breaks laws and is considered a crime making it very clear that the rules must be complied with.

### Wider stakeholder perspective:

- Standardisation across all companies – a level playing field is created.

- Sanction – the sanction is criminal and therefore a greater deterrent to transgression.

- Greater confidence in regulatory compliance.

### Arguments against a rules-based approach (and in favour of a principles-based approach)

### Organisation's perspective:

- Exploitation of loopholes – the exacting nature of the law lends itself to the manipulation of loopholes.

- Underlying belief – the belief is that you must only play by the rules set. There is no suggestion that you should **want** to play by the rules (i.e. no 'buy-in' is required).

- Flexibility is lost – there is no choice in compliance to reflect the nature of the organisation, its size or stage of development.

- Checklist approach – this can arise as companies seek to comply with all aspects of the rules and start 'box-ticking' leading to inefficient practices.

### Wider stakeholder perspective:

'Regulation overload' – the volume of rules and amount of legislation may give rise to increasing costs for businesses and for the regulators.

Legal costs – to enact new legislation to close loopholes.

Limits – there is no room to improve, or go beyond the minimum level set.

'Box-ticking' rather than compliance – this does not lead to well governed organisations.

# 5    Principles-based approach to corporate governance

## Best practice – policies and procedure

The UK uses a principle based approach to corporate governance which is required for listed entities but guidance for other entities. Entities should either comply or explain why they haven't applied the code

Obviously, best practice is intricately tied up with the size and resources of the entity in question. For listed entities, the most important issues of best practice are contained in the UK Corporate Governance Code. This was first issued in 1998 and has been updated at regular intervals since then.

The UK Corporate Governance Code can be seen in full on the FRC website at:

https://www.frc.org.uk/Our-Work/Codes-Standards/Corporate-governance/UK-Corporate-Governance-Code.aspx

The Code is not a rigid (or enforced) set of rules. Instead it consists of principles (main and supporting) and provisions.

In the UK all entities quoted on the stock exchange have to comply with the FSA listing rules and these include a requirement that all entities include in their annual report:

- a statement of how the entity has applied the main principles set out in the Code, and

- a statement as to whether the entity has complied with all relevant provisions set out in the Code.

The main provisions of the Code are:

## Leadership

- Every entity should be headed by an effective board with collective responsibility.

- There should be a clear division of responsibilities between the Chairman and the Chief Executive.

- No one individual should have unfettered powers of decision.

- Non-executive directors should constructively challenge and help develop proposals on strategy.

## Effectiveness

- The board should have the appropriate balance of skills, experience, independence and knowledge.

- There should be a formal, rigorous and transparent procedure for the appointment of new directors.

- All directors should receive induction and should regularly update and refresh their skills and knowledge.

- The board should be supplied with quality and timely information to enable it to discharge its duties.

- The board and individuals should be subject to a formal and rigorous annual evaluation of performance.

- All directors should be submitted for re-election at regular intervals.

### Accountability

- The board should present a fair, balanced and understandable assessment of the entity's position and prospects.

- The board is responsible for determining the nature and extent of the significant risks it is willing to take in achieving its strategic objectives.

- The board should maintain sound risk management and internal control systems.

- The board should establish formal and transparent arrangements for corporate reporting and risk management and internal control principles and for maintaining an appropriate relationship with the entity's auditor.

### Remuneration

- This should be sufficient to attract, retain and motivate directors of the quality required to run the entity successfully, but should not be excessive.

- This should be structured so as to link a significant proportion of the rewards to corporate and individual performance.

- There should be a formal and transparent procedure for developing policy on executive remuneration.

- No director should be involved in deciding his or her own remuneration.

### Relations with Shareholders

- There should be a dialogue with shareholders based on the mutual understanding of objectives.

- The board as a whole has responsibility for ensuring that a satisfactory dialogue with shareholders takes place.

- The board should use the AGM to communicate with investors and to encourage their participation.

 **The OECD Principles of Corporate Governance**

The OECD consists of 34 countries who want a free market economy with one set of rules for corporate governance.

Although there have always been well run entities as well as those where scandals have occurred, the fact that scandals do occur has led to the development of codes of practice for good corporate governance.

Often this is due to pressures exerted by stock exchanges. In 1999 the Organisation for Economic Co-operation and Development, OECD, assisted with the development of their 'Principles of Corporate

Governance.' These were intended to:

- assist member and non-member governments in their efforts to evaluate and improve the legal, institutional and regulatory framework for corporate governance in their countries.

- provide guidance and suggestions for stock exchanges, investors, corporations, and other parties that have a role in the process of developing good corporate governance.

The OECD principles were first published in 1999 and were revised in 2004. Their focus is on publicly traded entities. However, to the extent they are deemed applicable, they are a useful tool to improve corporate governance in non-traded entities.

There are six principles, each backed up by a number of sub principles. The principles, and those sub-principles relevant to the auditor, are reproduced on the following page.

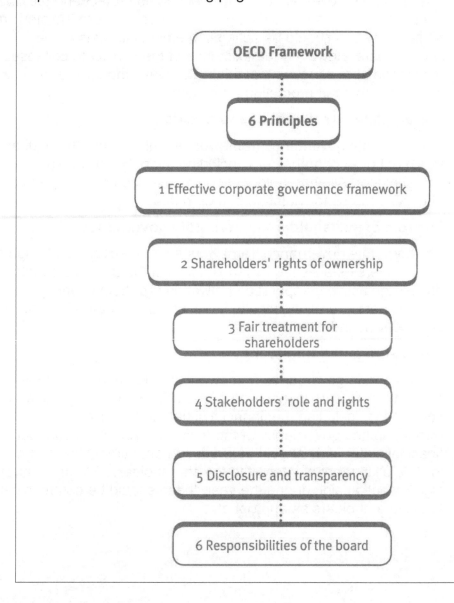

**The principles in detail**

**Structure of the Principles**

The six Principles:

(i) **Ensuring the basis for an effective corporate governance framework**

The corporate governance framework should promote transparent and efficient markets, be consistent with the rule of law and clearly articulate the division of responsibilities among different supervisory, regulatory and enforcement authorities. In other words, making sure everyone involved is aware of their individual responsibilities so no party is in doubt as to what they are accountable for.

(ii) **The rights of shareholders and key ownership functions**

The corporate governance framework should protect and facilitate the exercise of shareholders' rights. The directors are the stewards of the entity and should be acting in the best interests of the shareholders. However, the existence of the corporate collapses mentioned above proves that this isn't always the case and shareholders need protecting from such people.

(iii) **The equitable treatment of shareholders**

The corporate governance framework should ensure the equitable treatment of all shareholders, including minority and foreign shareholders. All shareholders should have the opportunity to obtain effective redress for violation of their rights.

(iv) **The role of stakeholders in corporate governance**

The corporate governance framework should recognise the rights of stakeholders established by law or through mutual agreements and encourage active co-operation between corporations and stakeholders in creating wealth, jobs, and the sustainability of financially sound enterprise.

(v) **Disclosure and transparency**

The corporate governance framework should ensure that timely and accurate disclosure is made on all material matters regarding the corporation, including the financial situation, performance, ownership and governance of the entity. Therefore, the annual financial statements should be produced on a timely basis and include all matters of interest to the shareholders. For any matters of significance arising during the year, these should be communicated to the shareholders as appropriate.

**(vi)  The responsibilities of the board**

The corporate governance framework should ensure the strategic guidance of the entity, the effective monitoring of management by the board, and the board's accountability to the entity and the shareholders. The introduction of audit committees and non-executive directors on the board is the usual way for monitoring management. Non-executive directors are not involved in the day to day running of the entity and are therefore more independent. They can evaluate the effectiveness of the executive board on its merits and make sure they are carrying out their duties properly.

## The status of the OECD principles

- The Principles represent a common basis that OECD Member countries consider essential for the development of good governance practice.

- They are intended to be concise, understandable and accessible to the international community.

- They are not intended to be a substitute for government or private sector initiatives to develop more detailed 'best practice' in governance.

## 6    Corporate governance in action

Corporate governance guidance generally incorporates the following:

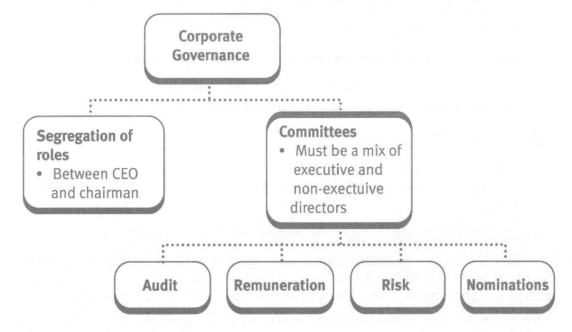

## The role of the board

 From the principles in the UK Corporate Governance Code (2016), the key roles and responsibilities of directors are to:

- provide entrepreneurial leadership of the company
- represent company view and account to the public
- decide on a formal schedule of matters to be reserved for board decision
- determine the company's mission and purpose (strategic aims)
- select and appoint the CEO, chairman and other board members
- set the company's values and standards
- ensure that the company's management is performing its job correctly
- establish appropriate internal controls that enable risk to be assessed and managed
- ensure that the necessary financial and human resources are in place for the company to meet its objectives
- ensure that its obligations to its shareholders and other stakeholders are understood and met
- meet regularly to discharge its duties effectively
- for listed companies:
  - appoint appropriate NEDs
  - establish remuneration committee
  - establish nominations committee
  - establish audit committee
- assess its own performance and report it annually to shareholders
- submit themselves for re-election at regular intervals. All directors in FTSE 350 companies should be put forward for re-election every year.

###  Independence of the board

The Code states as a principle that the board should include a balance of NEDs and executives. This is to reduce an unfavourable balance of power towards executives.

The board should consist of half independent NEDs excluding the chair.

One NED should be the senior independent director who is directly available to shareholders if they have concerns which cannot or should not be dealt with through the appropriate channels of chairman, CEO or finance director.

The primary fiduciary duty that NEDs owe is to the company's shareholders. They must not allow themselves to be captured or unduly influenced by the vested interests of other members of the company such as executive directors, trade unions or middle management.

There are also concerns over the recruitment of NED's and the challenge that this may bring to independence.

Recruiting those with previous industry involvement can result in a higher technical knowledge, a network of contacts and an awareness of what the strategic issues are within the industry. While these might be of some benefit to a NED's contribution, they can make the NED less independent as prior industry involvement might also reduce the NED's ability to be objective and uncontaminated by previously held views.

Accordingly, it is sometimes easier to demonstrate independence when NEDs are appointed from outside the industry.

In practice, many companies employ a mix of NEDs, and it is often this blend of talents and areas of expertise that makes a non-executive board effective.

### Reasons for NED independence

- To provide a detached and objective view of board decisions.

- To provide expertise and communicate effectively.

- To provide shareholders with an independent voice on the board.

- To provide confidence in corporate governance.

- To reduce accusations of self-interest in the behaviour of executives.

### Segregation of Roles

Best practice recommends that the roles of Chairman and Chief Executive Officer should be held be different people to reduce the power of prominent board members.

### Committees

The committees act as a control mechanism by having specialists to coordinate internal and external auditors, deal with remuneration, risk and nominations.

### Internal audit

Internal audit departments are employees of the entity who conduct audit procedures as per the instructions of the directors. They typically investigate the performance and effectiveness of internal control systems within the entity. They will recommend improvements to processes with the aim of reducing risk of fraud or error.

## Further detail

### Audit Committees

An audit committee is a committee consisting of non-executive directors which is able to view an entity's affairs in a detached and independent way and liaise effectively between the main board of directors and the external auditors.

**Best practice for listed entities:**

- The entity should have an audit committee of at least three non-executive directors (or, in the case of smaller entities, two).

- At least one member of the audit committee should have recent and relevant financial experience.

**The objectives of the audit committee**

- Increasing public confidence in the credibility and objectivity of published financial information (including unaudited interim statements).

- Assisting directors (particularly executive directors) in meeting their responsibilities in respect of financial reporting.

- Strengthening the independent position of an entity's external auditor by providing an additional channel of communication.

**The function of the audit committee**

- Monitoring the integrity of the financial statements.

- Reviewing the entity's internal financial controls.

- Monitoring and reviewing the effectiveness of the internal audit function.

- Making recommendations in relation to the appointment and removal of the external auditor and their remuneration.

- Reviewing and monitoring the external auditor's independence and objectivity and the effectiveness of the audit process.

- Developing and implementing policy on the engagement of the external auditor to supply non-audit services.

- Reviewing arrangements for confidential reporting by employees and investigation of possible improprieties ('whistleblowing').

**Benefits:**

- Improved credibility of the financial statements, through an impartial review of the financial statements, and discussion of significant issues with the external auditors.

- Increased public confidence in the audit opinion, as the audit committee will monitor the independence of the external auditors.

- Stronger control environment, as the audit committee help to create a culture of compliance and control.

- The internal audit function will report to the audit committee increasing their independence and adding weight to their recommendations.

- The skills, knowledge and experience (and independence) of the audit committee members can be an invaluable resource for a business.

- It may be easier and cheaper to arrange finance, as the presence of an audit committee can give a perception of good corporate governance.

- It would be less burdensome to meet listing requirements if an audit committee (which is usually a listing requirement) is already established.

**Problems:**

- Difficulties recruiting the right non-executive directors who have relevant skills, experience and sufficient time to become effective members of the committee.

- The cost. Non-executive directors are normally remunerated, and their fees can be quite expensive.

### Internal controls and risk management

One way of minimising risk is to incorporate internal controls into an entity's systems and procedures.

It is the director's responsibility to implement internal controls and monitor their application and effectiveness.

Auditors are not responsible for the design and implementation of their clients' control systems. Auditors have to assess the effectiveness of controls for reducing the risk of material misstatement of the financial statements. They incorporate this into their overall risk assessment, which allows them to design their further audit procedures.

## Test your understanding 1 – Practice questions

1   **An entity using a rules-based approach to corporate governance means .....**

   A   the entity must legally apply the rules.

   B   the entity does not have to legally apply the rules but must disclose if not applied.

   C   the entity does not have to legally apply the rules and need not disclose if not applied.

   D   the entity can ignore the rules.

2   **An entity using a principle-based approach to corporate governance, such as the UK Corporate Governance Code, means .....**

   A   the entity must comply with a distinct list of legally enforceable rules

   B   the entity should either comply with the principles if the code or explain why they haven't applied the code

   C   the entity must be a listed company

   D   the entity can ignore set regulations and apply governance in a fashion serving the best interests of the directors.

3   **Corporate governance rules were strengthened to:**

   A   protect shareholders.

   B   protect directors.

   C   protect auditors.

   D   protect employees.

4   Corporate Governance guidance includes the need for segregation of duties.

   **A practical example of the application of segregation of duty principles in the context of corporate governance would be:**

   A   the roles of the chairman and CEO are held by different people to reduce the power of prominent board members.

   B   the roles of employees are segregated to prevent fraud.

   C   the auditors are independent to employees.

   D   only 1 non-executive director can be on the audit committee.

5    Corporate governance rules suggests committees should be used within an entity.

**Which of the following is NOT a corporate governance driven committee?**

A    Nominations

B    Audit

C    Remuneration

D    Leadership

## 7    Chapter summary

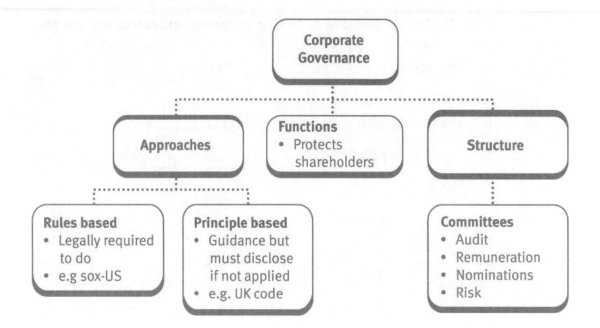

# Test your understanding answers

### Test your understanding 1 – Practice questions

1    A

2    B

The Corporate Governance Code is not rules based and so A is incorrect.

The principles of the Corporate Governance Code must be followed by listed entities but give best practice principles that can be applied voluntarily by private entities. Therefore, C is incorrect.

Principle–based governance codes are not to be applied to ensure the directors best interests. If this was the aim then ethical issues would arise and would reduce the credibility corporate governance principles.

3    A

4    A

Segregation of duties for employees does prevent fraud but would only be considered part of corporate governance best practice if the segregation involved the directors and board members. B is incorrect.

Independence of the auditor from an entity is an auditing ethical standard issues rather than relating to corporate governance. It is the responsibility of the audit firm to ensure independence not the entity being audited. As a result C is incorrect.

The audit committee should consist of only non-executive directors and should consist of at least 3 members (or 2 for SMEs).

5    D

# The Conceptual Framework

## Chapter learning objectives

| Lead | Component outcome |
| --- | --- |
| B1 Identify the main elements of financial statements | a. Identify the main elements of financial statements contained in the IFRS conceptual framework |

# 1 Session content

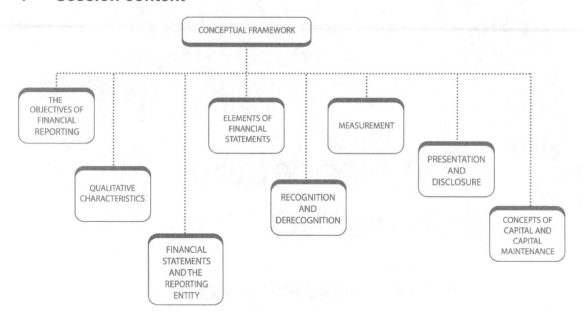

# 2 Introduction

Over time, transactions that entities enter into have become increasingly complex. Although the detail of the transactions may vary from situation to situation the basic accounting issues are often the same. As a result, the IASB developed a conceptual framework, which lays out the broad principles that should be applied when developing accounting standards and when determining an appropriate accounting treatment, **'The Conceptual Framework for Financial Reporting'** (the Framework).

 The Framework needs to be regularly updated to keep abreast with current market issues and transactions. In March 2018 a new version was issued. Knowledge of the contents of the new Framework is testable within the 2019 CIMA F1 syllabus.

# 3 Purpose and status of the Framework

According to the Framework, its purpose is to:

- assist the International Accounting Standards Board (Board) to develop IFRS Standards (Standards) that are based on consistent concepts

- assist preparers to develop consistent accounting policies when no IFRS Standard applies to a particular transaction or other event, or when an IFRS Standard allows a choice of accounting policy

- assist all parties to understand and interpret IFRS Standards.

The Framework is not an accounting standard and does not override the requirements of any IFRS Standards.

4    What does the Framework cover?

The Framework covers the following topics:

- The objectives of general purpose financial reporting
- Qualitative characteristics of useful financial information
- Financial statements and the reporting entity
- The elements of the financial statements
- Recognition and derecognition
- Measurement
- Presentation and disclosure
- Concepts of capital and capital maintenance.

This chapter covers each of these individual areas in detail.

 5    Objectives of general purpose financial reporting

The objective of financial reporting is to provide information about the reporting entity that is useful to users in making decisions relating to providing resources to the entity.

Users of the financial statements include:

– existing and potential investors

– lenders

– other creditors.

Decisions relating to providing resources to an entity include whether or not to:

– buy, sell or hold equity and debt instruments

– provide or settle loans and other forms of credit

– exercise the rights to vote on, or otherwise influence, management's actions that affect the use of the entity's economic resources.

To make such decisions, users will need information regarding the performance (profits), position (asset levels and claims against the entity), adaptability and prospects of an entity. This enables assessment of the stewardship of the directors and their utilisation of the entity's resources. Financial reports can provide significant elements of this detail.

## 6 Qualitative characteristics of useful financial information

For information to be useful it must possess the qualitative characteristics outlined in the Framework.

The Framework splits qualitative characteristics into two categories:

(i) Fundamental qualitative characteristics – **'must have'** characteristics.

- Relevance
- Faithful representation

(ii) Enhancing qualitative characteristics – **'would be nice to have'** characteristics.

- Comparability
- Verifiability
- Timeliness
- Understandability.

### Fundamental qualitative characteristics

### (i) Relevance

Information is relevant when it influences the economic decisions of users by helping them evaluate past, present or future events or confirming or correcting their past evaluations.

The relevance of information can be affected by its nature and materiality. Some items may be relevant to users simply because of their nature whereas some items may only become relevant once they are material. Hence, materiality is a threshold for the quality of information rather than a primary characteristic in its own right.

According to the Framework, information is material if its omission or misstatement could influence the decisions of users.

### Materiality

Materiality is an entity specific aspect of relevance and depends on the size of the item or error judged in the context of the entity's specific financial statements. Materiality will take different forms and values for different entities and, as a result, the Framework does not attempt to quantify it.

### (ii) Faithful representation

If information is to represent faithfully the transactions and other events that it purports to represent, they must be accounted for and presented in accordance with their substance and economic reality and not merely their legal form. This is described as the concept of applying substance over form.

To be a perfectly faithful representation, financial information would possess the following characteristics:

## Completeness

To be understandable information must contain all the necessary descriptions and explanations.

## Neutrality

Information must be neutral, i.e. free from bias. Financial statements are not neutral if, by the selection or presentation of information, they influence the making of a decision or judgement in order to achieve a predetermined result or outcome.

Neutrality is underpinned by the application of **prudence**. Prudence is an accounting mind-set which favours caution in situations of uncertainty and judgement. Practically applications of prudence can lead to judgemental liabilities being recorded more readily than uncertain assets.

## Free from error

Information must be free from error within the bounds of materiality. A material error or an omission can cause the financial statements to be false or misleading and thus unreliable and deficient in terms of their relevance.

Free from error does not mean perfectly accurate in all respects. For example, where an estimate has been used the amount must be described clearly and accurately as being an estimate. This phenomena is described as **measurement uncertainty**.

## Enhancing qualitative characteristics

There are 4 enhancing characteristics identified by the Framework. They are:

### (i) Comparability

Users must be able to compare financial statements over a period of time in order to identify trends in financial position and performance. Users must also be able to compare financial statements of different entities to be able to assess their relative financial position and performance.

In order to achieve comparability, similar items should be treated in a consistent manner from one period to the next and from one entity to another. However, it is not appropriate for an entity to continue accounting for transactions in a certain manner if alternative treatments exist that would be more relevant and reliable.

Disclosure of accounting policies should also be made so that users can identify any changes in these policies or differences between the policies of different entities.

### (ii)    Verifiability

Verifiability occurs if information can be independently confirmed or verified by knowledgeable third parties e.g. could the information be audited?

Verification can be direct or indirect. Direct verification means verifying through direct observation i.e. counting cash.

Indirect verification means checking the inputs (items included in the financial information) to a model, formula or other technique and recalculating the outputs (an expected value) using the same methodology and then comparing the result i.e. recalculating inventory amounts using the same assumption used by an entity such as first-in, first-out method.

### (iii)   Timeliness

Timeliness means having information available to decision makers in time to be capable of influencing their decisions. Generally, the older the information is the less useful it becomes.

### (iv)   Understandability

Information needs to be readily understandable by users. Information that may be relevant to decision making should not be excluded on the grounds that it may be too difficult for certain users to understand.

Understandability depends on:

- the way in which information is presented; and
- the capabilities of users.

It is assumed that users:

- have a reasonable knowledge of business and economic activities; and
- are willing to study the information provided with reasonable diligence.

For information to be understandable users need to be able to perceive its significance.

## 7    Financial statements and the reporting entity

The first two chapters of the Framework outline issues regarding general purpose financial information. The remaining chapters consider the financial statements specifically.

The Framework states that '**financial statements provide information about economic resources of the reporting entity, claims against the entity, and changes in those resources and claims, that meet the definitions of the elements of financial statements**' (Conceptual Framework para 3.1).

## Objectives of financial statements

'The objective of financial statements is to provide financial information about the reporting entity's assets, liabilities, equity, income and expenses that is useful to users of financial statements in assessing the prospects for future net cash inflows to the reporting entity and in assessing management's stewardship of the entity's economic resources' (Conceptual Framework, para 3.2).

That information is provided:

- in the statement of financial position, by recognising assets, liabilities and equity

- in the statement of financial performance by recognising income and expenses

- in other statements (statement of cash flows, statement of changes in equity) and notes.

### Going concern assumption

The Framework states '**financial statements are normally prepared on the assumption that the reporting entity is a going concern and will continue in operation for the foreseeable future**' (Conceptual Framework, para 3.9).

The foreseeable future is not strictly defined but can be generally considered as being a period of greater than 12 months. The financial statements are prepared under the assumption that the entity neither has an intention nor the need to liquidate or significantly reduce the scale of its operations.

If the business was not deemed to be a going concern, the financial statements would be prepared on the break-up basis e.g. all assets are valued using realisable values and no 'non-current' classifications can be used

The **accruals concept** is no longer considered to be an underlying assumption of the financial statements. However, it is still considered by the Framework as an important concept used within general purpose financial information.

The accruals concept states events should be dealt with in the accounting period they occur, rather than the period in which cash flows occur.

### The reporting entity

The Framework defines a reporting entity as an entity that chooses to or is required to prepare financial statements.

A reporting entity can be a single entity or can comprise of more than one entity.

If an entity (parent) has control over another entity (subsidiary), two options for the preparation of the financial statements exist. If a reporting entity comprises both the parent and its subsidiaries, the reporting entity's financial statements are referred to as 'consolidated financial statements'. If a reporting entity is the parent alone, the reporting entity's financial statements are referred to as 'unconsolidated financial statements'.

**8      The elements of financial statements**

The elements of financial statements are:

- Assets
- Liabilities
- Equity
- Income
- Expenses.

 **Assets**

The Framework defines an asset as **'a present economic resource controlled by the entity as a result of past events.**

**An economic resource is a right that has the potential to produce economic benefits'** (Conceptual Framework, para 4.2).

 **Liabilities**

The Framework defines a liability as **'a present obligation of the entity to transfer an economic resource as a result of past events'** (Conceptual Framework, para 4.2).

**Equity**

The Framework defines equity as **'the residual interest in the assets of the entity after deducting all its liabilities'** (Conceptual Framework, para 4.2).

**Income**

The Framework defines income as **'increases in assets or decreases in liabilities that result in increases in equity, other than those relating to contributions from equity participants'** (Conceptual Framework, para 4.2).

Examples include sales, gains on disposal of non-current assets and unrealised gains.

**Expenses**

The Framework defines expenses as **'decreases in assets or increases in liabilities that result in decreases in equity, other than those relating to distributions to equity participants'**(Conceptual Framework, para 4.2).

Examples include expenses that arise in the ordinary course of activities (such as wages, purchases and depreciation) and losses (such as losses on disposal of non-current assets and unrealised losses e.g. losses on revaluation).

## Assets, liabilities and equity interest

### Assets

The Framework defines an asset as **'a present economic resource controlled by the entity as a result of past events.**

**An economic resource is a right that has the potential to produce economic benefits'** To explain further the parts of the definition of an asset:

- **Right** – a right that generates economic resource could take many forms. For instance, an entity may have the right to receive cash, to receive goods or services or to use an asset. Rights are often created through contracts and legislation but can also be created through another entity's past practice.

- **Potential to produce future economic benefit** – The right must have the potential for economic resource.  For that potential to exist, it does not need to be certain, or even likely, that the right will produce economic benefits. It is only necessary that the right already exists and that, in at least one circumstance, it would produce for the entity economic benefits beyond those available to all other parties. However, whether the resource is recognised as an asset is dependent upon the recognition criteria outlined within the Framework (see section 9 below).

- **Control** – An entity controls an economic resource if it has the present ability to direct the use of the economic resource and obtain the economic benefits that may flow from it. Control is the ability to obtain the economic benefits and to restrict the access to others (e.g. by an entity being the sole user of its plant and machinery, or by selling surplus plant and machinery). An asset does not have to be legally owned, the key factor is whether the entity has control over the future economic benefits that the item will provide. A leased vehicle could therefore be an asset.

### Liabilities

The Framework defines a liability as **'a present obligation of the entity to transfer an economic resource as a result of past events'**

For a liability to exist all three of the following will be satisfied:

- **Obligation** – An obligation is a duty or responsibility that an entity has no practical ability to avoid. These may be legal or constructive. A constructive obligation is an obligation which is the result of expected practice rather than required by law or legal contract.

- **Transfer of economic resource** – this could be a transfer of cash, of other property or the provision of a service.

- **Present obligation as a result of past events** – a present obligation exists as a result of past events only if:
  - the entity has already obtained economic benefits or taken an action and,
  - as a consequence, the entity may have to transfer an economic resource that it would not otherwise have had to transfer.

e.g. acceptance of a loan into an entity's bank account creates the right to demand repayment of the balance and, as such, a liability exists.

### Equity

Equity is the residual amount after deducting all liabilities of the entity from all of the entity's assets.

Equity may be sub-classified in the financial statements into share capital, retained earnings and other reserves.

## 9 Recognition and derecognition

According to the Framework, recognition is **'the process of capturing for inclusion in the statement of financial position or the statement(s) of financial performance an item that meets the definition of one of the elements of financial statements – an asset, a liability, equity, income or expenses'**(Conceptual Framework, para 5.1).

### Recognition criteria

To be recognised in the financial statements, items must:

- **meet the definitions of one of the elements** of the financial statements
- provides **relevant** information regarding the particular element
- provides a **faithful representation** of the particular element

### Relevance

Indications that the information regarding an element is **not relevant** include:

- it is uncertain whether an asset or liability exists or,
- an asset or liability exists, but the probability of an inflow or outflow of economic benefits is low

### Faithful representation

Whether the information regarding an element would provide a faithful representation is linked to the ability to measure the element. If there is very high **measurement uncertainty** (e.g. an exceptionally wide range of possible outcomes with probabilities that are exceptionally difficult to estimate) then it could be argued that the inclusion of the element would not provide a faithful representation.

## Derecognition

Derecognition is the removal of all or part of a recognised asset or liability from an entity's statement of financial position. Derecognition normally occurs when that item no longer meets the definition of an asset or of a liability.

### Asset

Derecognition normally occurs when the entity loses control of all or part of the recognised asset.

### Liability

Derecognition normally occurs when the entity no longer has a present obligation for all or part of the recognised liability.

## 10 Measurement of the elements of financial statements

The Framework requires that the elements recognised in financial statements are quantified in monetary terms. This requires the selection of a measurement basis.

There are a number of different ways of measuring the elements including:

### Historical cost

Historical cost measures provide monetary information derived from the price of the transaction at the date the transaction occurs.

Unlike current value, historical cost does not reflect changes in values, except to the extent that those changes relate to impairment of an asset (which would reduce the asset) or a liability becoming onerous (which would increase the liability).

### Asset

The historical cost of an asset is the value of the costs incurred in acquiring or creating the asset, comprising the consideration paid plus transaction costs.

### Liability

The historical cost of a liability is the value of the consideration received to incur or take on the liability minus transaction costs.

### Current value

Current value measures provide monetary information about assets, liabilities and related income and expenses, using information updated to reflect conditions at the measurement date.

Current value measurement bases include:

– Fair value

– Value in use

– Current cost.

### Fair value

Fair value is the price that would be received to sell an asset, or paid to transfer a liability, in an orderly transaction between market participants at the measurement date.

### Value in use and fulfilment values

Assets can use the **value in use** as a measurement basis. Value in use is the present value of the cash flows, or other economic benefits, which an entity expects to derive from the use of an asset and from its ultimate disposal.

Liabilities can use the **fulfilment value** as a measurement basis. Fulfilment value is the present value of the cash, or other economic resources, that an entity expects to be obliged to transfer as it fulfils a liability.

### Current cost

The current cost of an asset is the cost to acquire an equivalent asset at the measurement date, plus the transaction costs that would be incurred at that date.

The current cost of a liability is the consideration that would be received for an equivalent liability at the measurement date minus the transaction costs that would be incurred at that date.

### Historical cost accounting

The historical cost approach has the following features:

- Accounting transactions are recorded at their original historical monetary cost.

- Items or events for which no monetary transaction has occurred are usually ignored altogether.

- Profit for the period is found by matching income against the cost of items consumed in generating the income for the period (such items include non-current assets which depreciate through use, obsolescence or the passage of time).

### Advantages of historical cost accounting

- Easy to understand

- Straightforward to produce

- Historical cost accounts are objective and free from bias

- Historical cost values are reliable and original values can be verified based on original invoices/accompanying documents

- Historical cost accounts do not record gains until they are realised

## Disadvantages of historical cost accounts

In periods in which prices change significantly, historical cost accounts have many deficiencies:

- the carrying amount of non-current assets is often substantially below current value

- Inventory in the statement of financial position reflects prices at the date of purchase or manufacture rather than those current at the year-end

- Statement of profit or loss expenses do not reflect the current value of assets consumed so profit in real terms is exaggerated

- No account is taken of the effect of increasing prices on monetary items (items designated or settled in cash); and

- The overstatement of profits and the understatement of assets can reduce the relevance of accounting ratio analysis (e.g. return on capital employed (ROCE))

As a result of the above, users of accounts can find it difficult to assess an entity's progress from year to year or to compare the results of different operations.

### Example of the deficiencies of historical cost accounts

Entity A acquires a new machine in 20X4. This machine costs $50,000 and has an estimated useful life of ten years.

Entity B acquires an identical one-year old machine in 20X5. The cost of the machine is $48,000 and it has an estimated useful life of nine years.

Depreciation charges (straight-line basis) in 20X5 are as follows.

| | |
|---|---|
| Entity A | $50,000/10 = $5,000 |
| Entity B | $48,000/9 = $5,333 |

CVs at the end of 20X5 are:

| | |
|---|---|
| Entity A $50,000 – $10,000) | = $40,000 |
| (2 × $5,000) | |
| Entity B $48,000 – $5,333 | = $42,667 |

Both entities are using identical machines during 20X5, but the statements of profit or loss will show quite different profit figures because of adherence to historical cost.

### Factors to consider when selecting a measurement base

An entity should select the base that would provide the most relevant and faithful representation of the element being measured in line with the fundamental qualitative characteristics.

The characteristics of the asset and liability being measured should be considered when selecting the measurement base. For example, if the asset is volatile in price and highly sensitive to market factors, then a current value approach would be more relevant. If an asset was to be held in the long-term and is stable in value it could considered that historical cost provides the more relevant (and less costly) information.

As ever, judgement is to be applied when selecting an appropriate measurement base and the Framework does not attempt to select the appropriate measures for specific elements within specific entities.

## 11 Presentation and disclosure

The Framework includes a chapter covering presentation and disclosure within the financial statements.

The chapter includes sections on:

- the objective of presentation and disclosure
- the classification of:
  (i) assets and liabilities
  (ii) equity
  (iii) income and expenses
- aggregation

### Objective of presentation and disclosure

The chapter considers how the presentation and disclosure of information within the financial statements adds to the fundamental and enhancing qualitative characteristics of the information.

By considering consistent presentation and the inclusion of extra disclosures, the relevance, understandability and comparability of the financial statements are improved.

### Classification

Classification is the sorting of assets, liabilities, equity, income or expenses on the basis of shared characteristics for presentation and disclosure purposes.

A specific area to note from this section is that the Framework outlines that income and expenses are classified and included either:

- in the statement of profit or loss or
- outside the statement of profit or loss, in other comprehensive income.

The Framework states that, as the statement of profit or loss is the primary source of information about an entity's financial performance for the period, all income and expenses are, in principle, to be included in that statement.

However, in exceptional circumstances, the Board may decide to exclude from profit or loss income or expenses that arise from a change in the current value of an asset or liability and instead include them in other comprehensive income. This is only allowed if the result gives a more relevant view or a more faithful representation to the statement of profit or loss.

## Aggregation

According to the Framework, aggregation makes information more useful by summarising a large volume of detail. However, aggregation conceals some of that detail. Hence, a balance needs to be found so that relevant information is not obscured either by a large amount of insignificant detail or by excessive aggregation.

## 12 Concepts of capital and capital maintenance

There are two concepts of capital:

- **A financial concept of capital.** With this method capital = net assets or equity of the entity. This concept should be used if the main concern of the user of the financial statements is the maintenance of the nominal value invested capital. This is used by most entities to prepare financial statements.

- **A physical concept of capital.** With this method capital = productive capacity of the entity (measured as units of output per day). This method should be used if the main concern of the user of the financial statements is the operating capacity of the entity.

Capital maintenance means preserving the value of the capital of the entity, and reporting profit only if the capital of the entity has been increased by activities and events in the accounting period.

 **Capital maintenance**

Capital maintenance is a theoretical concept which tries to ensure that excessive dividends are not paid in times of changing prices.

Capital maintenance concepts can be classified as follows:

- Physical capital maintenance (PCM), alternatively known as operating capital maintenance (OCM).

- Financial capital maintenance (FCM).

**Physical capital maintenance (PCM)**

PCM sets aside profits in order to allow the business to continue to operate at current levels of activity. In practice, this tends to mean adjusting opening capital by **specific** price changes

**Example:**

An entity starts trading on 1 January X1 with contribution of $2,000 from owners. This is used to purchase 200 units at $10 each, which are sold for $2,200 cash. Opening capital is $2,000 and closing is $2,200 so profit is usually measured as $200.

However, over the year, the price of the units has increased to $10.75 (a specific price change hitting the business, rather than general). This is a price increase of 7.5% (10.75 – 10.00/10.00).

Therefore increase opening capital by 7.5% to $2,150 (1.075 × 2,000)

Profit is therefore $2,200 – $2,150 = $50

Even if the profit is paid out, the entity is left with cash of $2,150. This is enough to buy 200 more units at $10.75 each. In other words, the productive capacity of the business has been maintained.

**Financial capital maintenance (FCM)**

FCM sets aside profits in order to preserve the value of shareholders' funds in 'real terms', i.e. after inflation.

Can measure the increase in monetary terms or in terms of constant purchasing power:

- Monetary terms

   An entity starts trading on 1 January X1 with contribution of $2,000 from owners. This is used to purchase 200 units at $10 each, which are sold for $2,200 cash.

   Opening capital is $2,000 and closing is $2,200 so profit is usually measured as $200.

- Constant purchasing power

   Inflation over time makes comparisons difficult so constant purchasing power adjusts for general indices of inflation – e.g. retail prices index.

   If increase in RPI is 5%

   Increase opening capital by 5% to $2,100 (1.05 × 2,000)

   So profit is only $2,200 – $2,100 = $100.

## 13 The Framework and the standard-setting process

The Framework provides a point of reference to the IASB when developing individual standards. Since the standards will then be developed with reference to a common set of concepts the standards themselves will become more consistent.

The IFRS Interpretations Committee issues guidance where issues have arisen which are not specifically covered by a standard. The IFRS Interpretations Committee can therefore ensure its guidance is consistent with agreed underlying principles by referring to the Framework.

### Test your understanding 1 – Qualitative characteristics

The International Accounting Standards Board's (IASB's) The Conceptual Framework for Financial Reporting identifies fundamental and enhancing qualitative characteristics of financial information.

**Required:**

Identify and explain the TWO fundamental qualitative characteristics of financial information listed in the IASB's Framework.

### Test your understanding 2 – IASB objectives

The Conceptual Framework for Financial Reporting (Framework) has a number of purposes, including:

- to assist the International Accounting Standards Board (Board) to develop IFRS Standards that are based on consistent concepts

- to assist preparers to develop consistent accounting policies when no IFRS Standard applies to a particular transaction or other event, or when an IFRS Standard allows a choice of accounting policy

- to assist all parties to understand and interpret the IFRS Standards.

**Required:**

Discuss how the Framework can help the IASB achieve these objectives.

**Test your understanding 3 – Practice questions**

1    In the Conceptual Framework for Financial Reporting, which of the following is not a qualitative characteristic of useful financial information?

A    Relevance

B    Faithful representation

C    Materiality

D    Understandability

2    According to The Conceptual Framework for Financial Reporting, which of the following items is an underlying assumption when preparing a set of financial statements?

A    Prudence

B    Going Concern

C    Accruals

D    Comparability

3    Which of the following items best defines relevant financial information to the users of financial statements?

A    Information that is free from material error, bias and is a faithful representation

B    Information that has been prudently prepared

C    Information that is comparable from one period to the next

D    Information that influences the decisions of users

4    Which of the following criteria need to be satisfied in order for an item to be recognised in the financial statements?

(i)    It meets the definition of an element of the financial statements

(ii)   It is probable that future economic benefits will flow to or from the entity

(iii)  It provides relevant information regarding the item

(iv)  The item has a cost or value that can be reliably measured

A    (i) and (ii)

B    (i) and (iii)

C    (i) and (iv)

D    (i), (iii) and (iv)

5    **Which of the following measurement bases could be used by an entity to recognise an asset according to The Conceptual Framework for Financial Reporting?**

A    Historical cost

B    Current cost

C    Value in use

D    Any of the above

6    The IASB's Framework identifies qualitative characteristics.

(i)    Relevance

(ii)    Comparability

(iii)    Verifiability

(iv)    Understandability

(v)    Faithful representation.

**Which of the above are not listed as enhancing characteristics?**

A    (i), (iv) and (v)

B    (ii), (iii) and (iv)

C    (ii) and (iii)

D    (i) and (v)

7    The Conceptual Framework for Financial Reporting provides definitions of the elements of financial statements. One of the elements defined by the Framework is 'expenses'.

**Which of the following represents the definition of 'expenses' as per the Framework?**

A    A present economic resource controlled by the entity as a result of past events

B    The residual interest in the assets of the entity after deducting all its liabilities

C    Decreases in assets or increases in liabilities that result in decreases in equity, other than those relating to distributions to equity participants

D    A right that has the potential to produce economic benefits

8   The International Accounting Standards Board's (IASB) Conceptual Framework for Financial Reporting sets out two fundamental qualitative characteristics of financial information, relevance and faithful representation.

**Which of the following characteristics would you expect information to possess if it is to have faithful representation? Select all that apply.**

A   Neutrality

B   Relevance

C   Prudence

D   Accruals

E   Completeness

9   According to the International Accounting Standards Board's Conceptual Framework for Financial Reporting, the objective of financial statements is:

'to provide financial information about the reporting entity's assets, liabilities, equity, income and expenses that is useful to _____ of financial statements in assessing the prospects for future net cash inflows to the reporting entity and in assessing management's _____ of the entity's economic resources'

**From the options below, fill in the missing information.**

**Directors, users, shareholders, utilisation, stewardship, performance**

10   The Conceptual Framework for Financial Reporting lists the qualitative characteristics of financial statements.

(i)     Comparability,

(ii)    Verifiability,

(iii)   Timeliness,

(iv)   Understandability,

(v)    Relevance,

(vi)   Faithful representation.

**Which TWO of the above are NOT included in the enhancing qualitative characteristics listed by the Framework?**

A   (i) and (vii)

B   (ii) and (v)

C   (iv) and (v)

D   (v) and (vi)

11  According to the International Accounting Standards Board's Conceptual Framework for Financial Reporting, which of the following are types of capital maintenance? Select all that apply.

A  Human

B  Physical

C  Spiritual

D  Neutral

E  Intellectual

F  Financial

12  To be recognised in the financial statements, items must:

–  meet the definitions of the _____ of the financial statements

–  provide _____ information regarding the particular transaction

–  provide a _____ of the particular transaction

**From the options below, fill in the missing information.**

**elements, users, components, relevant, free from error, faithful representation, financial, disclosure**

13  According to the Conceptual Framework for Financial Reporting, which of the following statements are true?

A  All income and expenses must always be included within profit or loss

B  Aggregation of information is forbidden

C  Classification sorts transactions based on shared characteristics

D  Disclosures notes are not considered to be part of the financial statements

## 14 Summary diagram

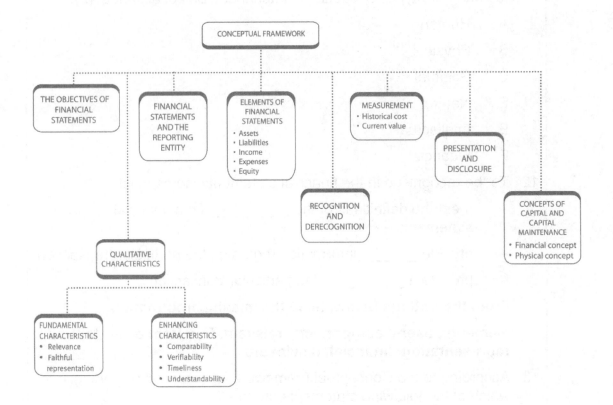

Test your understanding answers

### Test your understanding 1 – Qualitative characteristics

The two principal qualitative characteristics are:

**Relevance** – Information is relevant when it influences the economic decisions of users by helping them evaluate past, present or future events or confirming or correcting their past evaluations.

The relevance of information can be affected by its nature and materiality. Some items may be relevant to users simply because of their nature whereas some items may only become relevant once they are material. Hence, materiality is a threshold quality of information rather than a primary characteristic.

According to the Framework, information is material if its omission or misstatement could influence the decisions of users.

**Faithful representation** – If information is to represent faithfully the transactions and other events that it purports to represent, they must be accounted for and presented in accordance with their substance and economic reality and not merely their legal form.

To be a faithful representation of financial performance and position, the following characteristics should be evident:

**Completeness** – To be understandable information must contain all the necessary descriptions and explanations.

**Neutrality** – Information must be neutral, i.e. free from bias. Financial statements are not neutral if, by the selection or presentation of information, they influence the making of a decision or judgement in order to achieve a predetermined result or outcome.

**Free from error** – Information must be free from error within the bounds of materiality. A material error or an omission can cause the financial statements to be false or misleading and thus unreliable and deficient in terms of their relevance.

Free from error does not mean perfectly accurate in all respects. For example, where an estimate has been used the amount must be described clearly and accurately as being an estimate.

### Test your understanding 2 – IASB objectives

A conceptual Framework provides guidance on the broad principles of financial reporting. It highlights how items should be recorded, on how they should be measured and presented. The setting of broad principles could assist in the development of accounting standards, ensuring that the principles are followed consistently as standards and rules are developed.

A conceptual Framework can provide guidance on how similar items are treated. By providing definitions and criteria that can be used in deciding the recognition and measurement of items, conceptual Frameworks can act as a point of reference for those setting standards, those preparing and those using financial information.

The existence of a conceptual Framework can remove the need to address the underlying issues over and over again. Where underlying principles have been established and the accounting standards are based on these principles, there is no need to deal with them fully in each of the standards. This will save the standard-setters time in developing standards and will again ensure consistent treatment of items.

Where a technical issue is raised but is not specifically addressed in an accounting standard, a conceptual Framework can help provide guidance on how such items should be treated. Where a short-term technical solution is provided by the standard-setters, the existence of a conceptual Framework will ensure that the treatment is consistent with the broad set of agreed principles

**Test your understanding 3 – Practice questions**

1   C

2   B

3   D

4   B

5   D

6   D

7   C

Option A is the definition of an asset.

Option B is the definition of equity.

Option D is the definition of an economic resource.

8   A and E

The characteristics of faithful representation are completeness, neutrality and free from error.

9   The objective of financial statements is to provide financial information about the reporting entity's assets, liabilities, equity, income and expenses that is useful to **users** of financial statements in assessing the prospects for future net cash inflows to the reporting entity and in assessing management's **stewardship** of the entity's economic resources'

10   D

11   B, F

12   elements, relevant, faithful representation

'To  be recognised in the financial statements, items must:

– meet the definitions of the **elements** of the financial statements

– provide **relevant** information regarding the particular transaction

– provide a **faithful representation** of the particular transaction'

13   C

Income and expenses can, in exceptional circumstances, be classified under other comprehensive income. A is incorrect.

Significant amounts of content within the financial statements are aggregated otherwise the content would be unwieldy. Option B is incorrect.

Disclosure notes are considered part of the financial statements. Option D is incorrect.

# Introduction to Single Entity Accounts

## Chapter learning objectives

| Lead | Component outcome |
|---|---|
| B3. Apply financial reporting standards to prepare basic financial statements | Apply financial reporting standards to prepare: |
| | a. Statement of financial position |
| | b. Statement of profit or loss and other comprehensive income |
| | c. Statement of changes in equity |

# 1    Session content

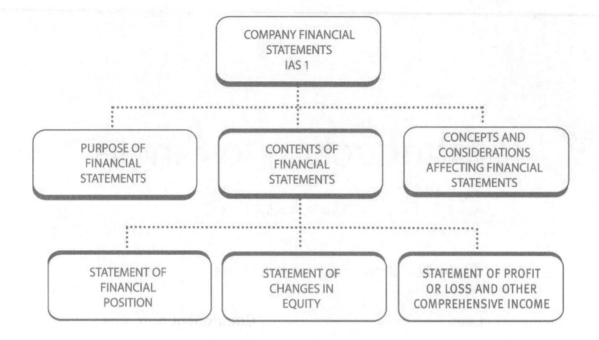

## 2    IAS 1 *Presentation of Financial Statements*

All entities preparing their financial statements in accordance with International Accounting Standards should follow the requirements of IAS 1 *Presentation of Financial Statements*. IAS 1 prescribes what a set of financial statements should contain and how they should be presented.

### Purpose of financial statements

According to IAS 1 *Presentation of Financial Statements* the objective of financial statements is to provide information about the financial position, performance and cash flows of an enterprise that is useful in making economic decisions. The financial statements will also show how effectively management have looked after the resources of the entity, i.e. it will help users assess the stewardship of management.

### Contents of financial statements

IAS 1 defines a complete set of financial statements as:

- **'a statement of financial position**
- **either:**
  - **a statement of profit or loss and other comprehensive income, or**
  - **a statement of profit or loss plus a statement showing other comprehensive income**

- **a statement of changes in equity**

- **a statement of cash flows**

- **accounting policies note and other explanatory note' (IAS 1, para 10)**

IAS 1 does not require the above titles to be used by entities. It is likely that many entities in practice will continue to use the previous terms of balance sheet rather than statement of financial position and cash flow statement rather than statement of cash flows.

Entities are also encouraged to present a financial review by management which describes and explains the main features of the entity's financial performance and financial position.

This chapter looks at the formats of the statement of profit or loss and other comprehensive income, statement of financial position and statement of changes in equity. The statement of cash flow is considered in a later chapter. Notes to the financial statements are considered with their relevant standards, where appropriate.

### Responsibility for financial statements

The board of directors (and/or other governing body) of an entity is responsible for the preparation and presentation of its financial statements.

### 3 Concepts and other considerations affecting financial statements

### Fair presentation

IAS 1 *Presentation of Financial Statements* states that '**Financial statements shall present fairly the financial position, financial performance and cash flows of an entity**' (IAS 1, para 15). Entities that comply with all relevant IAS's will virtually always achieve this objective.

A fair presentation requires that entities:

- show a faithful representation of the effects of transactions

- select definitions and recognition criteria set down in accordance with the conceptual framework and apply accounting policies in accordance with IAS 8 *Accounting Policies, Changes in Accounting Estimates and Errors* (not within the F1 syllabus)

- present information in a manner which provides relevant, reliable, comparable and understandable information;

- provide additional disclosures if the requirements of an IFRS Standard or IAS are insufficient to enable users to understand the impact of the transaction on the financial position and performance

If, however, an entity feels that compliance with an IFRS Standard would be misleading and that it is necessary to depart from the requirements of an IFRS Standard in order to show a fair presentation, the entity should make the following disclosures:

- that management have concluded that the financial statements do present fairly the financial position, financial performance and cash flows

- that the entity has complied with IFRS Standards except that it has departed from an IFRS Standard in order to show a fair presentation

- the IFRS Standard that has been departed from, the nature of the departure i.e. the treatment that the IFRS Standard would require and the reason why such treatment would be misleading and the treatment adopted instead

- the financial impact of the departure on net profit/loss, assets, liabilities, equity and cash flows

However, departing from the provisions of the standards in the interests of fair presentation, would be very rare.

## Going concern

According to IAS 1 *Presentation of Financial Statements* financial statements should be prepared on the going concern basis unless management intend to liquidate the business or to cease trading.

Preparing financial statements on the going concern basis means preparing them on the assumption that the entity will continue to trade for the foreseeable future.

## Accruals basis

IAS 1 *Presentation of Financial Statements* requires entities to prepare their financial statements (except for cash flow information) using the accruals basis of accounting.

This means that transactions should be recorded in the accounting period to which they relate regardless of whether or not cash has been received or paid.

This concept also means that expenses should be recognised in the statement of profit or loss and other comprehensive income so as to match against directly related income.

## Consistency

Presentation and classification of items should be consistent from one period to the next.

Changes are allowed, if required by an IFRS or if it is deemed more appropriate to change the presentation of information.

## Materiality and aggregation

Each material class of similar items should be presented separately in the financial statements. Immaterial amounts should be aggregated with amounts of a similar nature and need not be disclosed separately.

Omissions or misstatements of items are material if they could influence the economic decisions of users. Materiality depends on the size and nature of the omission or misstatement.

## Off-setting

Assets and liabilities, and income and expenses, should not be offset except when offsetting is required or allowed by an IFRS.

## Comparative information

Comparative information should be disclosed in respect of the previous period for all amounts reported in the financial statements unless an IFRS requires or allows otherwise.

### Other requirements

Financial statements should be presented at least annually and should be issued on a timely basis (within 6 months of the end of the reporting period for public entities and 9 months for private entities) to be useful to users.

IAS 1 does not specify the format of financial statements, but it does provide an appendix which sets out illustrative formats for the statements to be included in financial statements. In addition, it provides guidance on the items that should be disclosed in these statements and those that can be relegated to the notes that accompany the statements (see below suggested formats).

## The statement of financial position

The suggested format for the statement of financial position (SOFP) is as follows:

**XYZ Statement of Financial Position as at 31 December 20X0**

|  | $000 | $000 |
|---|---|---|
| **Assets** | | |
| **Non-current assets** | | |
| Property, plant and equipment | X | |
| Goodwill | X | |
| Other non-current assets | X | |
|  | — | |
|  | | X |
| **Current assets** | | |
| Inventories | X | |
| Trade and other receivables (e.g. prepayments) | X | |
| Cash and cash equivalents | X | |
|  | — | |
|  | | X |
| **Non-current assets held for sale** | | X |
|  | | — |
| Total assets | | X |
|  | | — |
| **Equity and liabilities** | | |
| **Capital and reserves** | | |
| Issued share capital | X | |
| Share premium | X | |
| Revaluation reserve | X | |
| Retained earnings | X | |
|  | — | |
| Total equity | | X |
| **Non-current liabilities** | | |
| Long-term borrowings | X | |
| Provisions | X | |
|  | — | |
|  | | X |
| **Current liabilities** | | |
| Trade and other payables | X | |
| Short-term borrowings | X | |
| Current tax payable | X | |
|  | — | |
|  | | X |
|  | | — |
| Total equity and liabilities | | X |
|  | | — |

The format requires comparative figures for the previous year, these have been omitted as you will not need to prepare comparatives in questions.

Assessment on single entity accounts will be in the form of OTQ's. They will only test one or two principles at a time. You will not be expected to prepare a set of financial statements in totality.

### Information to be presented in the SOFP

IAS 1 *Presentation of Financial Statements* requires that, as a minimum, the following line items appear in the statement of financial position (where there are amounts to be classified within these categories):

(a)   property, plant and equipment

(b)   investment property

(c)   intangible assets

(d)   financial assets (excluding amounts shown under (e), (h) and (i))

(e)   investments accounted for using the equity method

(f)   biological assets

(g)   inventories

(h)   trade and other receivables

(i)   cash and cash equivalents

(j)   the total of assets classified as held for sale in accordance with IFRS 5 *Non-current Assets Held for Sale and Discontinued Operations*

(k)   trade and other payables

(l)   provisions

(m)   financial liabilities (excluding amounts shown under (k) or (l))

(n)   liabilities and assets for current tax as defined in IAS 12 *Income Taxes*

(o)   deferred tax liabilities and deferred tax assets, as defined in IAS 12 *Income Taxes*

(p)   liabilities included in disposal groups classified as held for sale in accordance with IFRS 5 *Non-current Assets Held for Sale and Discontinued Operations*

(q)   non-controlling interest, presented within equity

(r)   issued capital and reserves attributable to owners of the parent

The above list includes items that the IASB believes are so different in nature or function that they should be separately disclosed, but does not require them to appear in a fixed order or format.

NB. Some of these classes of transactions are not covered within the F1 syllabus but are included for completeness purposes.

Additional line items, headings and subtotals should be shown in the statement of financial position if another IFRS requires it or where it is necessary to show a fair presentation of the financial position. In deciding whether additional items should be separately presented, management should consider:

- the nature and liquidity of assets and their materiality (e.g. the separate disclosure of monetary and non-monetary amounts and current and non-current assets)

- their function within the entity (e.g. the separate disclosure of operating assets and financial assets, inventories and cash) and

- the amounts, nature and timing of liabilities (e.g. the separate disclosure of interest-bearing and non-interest-bearing liabilities and provisions and current and non-current liabilities).

Assets and liabilities that have a different nature or function within an entity are sometimes subject to different measurement bases, for example, plant and equipment may be carried at cost or held at a revalued amount (in accordance with IAS 16 *Property, Plant and Equipment*). The use of these different measurement bases for different classes of items suggests separate presentation is necessary for users to fully understand the accounts.

## Information to be presented in either the SOFP/notes

Further sub-classifications of the line items should be presented either in the statement of financial position or in the notes. The size, nature and function of the amounts involved, or the requirements of another IFRS will normally determine whether the disclosure is in the statement of financial position or in the notes.

The disclosures will vary for each item, but IAS 1 *Presentation of Financial Statements* gives the following examples:

(a) tangible assets are analysed (IAS 16 *Property, Plant and Equipment*) by class e.g. property, plant and equipment, land and buildings, etc.

(b) receivables are analysed between:

- amounts receivable from trade customers

- receivables from related parties

- prepayments

- other amounts

(c) inventories are classified (IAS 2 *Inventories*) into merchandise, production supplies, materials, work in progress and finished goods

(d) provisions are analysed showing provisions for employee benefits separate from any other provisions

(e) equity capital and reserves are analysed showing separately the various classes of paid-in capital, share premium and reserves

## Share capital and reserves disclosures

IAS 1 *Presentation of Financial Statements* also requires that the following information on share capital and reserves be made either in the statement of financial position or in the notes:

(a) for each class of share capital:

- the number of shares authorised

- the number of shares issued and fully paid, and issued but not fully paid

- par value per share, or that the shares have no par value

- a reconciliation of the number of shares outstanding at the beginning and at the end of the year, the rights, preferences and restrictions attaching to that class, including restrictions on the distribution of dividends and the repayment of capital,

- shares in the entity held by the entity itself or by subsidiaries or associates of the entity, and

- shares reserved for issuance under options and sales contracts, including the terms and amounts

(b) a description of the nature and purpose of each reserve within owners' equity

IAS 1 *Presentation of Financial Statements* requires the following to be disclosed in the notes:

- the amount of dividends that were proposed or declared after the reporting period but before the financial statements were authorised for issue

- the amount of any cumulative preference dividends not recognised.

Note: IAS 1 and IAS 10 *Events After the Reporting Period* do not allow proposed dividends to be included as a liability in the statement of financial position, unless the dividend was declared before the end of the reporting period.

**Current/Non-current distinction**

**Current assets**

An asset should be classified as a current asset when it is any of the following:

- is expected to be realised in, or is intended for sale or consumption in the entity's normal operating cycle

- is held primarily for trading purposes

- is expected to be realised within 12 months of the end of the reporting period or

- is cash or cash equivalent

All other assets should be classified as non-current assets.

**Current liabilities**

A liability should be classified as a current liability when it:

- is expected to be settled in the entity's normal operating cycle

- is due to be settled within 12 months of the end of the reporting period

- is held primarily for the purpose of being traded or

- the entity does not have an unconditional right to defer settlement of the liability for at least 12 months after the end of the reporting period

All other liabilities should be classified as non-current liabilities.

## 4 Statement of changes in equity

The statement of changes in equity (SOCIE) provides a summary of all changes in equity..

This includes the effect of share issues and dividends.

This statement is useful since the total change in equity reflects the increase or decreases in the net assets of the enterprise in the period and so reflects the change in the wealth of the enterprise in the period.

## XYZ Statement of changes in equity for the year ended 31 December 20X0

| | Share capital $000 | Share premium $000 | Revaluation reserve $000 | Retained earnings $000 | Total $000 |
|---|---|---|---|---|---|
| Balance at 31 December 20W9 | X | X | X | X | X |
| Transfer to retained earnings | | | (X) | X | – |
| Total comprehensive income for the period | | | X | X | X |
| Dividends | | | | (X) | (X) |
| Issue of share capital | X | X | | | X |
| At 31 December 20X0 | X | X | X | X/(X) | X |

### Dividends and shares

Share capital in the SOFP may include both ordinary/equity and preference shares.

**Ordinary/equity shares**

- Ordinary/equity shareholders (The terms ordinary and equity are used interchangeably) own a percentage of the entity's net assets.

- Voting rights are attached to the shares.

- A year-end dividend may be paid to shareholders based on the performance of the entity.

- The dividend is paid as an amount per share.

- A dividend will first be proposed by directors, then declared (confirmed) and then paid.

- Ordinary/equity dividends should only be accounted for when declared.

- Dividends may be interim, i.e. paid part way through the year and final, i.e. declared and/or paid at year-end.

Ordinary/equity shares will be accounted for as follows:

Debit      Cash/Bank

Credit      Share capital (nominal value)

Credit      Share premium (excess of proceeds above nominal value)

Ordinary/equity dividends will be accounted for as follows:

Debit      Retained earnings (shown in SOCIE)

Credit      Cash/Bank

### Preference shares

- Preference shareholders own a percentage of the entity's share capital.

- Voting rights are not attached to the shares.

- A year-end dividend will be paid to shareholders based on a percentage of the investment.

- Preference dividends should be accounted for on an accruals basis.

Preference dividends will be accounted for as follows:

If classified as equity instruments:

Debit      Retained earnings (SPL)

Credit      Cash (SOFP)

If classified as liability instruments:

Debit      Finance Cost (SPL)

Credit      Accruals (SOFP)

---

### Test your understanding 1 – SOCIE

An entity Apple has the following balances at 1 January 20X1:

| | $ |
|---|---:|
| Share capital ($1 nominal value) | 100,000 |
| Share premium | 50,000 |
| Retained earnings | 200,000 |

During the year Apple issued 50,000 shares at $1.20 and paid all shareholders a dividend of $0.10 per share.

Profit after tax amounted to $120,000.

**Required:**

Prepare the statement of changes in equity for the year ended 31 December 20X1 for Apple.

# 5    Statement of profit or loss and other comprehensive income

The Conceptual Framework sets out the need for a statement of performance. It does not define whether this is a single statement or two separate statements.

IAS 1 *Presentation of Financial Statements* applies The Framework's requirements for a statement of performance by allowing a choice of two presentations of profit or loss and other comprehensive income:

- A statement of profit or loss and other comprehensive income; or

- A statement of profit or loss showing the profit or loss for the period PLUS a separate statement of other comprehensive income, which will also include a total for total comprehensive income.

**Total comprehensive income** is the profit or loss for the period, plus other comprehensive income.

**Other comprehensive income (OCI)** is income and expenses that are not recognised in profit or loss (i.e. they are recorded in reserves rather than as an element of the profit for the period).

In F1, other comprehensive income mainly includes any change in the revaluation reserve. Further detail on OCI can be found later in this chapter.

The statement of profit or loss and other comprehensive income would be presented as one statement as follows:

**XYZ Statement of profit or loss and other comprehensive Income for the year ended 31 December 20X0**

|  | $000 |
|---|---|
| Revenue | X |
| Cost of sales | (X) |
|  |  |
| Gross profit/(loss) | X/(X) |
| Distribution costs | (X) |
| Administrative expenses | (X) |
|  |  |
| Profit/(loss) from operations | X/(X) |
| Income from investments | X |
| Finance cost | (X) |
|  |  |
| Profit/(loss) before tax | X/(X) |
| Income tax expense | (X) |
|  |  |
| Profit/(loss) for the period | X/(X) |
| **Other comprehensive income** |  |
| e.g. Gain/loss on revaluation | X |
|  |  |
| **Total comprehensive income for the year** | X |

This analysis of expenses is based on the function method. This presentation method is the format most likely to appear in the OTQ's and case study.

The alternative method for presentation of expenses is to categorise by the nature of expenses. This is commonly associated with manufacturing entities but is not widely utilised.

**Nature of expenses method**

In this method expenses are presented according to their nature rather than their function as follows:

**XYZ Statement of profit or loss and other comprehensive Income for the year ended 31 December 20X0**

| | $000 |
|---|---|
| Revenue | X |
| Other operating income | X |
| Changes in inventory of WIP and finished goods | (X) |
| Work performed by the entity and capitalised | X |
| Raw material and consumables used | (X) |
| Employee benefits expense | (X) |
| Depreciation and amortisation expense | (X) |
| Impairment of property, plant and equipment | (X) |
| Other expenses | (X) |
| Finance costs | (X) |
| | ___ |
| Profit/(loss) before tax | X/(X) |
| Income tax expense | (X) |
| | ___ |
| Profit/(loss) for the period | X/(X) |
| **Other comprehensive income** | |
| Gain/loss on revaluation | X |
| | ___ |
| **Total comprehensive income for the year** | X |

**Material items**

- When items of income and expenses are material, their nature and amount shall be disclosed separately before operating profit.

- This may either be done on the face of the statement of profit or loss and other comprehensive income or in the notes.

- Examples:

  - inventory write-offs

  - impairment losses

  - restructuring costs

  - disposals of property, plant and equipment

  - litigation settlements

The statement of profit or loss used to be called the income statement. The current revised IAS 1 states either title can be used. For assessment purposes always use the current title of statement of profit or loss.

> **Other comprehensive income**
>
> IAS 1 requires other comprehensive income to be split between two headings:
>
> - items that will not be reclassified to profit or loss and
>
> - items that may be reclassified subsequently to profit or loss
>
> F1 students will mainly deal with gains or losses arising from revaluations of property, plant and equipment in other comprehensive income and these should be shown as 'items that will not be reclassified to profit or loss'.
>
> Items that may be reclassified subsequently to profit or loss could be exchange differences on translating foreign operations, fair value through profit or loss financial assets, cash flow hedges and income tax relating to any items reclassified (covered in the F2 syllabus).

## Alternative presentation – two separate statements

An entity may present two statements instead of one: a separate statement of profit or loss and a statement of total comprehensive income.

### Statement 1 – Statement of profit or loss

A recommended format for the statement of profit or loss would be as follows:

**XYZ Statement of profit or loss for the year ended 31 December 20X0**

|  | $000 |
|---|---|
| Revenue | X |
| Cost of sales | (X) |
|  |  |
| Gross profit/(loss) | X/(X) |
| Distribution costs | (X) |
| Administrative expenses | (X) |
|  |  |
| Profit/(loss) from operations | X/(X) |
| Income from investments | X |
| Finance cost | (X) |
|  |  |
| Profit/(loss) before tax | X/(X) |
| Income tax expense | (X) |
|  |  |
| Profit/(loss) for the period | X/(X) |

### Statement 2 – Statement of profit or loss and other comprehensive income

A recommended format for the presentation of total comprehensive income as a separate statement would be:

**XYZ Statement of profit or loss and other comprehensive income for the year ended 31 December 20X0**

|  |  |
|---|---|
| Profit/(loss) for the period | X/(X) |
| **Other comprehensive income** |  |
| e.g. Gain/loss on revaluation | X/(X) |
|  |  |
| **Total comprehensive income for the year** | X |

## Information to be presented in the SPL

IAS 1 *Presentation of Financial Statements* requires that certain information (as a minimum) is presented in the statement of profit or loss, including:

(a)  revenue

(b)  finance costs

(c)  share of profits and losses of associates and joint ventures (beyond the scope of this syllabus),

(d)  tax expense

(e)  a single amount for the total of discontinued operations (see later in publication for more detail)

Additional line items, headings and subtotals should be shown in the statement of profit or loss if another IFRS requires it or where it is necessary to show a fair presentation of the financial position.

Materiality, the nature and function of the item are likely to be the main considerations when deciding whether to include an additional line item in the statement of profit or loss.

## Notes to the financial statements

Notes to the financial statements normally include narrative descriptions or more detailed analysis of items in the financial statements, as well as additional information such as contingent liabilities and commitments.

IAS 1 also provides guidance on the structure of the accompanying notes to financial statements, the accounting policies and other required disclosures.

The notes to the financial statements of an entity should:

(a)  present information about the basis of preparation of the financial statements and the specific accounting policies adopted for significant transactions

(b)  disclose the information required by other IFRSs that is not presented elsewhere in the financial statements

(c)  provide additional information which is not presented elsewhere in financial statements but is relevant to an understanding of any of them

Notes to the financial statements should be presented in a systematic manner and any item in the financial statements should be cross-referenced to any related information in the notes.

Notes are normally provided in the following order, which assists users in understanding the financial statements and comparing them with those of other entities:

(a) statement of compliance with IFRSs

(b) summary of the significant accounting policies applied

(c) supporting information for items presented in each financial statement in the order in which each line item and each financial statement is presented

(d) other disclosures, including:

    – contingent liabilities, commitments and unrecognised contractual commitments other financial disclosures

    – non-financial disclosures

## Accounting policies

The summary of significant accounting policies in the notes to the financial statements should describe the following:

- the measurement basis (or bases) used in preparing the financial statements and

- each specific accounting policy that is necessary for a proper understanding of the financial statements

### Test your understanding 2 – Practice questions

1 **Which of the following best describes the purpose of financial statements according to IAS 1 *Presentation of Financial Statements*?**

    A    To provide information that enables users to assess the stewardship of management

    B    To provide information about the financial position, financial performance and cash flows of an enterprise

    C    To provide a summary of all financial transactions entered into in the accounting period

    D    To provide an statement of profit or loss and other comprehensive income and a statement of financial position

2 **Which of the following are concepts that should be applied when preparing financial statements according to IAS 1 *Presentation of Financial Statements*?**

(i) Going concern

(ii) Accruals

(iii) Consistency

(iv) Off-setting

A (i) and (ii)

B (i) and (iii)

C (i), (ii) and (iv)

D All of them

3 **Which of the following items must be shown on the face of the statement of profit or loss and other comprehensive income according to IAS 1 *Presentation of Financial Statements*?**

(i) Revenue

(ii) Cost of sales

(iii) Gross profit

(iv) Finance costs

(v) Income tax expense

A All of them

B (i), (ii), (iii) and (iv)

C (i), (iv) and (v)

D (i), (ii) and (iii)

4 **Which of the following items would be shown in the statement of changes in equity?**

(i) Profit for period

(ii) Dividends paid

(iii) Dividends proposed after the reporting period

(iv) Issue of shares

(v) Revaluation surplus

A (i), (ii), (iv) and (v)

B (i), (ii), (iii) and (iv)

C (i), (iii), (iv) and (v)

D All of them

5   **Which of the following items would be shown as other comprehensive income on the statement of profit or loss and other comprehensive income?**

(i)     Profit for period

(ii)    Dividends paid

(iii)   Dividends proposed

(iv)    Issue of shares

(v)     Revaluation surplus

A     (i), (ii), (iv) and (v)

B     (i), (ii), and (iv)

C     (v)

D     All of them

6   **According to IAS 1 *Presentation of Financial Statements*, which of the following must be recognised in the statement of profit or loss?**

A     Depreciation

B     Equity dividends paid

C     Revaluation gains

D     Transfer from a revaluation reserve to retained earnings when a revalued asset is sold

7   **According to IAS 1 *Presentation of Financial Statements* which of the following will appear separately in an entity's statement of changes in equity?**

A     Other income and dividends paid

B     Other income, surplus arising on a revaluation and proceeds from a share issue

C     Dividends paid, dividends received and proceeds from a share issue

D     Dividends paid and proceeds from a share issue

8    **Which of the following assets would be classified as current according to IAS 1 Presentation of Financial Statements definition?**

Asset A which is expected to be sold within the next 12 months

Asset B which is not expected to be sold within the next 12 months but expected to be realised with the entity's normal operating cycle

Asset C which is held primarily for the purpose of being traded but for which there is currently no anticipated sale date

A    Asset A only

B    Asset A and Asset B

C    Asset A and Asset C

D    All of them

## 6 Summary diagram

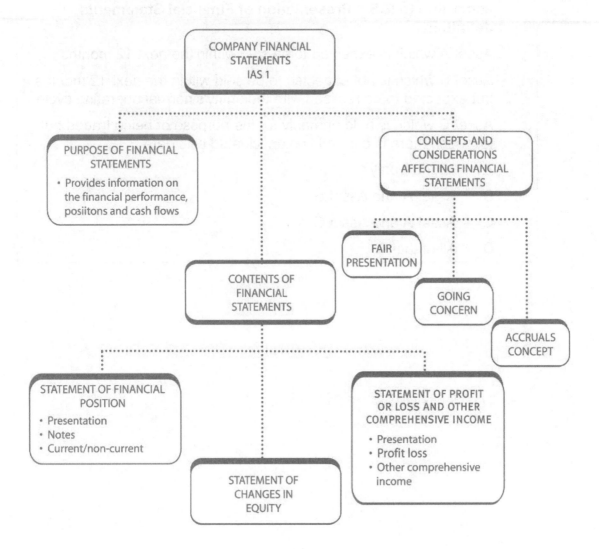

# Test your understanding answers

## Test your understanding 1 – SOCIE

**Apples statement of changes in equity for the year ended 31 December 20X1**

| | Share capital | Share premium | Retained earnings | Total |
|---|---|---|---|---|
| | $ | $ | $ | $ |
| Balance at 1 January 20X1 | 100,000 | 50,000 | 200,000 | 350,000 |
| Profit for the year | – | – | 120,000 | 120,000 |
| Issue of share capital (W1) | 50,000 | 10,000 | | 60,000 |
| Dividends paid (W2) | – | – | (15,000) | (15,000) |
| Balance at 31 December 20X1 | 150,000 | 60,000 | 305,000 | 515,000 |

(W1) Share issue = 50,000 × $1 = $50,000 share capital and 50,000 × $0.20 = $10,000 share premium.

(W2) Dividend of $0.10 per share is based on 150,000 shares (100,000 b/wd plus 50,000 issued during the year)

## Test your understanding 2 – Practice questions

1  B

2  D

3  C

4  A

5  C

6  A – All other items will be shown in the SOCIE and not the statement of profit or loss. The revaluation gain (option C) will also be shown as other comprehensive income.

7  D – Other income and dividends received form part of the statement of profit or loss

8  D

# Non-current assets – IAS 16 Property, plant and equipment and IAS 36 Impairment of assets

## Chapter learning objectives

| Lead | Component outcome |
|------|-------------------|
| B2. Explain specific IFRS financial reporting standards | Explain the specific financial reporting standards related to:<br><br>a. Non-current assets<br><br>c. Impairment |

# 1 Session content

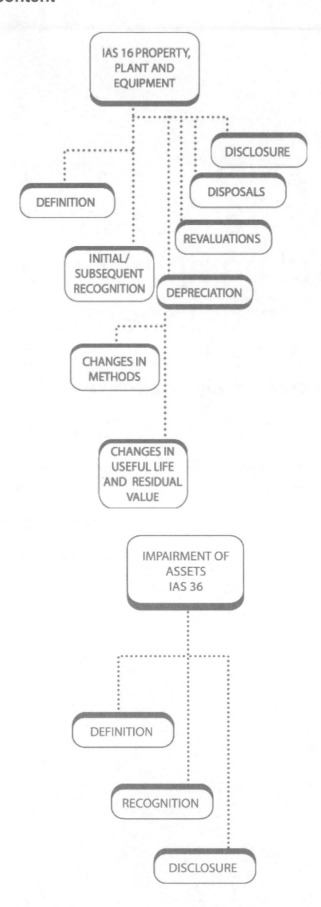

## 2    IAS 16 Property, plant and equipment: definitions

### Property, plant and equipment

Property, plant and equipment are tangible assets that:

- are held by an entity for use in the production or supply of goods or services, for rental to others, or for administrative purposes, and

- are expected to be used during more than one period.

You should know these definitions from your earlier studies. Please review to ensure that you have sound knowledge of all of the following.

The following definitions are taken from IAS 16 *Property, Plant and Equipment*:

### Carrying amount

**'The amount at which an asset is recognised, after deducting any accumulated depreciation and impairment losses.** (IAS 16, para 6).

### Cost

**'The amount paid and the fair value of other consideration given to acquire an asset at the time of its acquisition or construction'** (IAS 16, para 6).

### Depreciable amount

**'The cost or valuation of an asset less its residual value'** (IAS 16, para 6).

### Depreciation

**'The systematic allocation of the depreciable amount of an asset over its useful life'** (IAS 16, para 6).

### Fair value

**'The amount for which an asset can be exchanged between knowledgeable, willing parties in an arm's length transaction'** (IAS 16, para 6).

### Impairment loss

**'The amount by which the carrying amount exceeds its recoverable amount'** (IAS 16, para 6).

### Recoverable amount

**'The higher of an asset's net realisable value and its value in use'** (IAS 16, para 6).

### Residual value

'The residual value of an asset is the amount that the entity would currently obtain from disposal of the asset, after deducting the estimated costs of disposal, assuming that the asset was already at the point where it would be disposed of (using the age and condition that would be assumed to apply at the time of disposal)' (IAS 16, para 6).

### Useful life

'The period over which the asset is expected to be available for use by the entity or the volume of output expected from the asset' *(IAS 16, Para 6).*

## 3 Initial recognition

In accordance with IAS 16 **Property, Plant and Equipment** an asset should be recognised as an asset when:

- it is probable that future economic benefits will flow to the entity and

- the cost of the asset can be measured reliably.

In accordance with IAS 16 *Property, Plant and Equipment*, the asset should initially be measured at its cost. This should include:

- its purchase price

- directly attributable costs to bring the asset to the location and condition necessary for it to be capable of operating for its intended use, i.e. site preparation, initial delivery costs, installation costs, testing costs, professional fees

- the initial estimate of the cost of dismantling and removing the item and restoring the site, where there is an obligation to incur such costs

The cost of a self-constructed asset is determined using the same principles.

### Subsequent expenditure

In accordance with IAS 16 *Property, Plant and Equipment,* subsequent expenditure should be capitalised when:

- the expenditure improves the future economic benefits that the asset will generate

- it replaces a component of an asset and the carrying amount of the component replaced is derecognised, e.g. overhaul of a furnace or a roof (where both are separately identified as assets)

- it is the cost of a major inspection for faults and the carrying amount of the previous inspection is derecognised

The costs of day-to-day servicing should be recognised in the statement of profit or loss as incurred.

## Illustration 1 – Initial measurement

Which one of the following should be accounted for as capital expenditure?

A    The cost of painting a building

B    Maintenance of a machine which keeps production at the same level

C    The purchase of a car by a garage for resale

D    Legal fees incurred on the purchase of a building

## Solution

The answer is D because the legal fees are part of the initial cost of the asset. They are directly attributable costs to bring the asset to the location and condition necessary for it to be capable of operating for its intended use.

A and B are examples of revenue expenses. They are maintenance costs and must be charged to the statement of profit or loss as an expense.

C would normally be an example of an asset to capitalise. However, as the business is a garage and the car is being bought for resale, it must be treated as a purchase expense (inventory) and not a non-current asset.

The car is not a resource for running the business but an item purchased with the intention to sell.

## Case Study Question

**2015 CIMA Professional Qualification Syllabus, Operational Level Case Study Exam, August 2016 – Question (Modified)**

Pene Lopez calls you into her office and says the following to you:

"Thomas wants us to produce a monthly report that puts a monetary value on the cost of quality. David used to produce one at his previous employment. He claims that it really does emphasise the importance of getting it "right first time".

Now that the building work in the old grain barn is complete and the Upper Class Pets' production running smoothly within it, Thomas wants a final total of the expenditure involved. He wants us to capitalise as much of the expenditure on the building work as we can. I have produced a schedule of the expenditure and will give it to you in a moment.

I have to be in meetings all day and as Cormac is on leave I want you to provide the draft of a briefing paper for Thomas in which you:

- firstly, explain quality costs using the extracts from the minutes that I left on your desk to give examples of the different categories of quality costs. I know that you can't quantify any of these costs right now, but please explain how we could get the information that we need to do so

- secondly, explain, with reference to the relevant international financial reporting standard rules, what expenditure can be capitalised and what cannot.

Thank you"

Pene Lopez then hands you the schedule she prepared of the expenditure to convert the grain store into a production unit for UCP products. This schedule can be found below.

**Schedule of expenditure for the new production facility**

|  |  | TS |
|---|---|---|
| Architects fees/legal |  | 3,500 |
| Site preparation | Levelling the floor of the store and testing for ground contamination | 4,200 |
| Building contractor's cost |  | 420,000 |
| Purchase price of new plant and equipment |  | 96,000 |
| Import duties paid in respect of the plant and equipment |  | 8,500 |
| Installation cost in respect of plant and equipment | Work undertaken by our maintenance staff and selected production workers | 6,100 |
| Training costs | Costs required to train installation workers | 1,700 |
| Share of general overheads |  | 4,000 |
| Marketing to get new customers | Additional work undertaken to fill the new facility to capacity | 3,000 |

**(note – for the purpose of this illustration quality costs have not been discussed as this is not relevant to the F1 exam)**

© Copyright CIMA – 2015 CIMA Professional Qualification Operational Level F1 Financial Reporting and Taxation Case Study Exam February 2017

## Case Study Suggested Answer

### 2015 CIMA Professional Qualification Syllabus, Operational Level Case Study Exam, February 2017 – Suggested Answer

**Note this is an extract from the suggested answer and focuses solely on the areas of the case study relevant to the F1 exam, the quality costs are not discussed below.**

### ACCOUNTING TREATMENT OF NEW PRODUCTION FACILITY COSTS

IAS 16: *Property, Plant and Equipment* states that expenditure associated with an item of property plant and equipment can be capitalised if it is either part of the purchase price (including import duties) or directly attributable to getting the asset ready for its intended use.

From the schedule the purchase price of the new plant and equipment, import duties and building contractor's cost all into this first category.

The costs that are directly attributable costs include: the architects fees, the site preparation costs, and the installation of the plant and equipment. All of these costs are necessary to build and to ensure that the machines work correctly.

The training costs however cannot be capitalised as they do not meet the definition of an asset. Although the training may lead to future economic benefit for our business, we cannot control it as the staff are free to leave the business at any time.

The cost of marketing and general overhead are not likely to be directly attributable and will have to be expensed as they are incurred. The marketing is an event that bears no relation to the construction of the new facility and the overhead is an apportionment rather than directly incurred, which in accordance with IAS 16 cannot be capitalised.

© Copyright CIMA – 2015 CIMA Professional Qualification Operational Level F1 Financial Reporting and Taxation Case Study Exam February 2017

**Illustration 2 – Subsequent measurement**

Which ONE of the following items would we recognise as subsequent expenditure on a non-current asset and capitalise as required by IAS 16 Property, Plant and Equipment?

A   A furnace was purchased five years ago, when the furnace lining was separately identified in the accounting records. The furnace now requires re-lining at a cost of $200,000. When the furnace is re-lined it will enable the business to use the furnace for a further five years.

B   An office building was badly damaged in a fire. The cost to restore the building to its original condition will be $250,000.

C   A delivery vehicle has broken down and when inspected it was discovered a new engine would be required estimated at $5,000.

D   A factory is closed for two weeks each year to enable the entity to undertake routine maintenance and repairs costing $75,000.

 **Solution**

The answer is A.

By re-lining the furnace we are enhancing the original asset. By extending its useful life, the benefits are being increased beyond the assets original performance.

All other options are revenue expenses to be charged to the statement of profit or loss because they are simply repairs to the original asset.

## Measurement after initial recognition

IAS 16 requires that entities either apply the cost model or the revaluation model

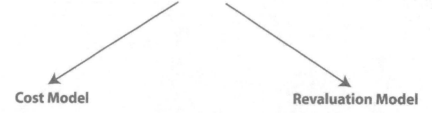

**Cost Model**

Carrying value = Cost

Less: Accumulated depreciation

Less: Accumulated impairment losses

**Revaluation Model**

Carrying value = Fair Value

Less: Accumulated depreciation

Less: Accumulated impairment losses

An entity may decide to use a combination of these two models for measuring assets but must make sure that each class of assets uses the same model, i.e. use the cost model for plant and machinery and the revaluation model for land and buildings.

## Depreciation

IAS 16 *Property, Plant and Equipment* defines depreciation as **'the systematic allocation of the depreciable amount of an asset over its useful life'** (IAS 16, para 6).

Depreciable amount is the cost/valuation less residual value.

The depreciation charge should be recognised in the statement of profit or loss unless it is included in the carrying amount of an asset, e.g. depreciation on equipment used for development activities.

Land will not be depreciated since it has an unlimited life. Buildings, however, do have a finite life and so should be depreciated.

Therefore, if we are given a total for land and buildings we must remember to remove the land element from the total **before** we calculate the depreciation on the building.

For example, total for land and buildings amounts to $100,000. This includes land at cost of $20,000. Buildings should be depreciated at 10% on a straight line basis. The depreciation would be calculated as ($100,000 – $20,000) × 10% = $8,000 a year.

Repair and maintenance does not negate the need to depreciate the asset.

If the residual value is greater than the carrying amount, the depreciation charge is zero.

 **How do we calculate depreciation?**

Depreciation can be calculated using the straight line or the reducing balance method.

The straight line method is based on cost and will be calculated as a % of cost. Each year the depreciation charge will be the same. However, if the % is not given it can be calculated as:

$$\frac{\text{Cost} - \text{residual value}}{\text{useful economic life}}$$

Residual value is the amount the entity would expect to receive from disposal of the asset at the end of its useful life to the business.

The reducing balance method is based on the carrying amount of the asset (CA). This is usually expressed as a %. It does not take into account any estimated residual value.

When the depreciation is calculated the double entry will be:

Dr Depreciation expense (SPL)

Cr Accumulated depreciation (SOFP)

## Changes in depreciation method

In accordance with IAS 16 Property, Plant and Equipment, depreciation methods should be reviewed periodically. If it is decided that there has been a change in the pattern of consumption of benefits, the depreciation method should be changed to reflect this, e.g. a change from the straight line method to the reducing balance method.

Any change in the depreciation method should be treated as a change in accounting estimate and so the new method should be applied in the current and future accounting periods (for reference, this treatment applies IAS 8 Accounting Policies, Changes in Accounting Estimates and Errors. IAS 8 is outside the scope of the F1 syllabus). Changes in depreciation methods do not represent a change in accounting policy and so depreciation charges of earlier periods should not be altered.

### Illustration 3 – Changes in depreciation method

An asset was purchased two years ago for $100,000.

The directors chose to depreciate the asset using the reducing balance method and so used a rate of 20% per annum.

The directors have decided that a fairer presentation would be given if the depreciation method was changed to the straight line basis and will implement the new depreciation method in the year ended 30 June 20X1.

At this time the directors estimated that the useful life was eight years and that the residual value was $10,700.

**Calculate the depreciation charge for the year ended 30 June 20X1 in respect of this asset.**

### Solution

The original depreciation charge was:

Year 1 = Carrying amount × reducing balance depreciation rate = $100,000 × 20% = $20,000

Year 2 = Carrying amount × reducing balance depreciation rate = $80,000 × 20% = $16,000

The asset has been depreciated for 2 years when the change of depreciation method occurs and therefore carrying amount would be:

$100,000 – ($20,000 + $16,000) = $64,000

The carrying amount at the date of the change must be used to recalculate the new depreciation charge.

$$\frac{\text{Carrying amount 30 June X1} - \text{residual value}}{\text{Remaining useful economic life}} = \frac{\$64,000 - \$10,700}{8} = \$6,663 \text{ p.a.}$$

## Test your understanding 1 – Methods

An asset was purchased two years ago for $150,000. The directors chose to depreciate the asset using the reducing balance method and so used a rate of 25% per annum. The directors have decided that a fairer presentation would be given if the depreciation method was changed to the straight line basis and will implement the new depreciation method in the year ended 30 June 20X1. At this time the directors estimated that the remaining useful life was eight years and that the residual value was $8,500.

**Calculate the depreciation charge for the year ended 30 June 20X1 in respect of this asset.**

## Changes in useful life and residual value

On acquiring an asset, its useful life and residual value will be estimated. Subsequently, it may be appropriate to revise these estimates

Again, any change in the useful life or residual value will result in adjustments to the depreciation charge for current and future periods but no changes should be made to past accounting periods, i.e. it is a change in accounting estimate.

## Illustration 4 – Changes in useful life

An asset was purchased three years ago for $50,000 at which time it was thought that the asset had a residual value of $5,000 and a useful economic life of ten years. The directors have decided that as a result of using the asset more than was originally planned the remaining useful economic life is only five years as at 1 July 20X0. Their estimate of residual value has remained unchanged. The asset is depreciated on the straight line basis.

**Calculate the depreciation charge for the year ended 30 June 20X1 in respect of this asset.**

## Solution

The original depreciation was:

$$\frac{\text{Cost} - \text{residual value}}{\text{Useful economic life}} = \frac{\$50,000 - \$5,000}{10} = \$4,500 \text{ p.a.}$$

The asset has been depreciated for 3 years when the change of UEL life occurs and therefore carrying amount would be:

$50,000 – (3 × \$4,500) = \$36,500$

The carrying amount at the date of the change must be used to recalculate the new depreciation charge.

$$\frac{\text{Carrying amount} - \text{residual value}}{\text{Useful economic life}} = \frac{£36,500 - \$5,000}{5} = \$6,300 \text{ p.a.}$$

## Test your understanding 2 – Changes in useful life of an asset

An asset was purchased on 1 July 20X1 for \$75,000 at which time it was thought that the asset had a residual value of \$5,000 and a useful economic life of seven years. The directors have decided that as a result of not using the asset as much as was originally planned the remaining useful economic life is ten years as at 1 July 20X5. Their estimate of residual value has remained unchanged. The asset is depreciated on the straight line basis.

**Calculate the depreciation charge for the year ended 30 June 20X6 in respect of this asset.**

## 4 Revaluations

As discussed previously in the chapter, IAS 16 *Property, Plant and Equipment*, allows the treatment of assets to be shown at their revalued amount less accumulated depreciation and accumulated impairment losses.

The revalued amount of an asset is the asset's fair value at the date of revaluation.

IFRS 13 *Fair Value Measurement*, published in May 2011 and applicable for accounting periods commencing from 1 January 2013, sets out a single framework for measuring fair value.

IFRS 13 defines fair value as **'the price that would be received to sell an asset or transfer a liability in an orderly transaction between market participants at the measurement date'** (IFRS 13, B2).

Revaluing to fair value, means that the item of property plant and equipment will reflect the current value of the asset at the point the revaluation occurs.

Key revaluation issues to remember include:

- If an asset is revalued, any accumulated depreciation up to the date of the revaluation should be reversed. This will increase the revaluation surplus. The revaluation surplus is also described as the revaluation surplus.

- Depreciation will then be calculated based on the revalued amount.

- Revaluations must be made for the whole of the class of assets, i.e. if we revalue one building we must revalue the whole of the class of buildings at the same time.

- The frequency of revaluations will depend upon the volatility of the fair values of the asset class. The more volatile, the more frequent the revaluation.

### Steps to account for a revaluation:

1 Restate asset cost to the revalued amount.

2 Remove any existing accumulated depreciation.

3 Transfer the increase in the cost account and the existing accumulated depreciation to the revaluation surplus account within equity.

4 Recalculate current year's depreciation on the revalued amount if applicable.

### Upwards revaluations of PPE

### Accounting entries:

Dr   Asset cost (revalued amount – original cost)

Dr   Accumulated depreciation (depreciation up to the revaluation date – at this point the balance of this account will be nil)

Cr   Revaluation surplus (revalued amount – previous carrying amount)

if an asset increases in value we will increase the asset cost account (Dr) to the revalued amount and increase the revaluation surplus (Cr). This revaluation surplus will appear in the equity section of the statement of financial position.

An entity is allowed to gradually release this reserve into retained earnings over the life of the asset by reducing the revaluation surplus (Dr) and increasing the retained earnings (Cr). This movement would be seen in the statement of changes in equity. However, in the examination, the question will make it explicitly clear if the transfer within equity is required to be performed. If it is not mentioned, it is not necessary.

## Release of the revaluation surplus

On revaluation of an asset, it is permissible to either leave the revaluation surplus as it is until the revalued asset is sold or, if it is a depreciating asset, to release the revaluation surplus into retained earnings gradually over the life of the asset.

If an asset is revalued upwards, future depreciation charges will increase and profits will reduce, despite there being no changes to the operations of the entity. As a result the entity may opt to perform the transfer between equity between revaluation surplus and retained earnings for the amount of excess depreciation charged.

The transfer equals the difference in the depreciation charge on the basis of the original asset value and on the basis of the revalued amount.

For example, an entity acquired an asset costing $100,000 on 1 January 20X5 with a useful life of ten years. The asset was revalued to $150,000 on 31 December 20X9. The useful life is unchanged.

At the revaluation date we must increase the asset value to $150,000 and remove any accumulated depreciation, i.e. $100,000/10 = $10,000 depreciation per year multiplied by 5 years, (remember we always depreciate as normal up to the revaluation date).

| | | |
|---|---|---|
| Debit | Accumulated depreciation ($10,000 × 5 years) | $50,000 |
| Debit | Asset cost ($150,000 – $100,000) | $50,000 |
| Credit | Revaluation surplus | $100,000 |

The revaluation surplus reflects the increase in the carrying amount of the asset, i.e. $100,000 – $50,000 = $50,000 increasing to $150,000.

The new depreciation charge will be based on the revalued amount of $150,000 over the remaining life of the asset of 5 years, i.e. $30,000 p.a. This is an increase in depreciation of $20,000, compared with the original depreciation amount of $10,000 p.a. This means each year we could release $20,000 from the revaluation surplus to retained earnings as follows:

| | | |
|---|---|---|
| Debit | Revaluation surplus | $20,000 |
| Credit | Retained earnings | $20,000 |

By doing this we are recognising the revaluation surplus over the remaining life of the asset, i.e. $100,000/5 years = $20,000 p.a.

This would be shown as a movement in the SOCIE.

We should only do this in a question if we are instructed to do so.

## Downwards revaluation of PPE

### Downward revaluation after previous revaluation upwards

Dr Revaluation surplus (only to reverse the previous revaluation upwards)

Dr P/L (with any excess once revaluation increase is reversed)

Cr PPE – Cost account

If an asset subsequently decreases in value we will reduce the cost account (Cr) to the new fair value and decrease the revaluation surplus (Dr) **up to the maximum we have previously revalued for that particular asset**.

Any excess amount must be charged to the statement of profit or loss as an expense for the year.

### Illustration 5 – Revaluation downwards

A piece of land was previously revalued upwards in year one by $10,000. In year 2, the land is considered to have reduced in value by $15,000.

We would reduce the cost by $15,000 (Cr). The other side of the entry will reduce the revaluation surplus by $10,000 (Dr) to reverse the balances held in revaluation surplus from the previous revaluation upwards and the difference of $5,000 will be charged to the statement of profit or loss in an appropriate expense category.

The journal entry required is:

Dr Revaluation surplus $10,000

Dr P/L $5,000

Cr PPE – Cost account $15,000

Any revaluations we make during the year that affect the revaluation surplus, upwards or downwards, must be shown on the face of the statement of profit or loss and other comprehensive income under the heading **'other comprehensive income'**.

The amount should reflect the movement made in the revaluation surplus during the year.

Therefore, using the above example we would show the $10,000 increase in year one in other comprehensive income, as a gain on revaluation, i.e. a positive figure.

In year two we would show the $10,000 decrease in other comprehensive income, as a loss on revaluation and the $5,000 expense would reduce profits.

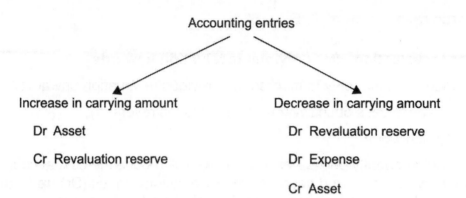

Accounting entries

**Increase in carrying amount**

Dr Asset

Cr Revaluation reserve

**Decrease in carrying amount**

Dr Revaluation reserve

Dr Expense

Cr Asset

The revaluation reserve may be
transferred to retained earnings
as the asset is used

Dr Revaluation reserve

Cr Retained earnings

Any remaining balance in the
revaluation reserve will be transferred
to retained earnings when the asset
is disposed

The revaluation reserve must exist
in relation to the same asset, in
order to Dr Revaluation reserve

Therefore this accounting entry
only applies where an asset was
previously revalued upwards

**Illustration 6 – Revaluations**

Land was purchased at a cost of $30,000. It was subsequently revalued
to:

Year 1        $40,000

Year 2        $33,000

Year 3        $24,000

**Show how each of the gains or losses will be recorded within the
revaluation surplus or the statement of profit or loss.**

## Solution

### Year 1

**The asset has increased in value from $30,000 to $40,000.**

| | |
|---|---|
| Dr Asset | $10,000 |
| Cr Revaluation surplus | $10,000 |

### Year 2

**The asset has decreased in value from $40,000 to $33,000. This decrease can be charged against the revaluation surplus because the surplus within equity already has $10,000 in it from year 1 for that particular asset.**

| | |
|---|---|
| Dr Revaluation surplus | $7,000 |
| Cr Asset | $7,000 |

### Year 3

**The asset has decreased in value from $33,000 to $24,000. The decrease cannot all be charged against the revaluation surplus because there is only $3,000 left after year 2 for that particular asset. The reserve is reduced to nil and then the balance of the decrease is charged against profits in the statement of profit or loss.**

| | |
|---|---|
| Dr Revaluation surplus | $3,000 |
| Dr Statement of profit or loss | $6,000 |
| Cr Asset | $9,000 |

## Illustration 7 – Revaluations

Asset A cost $50,000 on 1 January 20X4. This asset has a useful life of 10 years and is revalued to $25,000 on 31 December 20X9.

Asset B cost $50,000 on 1 January 20X7. This asset has a useful life of 5 years and is revalued to $17,000 on 31 December 20X9.

**Show how each of the gains or losses will be recorded within the revaluation surplus or the statement of profit or loss.**

## Solution

### Asset A

On 31 December 20X9 Asset A has a carrying amount of $20,000 (cost $50,000 – depreciation $30,000 ($50,000/10 = $5,000 p.a. multiplied by 6 years).

The cost account will reduce from $50,000 to £25,000.

The accumulated depreciation of $30,000 will be removed from the books.

Overall the carrying amount of the asset has increased from $20,000 to $25,000. This increase of $5,000 will be credited to the revaluation surplus.

We must remember next year's depreciation will be based on the revalued amount of £25,000 over the remaining life of 4 years.

| | |
|---|---|
| Cr Asset cost | $25,000 |
| Dr Accumulated depreciation | $30,000 |
| Cr Revaluation surplus | $5,000 |

### Asset B

On 31 December 20X9 Asset B has a carrying amount of $20,000 (cost $50,000 – depreciation $30,000 ($50,000/5 = $10,000 p.a. multiplied by 3 years).

The cost account will reduce from $50,000 to £17,000.

The accumulated depreciation removed from the books = $30,000.

Overall, the carrying amount of the asset decreased in value from $20,000 to $17,000. The decrease of $3,000 is charged against profits in the SPL. This asset has not been revalued in the past and therefore does not have a revaluation surplus you can use. You cannot use the reserve from Asset A.

We must remember next year's depreciation will be based on the revalued amount of £17,000 over the remaining life of 2 years.

| | |
|---|---|
| Dr Statement of profit or loss expense | $3,000 |
| Dr Accumulated depreciation | $30,000 |
| Cr Asset cost | $33,000 |

**Note:** The revaluation surplus relates to asset A. Therefore, only future downward valuations of asset A can be set against the revaluation surplus.

## Test your understanding 3 – Revaluations

Building A was purchased on 01/01/X3 costing $50,000. It has a useful economic life of 50 years and no residual value.

Building B was purchased on 01/01/X3 costing $100,000. It has a useful life of 40 years and no residual value.

The entity has a policy to revalue its assets every four years and has done so as follows:

**Building A**

Valuation at 31/12/X6 $69,000

**Valuation at 31/12/Y0 $84,000**

**Building B**

Valuation at 31/12/X6 $108,000

Valuation at 31/12/Y0 $64,000

**Show how the revaluations will be recorded, clearly showing the carrying amount of the assets at 31/12/Y1.**

## Further detail on revaluation decreases

### Revaluation downwards then upwards

Let us consider what happens when the decrease in value occurs first, followed by a subsequent increase in value for the asset.

For example, If an item of land decreases in value in year one by $10,000 we will reduce the cost account (Cr) to reflect the new fair value amount and charge the decrease immediately to the statement of profit or loss as an expense for the year.

Dr P/L $10,000

Cr Land $10,000

If the same land was revalued upwards by $15,000 the following year we can reverse our previous entry to the statement of profit or loss and then show the excess from the revaluation in the revaluation surplus.

Increase the asset cost account (Dr) by $15,000, reverse the previous charge to the statement of profit or loss expense of $10,000 (Cr) and then show the difference of $5,000 in the revaluation surplus (Cr).

Dr Land $15,000

Cr P/L $10,000

Cr Revaluation surplus $5,000

**Retirement and disposals**

An item of property, plant and equipment should be eliminated from the statement of financial position on disposal or when the asset is permanently withdrawn from use.

Gain/(loss) on disposal = Net disposal proceeds – carrying amount

Gains or losses on disposal should be recorded in the statement of profit or loss in an appropriate expense category. If we have a loss on disposal this will increase the expense and a profit will reduce the expense.

We will look at retired assets in more detail later when we look at IFRS 5 *Non-current Assets Held for Sale and Discontinued Operations*.

## Disposal of revalued assets

When a previously revalued asset is disposed of the gain on disposal is measured as the difference between the carrying amount on the SOFP and the proceeds received.

However, if the asset has been revalued in the past, it will have an unrealised gain in the revaluation surplus that must now be removed.

The amount should be transferred from the revaluation surplus to retained earnings. This movement will be seen in the SOCIE and will not affect this year's profit.

 **Illustration 8 – Disposal of a revalued asset**

An entity originally purchased a piece of land on 01/01/X7 for $100,000. On the 31/12/X8 the land was revalued to $150,000.

The land was sold for $180,000 on 31/12/Y1.

**Calculate the profit or loss on disposal to be shown in the statement of profit or loss and any revaluation adjustments that need to be made.**

 **Solution**

When the land was revalued the entries would be made as follows:

This asset increases in value from $100,000 to $150,000. The increase is credited to the revaluation surplus.

| | |
|---|---|
| Dr Asset | $50,000 |
| Cr Revaluation surplus | $50,000 |

When the asset was sold the carrying amount was $150,000.

The gain on disposal to the statement of profit or loss would be $30,000 ($180,000 – $150,000)

This would be accounted for by:

| | |
|---|---:|
| Dr Bank | $180,000 |
| Cr Land | $150,000 |
| Cr Profit or loss | $30,000 |

The revaluation surplus for the land would now be released into retained earnings as the gain is now realised.

| | |
|---|---:|
| Dr Revaluation surplus | $50,000 |
| Cr Retained earnings | $50,000 |

This would be shown on the SOCIE.

## Disclosure

IAS 16 *Property, Plant and Equipment*, requires the following disclosure requirements:

For each class of property, plant and equipment

- measurement bases, i.e. cost or valuation

- depreciation methods with useful life or depreciation rate

- gross carrying amount and accumulated depreciation at the beginning and end of the period

- reconciliation of additions, disposals, revaluations, impairments and depreciation

- when assets have been revalued:

    - basis of valuation

    - date of valuation

    - whether an independent valuer was used

    - carrying amount if no revaluation had taken place

    - revaluation surplus

## Property, plant and equipment (PPE)

The property, plant and equipment note (IAS 16) shows the movements in the year for each category of asset.

| | Land and buildings $000 | Plant and equipment $000 | Vehicles $000 | Total $000 |
|---|---|---|---|---|
| **Cost/Valuation** | | | | |
| At 1 January 20X0 | X | X | X | X |
| Additions | X | X | X | X |
| Surplus/(deficit) on revaluations | X/(X) | – | – | – |
| Disposals | (X) | (X) | (X) | (X) |
| At 31 December 20X0 | X | X | X | X |
| | | | | |
| **Accumulated Depreciation:** | | | | |
| At 1 January 20X0 | X | X | X | X |
| Charged during the year | X | X | X | X |
| Revaluations | (X) | – | – | (X) |
| Disposals | (X) | (X) | (X) | (X) |
| At 31 December 20X0 | X | X | X | X |
| | | | | |
| **Carrying amount** | | | | |
| At 1 January 20X0 | X | X | X | X |
| At 31 December 20X0 | X | X | X | X |

**Test your understanding 4 – PPE note**

A building was purchased many years ago for $200,000. It has been depreciated at 2% per annum (50 year life) on the straight line basis and the carrying amount of the asset at 1 July 20X0 is $132,000. The directors have had the asset valued at $750,000 and would like to incorporate this valuation into the financial statements for the year ended 30 June 20X1.

**Prepare a non-current asset note for the year ended 30 June 20X1 and calculate the revaluation surplus assuming that:**

**(a)   the valuation is as at 1 July 20X0.**

**(b)   the valuation is as at 30 June 20X1.**

## 5 IAS 36 Impairment of Assets

IAS 36 *Impairment of Assets* defines an impairment loss as **'the amount by which the carrying amount of an asset exceeds its recoverable amount'** (IAS 36, para 6).

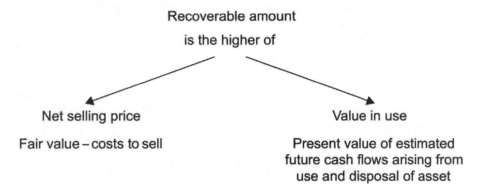

Recoverable amount

is the higher of

Net selling price

Fair value – costs to sell

Value in use

Present value of estimated future cash flows arising from use and disposal of asset

An entity should assess at each reporting date whether there is any indication that an asset may be impaired. If such indications exist, the recoverable amount should be estimated, i.e. an impairment review should be carried out. If no such indications exist, it is not necessary to carry out an impairment review.

The following situations may indicate that an asset has been impaired:

- decline in market value

- technological, legal or economic changes

- physical damage

- plans to dispose of asset.

### Procedures to check for impairment

At the end of each reporting period an entity should assess whether there are internal or external indications that the value of any asset is impaired.

In assessing whether there is any indication that an asset may be impaired, an entity shall consider the following indications:

**External sources of information:**

- During the period, an asset's market value has declined significantly more than would be expected as a result of the passage of time or normal use.

- Significant changes with an adverse effect on the entity have taken place during the period within the markets in which the entity operates or to which an asset is dedicated.

- Market interest rates have increased during the period. These increases are likely to affect the discount rate used in calculating an asset's value in use and so could decrease the asset's recoverable amount.

**Internal sources of information:**

- Evidence is available of obsolescence or physical damage of an asset.

- Significant changes with an adverse effect on the manner in which an asset is used or is expected to be used. Examples of such changes include the asset becoming idle, plans to discontinue or restructure the operation to which an asset belongs, and plans to dispose of an asset before the previously expected date.

- Evidence is available from internal reporting that indicates that the economic performance of an asset is, or will be, worse than expected.

## Recognition and measurement of an impairment loss

An impairment loss occurs when the recoverable amount of an asset is below its carrying amount,

An impairment loss should be recorded as an expense in the statement of profit or loss, unless the asset has previously been revalued upwards.

If the asset had previously been revalued, the impairment can be offset against the revaluation surplus.

### Cash-generating units

If there is an indication of impairment of an asset, the recoverable amount must be identified.

If it is not possible to estimate the recoverable amount of the individual asset (e.g. the asset does not produce its own cash flows to calculate value in use), then the entity will extrapolate their impairment calculations to incorporate groupings of assets rather than simply impairing individual assets.

These groups of assets are called cash-generating units.

A cash-generating unit is the smallest identifiable group of assets that generates independent cash inflows.

**Illustration 9 – Impairment**

The following information relates to three assets held by an entity:

|                    | A   | B   | C   |
| ------------------ | --- | --- | --- |
| Carrying amount    | 200 | 200 | 200 |
| Net selling price  | 220 | 125 | 140 |
| Value in use       | 160 | 150 | 190 |

**Calculate the impairment losses, if any, in respect of the three assets.**

 **Solution**

|                                                              | A   | B    | C    |
| ------------------------------------------------------------ | --- | ---- | ---- |
| Recoverable amount (higher of net selling price and value in use) | 220 | 150  | 190  |
| Carrying amount                                              | 200 | 200  | 200  |
| Impairment                                                   | NO  | (50) | (10) |

 **Test your understanding 5- Impairment**

The following information relates to three assets held by an entity:

|                    | A   | B   | C   |
| ------------------ | --- | --- | --- |
| Carrying amount    | 200 | 200 | 200 |
| Net selling price  | 250 | 175 | 160 |
| Value in use       | 180 | 150 | 180 |

**Calculate the impairment losses, if any, in respect of the three assets.**

### Disclosure

IAS 36 *Impairment of Assets* requires the following disclosure requirements:

For each class of property, plant and equipment:

- The amount of impairment losses recognised in the statement of profit or loss during the period and where it has been included, i.e. which expense category.

- The amount of reversals for impairment losses recognised in the statement of profit or loss during the period and where it has been included.

- The amount of impairment losses recognised directly in equity during the period.

- The amount of reversals of impairment losses recognised directly in equity during the period.

**Test your understanding 6 – Practice questions**

1   An entity purchased a property 15 years ago at a cost of $100,000 and has depreciated it at a rate of 2% per annum, using the straight line basis. The entity had the property professionally revalued at $500,000.

**What is the revaluation surplus that will be recorded in the financial statements in respect of this property?**

A   $400,000

B   $500,000

C   $530,000

D   $430,000

2   An entity owns two buildings, A and B, which are currently recorded in the books at carrying amounts of $170,000 and $330,000 respectively. Both buildings have recently been valued as follows:

Building A      $400,000

Building B      $250,000

The entity currently has a balance on the revaluation surplus of $50,000 which arose when building A was revalued several years ago. Building B has never been previously revalued.

**What double entry will need to be made to record the revaluations of buildings A and B?**

| | | | |
|---|---|---|---:|
| A | Dr | Non-current assets | $150,000 |
| | Dr | Statement of profit or loss | $80,000 |
| | Cr | Revaluation surplus | $230,000 |
| B | Dr | Non-current assets | $150,000 |
| | Dr | Statement of profit or loss | $30,000 |
| | Cr | Revaluation surplus | $180,000 |
| C | Dr | Non-current assets | $150,000 |
| | Cr | Revaluation surplus | $150,000 |
| D | Dr | Non-current assets | $150,000 |
| | Dr | Statement of profit or loss | $50,000 |
| | Cr | Revaluation surplus | $200,000 |

3    The following information relates to three assets held by an entity:

|  | Asset A $ | Asset B $ | Asset C $ |
|---|---|---|---|
| Carrying amount | 100 | 50 | 40 |
| Value in use | 80 | 60 | 35 |
| Fair value less cost to sell | 90 | 65 | 30 |

**What is the total impairment loss?**

A    $15

B    $30

C    $Nil

D    $1

4    On 1 April 20X0 Slow and Steady showed non-current assets that had cost $312,000 and accumulated depreciation of $66,000. During the year ended 31 March 20X1, Slow and Steady disposed of non-current assets which had originally cost $28,000 and had a carrying amount of $11,200.

The entity's policy is to charge depreciation of 40% on the reducing balance basis, with no depreciation in the year of disposal of an asset.

**What is the depreciation charge to the statement of profit or loss for the year ended 31 March 20X1?**

A    $113,600

B    $98,400

C    $93,920

D    $87,200

5    A building contractor decides to build an office building, to be occupied by his own staff. Tangible non-current assets are initially measured at cost.

**Which of the following expenses incurred by the building contractor cannot be included as a part of the cost of the office building?**

A    Interest incurred on a specific loan taken out to pay for the construction of the new offices

B    Direct building labour costs

C    A proportion of the contractor's general administration costs

D    Hire of plant and machinery for use on the office building site

6   **The purpose of depreciation is to:**

A   Allocate the cost less residual value on a systematic basis over the asset's useful economic life

B   Write the asset down to its market value each period

C   Charge profits for the use of the asset

D   Recognise that assets lose value over time

7   **Which of the following items of property, plant and equipment are NOT depreciated:**

A   Machinery

B   Land

C   Buildings with a life in excess of 30 years

D   Vehicles

8   Plant and machinery, costing $50,000, was purchased on 1 April 20X6. This was depreciated for 2 years at 20 per cent a year using the reducing balance method. On 1 April 20X8, some of the machinery (original cost $25,000) was sold for $12,000. Replacement machines were acquired on the same date for $34,000.

**What was the carrying amount of plant and machinery at March 20X9?**

9   Roming Co purchased property costing $440,000 on 1 January 20X5. The property is being depreciated over 50 years on a straight-line basis. The property was revalued on 1 January 20X9 at $520,000. The useful life was also reviewed at that date and is estimated to be a further 40 years.

**Prepare the accounting entries to record the revaluation and calculate the depreciation charge that will apply from 1 January 20X9.**

## 6    Summary diagram

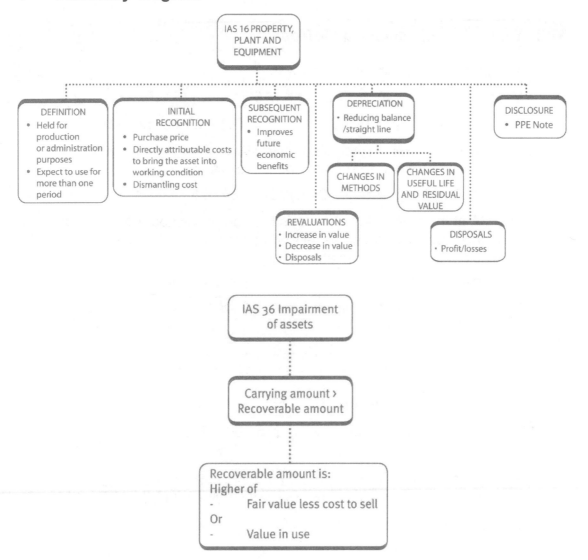

## Test your understanding answers

### Test your understanding 1 – Methods

The original depreciation charge was:

Year 1 = Cost $150,000 × 25% = $37,500

Year 2 = CA $112,500($150,000 – $37,500) × 25% = $28,125

The asset has been depreciated for 2 years when the change of depreciation method occurs and therefore CA would be:

Cost $150,000 – ($37,500 + $28,125) = $84,375

The CA at the date of the change is the carrying amount on the statement of financial position for the asset and must therefore be used to recalculate the new depreciation charge.

$$\frac{\text{CA} - \text{residual value}}{\text{Remaining useful economic life}} = \frac{\$84,375 - \$8,500}{8} = \$9,484 \text{ p.a.}$$

### Test your understanding 2 – Changes in useful life of an asset

The original depreciation charge was:

$$\frac{\text{CA} - \text{residual value}}{\text{Remaining useful economic life}} = \frac{\$75,000 - \$5,000}{7} = \$10,000 \text{ p.a.}$$

The asset has been depreciated for 4 years when the change of depreciation method occurs and therefore CA would be:

Cost $75,000 – $40,000 = $35,000

The CA at the date of the change is the carrying amount on the statement of financial position for the asset and must therefore be used to recalculate the new depreciation charge.

$$\frac{\text{CA} - \text{residual value}}{\text{Remaining useful economic life}} = \frac{\$35,000 - \$5,000}{10} = \$3,000 \text{ p.a.}$$

## Test your understanding 3 – Revaluations

### Asset A

The asset initially cost increases by $19,000, ($50,000 to $69,000).

Depreciation is $10,000 pa ($50,000/50). Therefore accumulated depreciation at 31/12/X6 will be $4,000.

After 4 years (31/12/X6) the carrying amount will be $46,000 ($50,000 – $4,000).

The asset increases in value from $46,000 to $69,000. The increase of $23,000 is credited to the revaluation surplus.

| | |
|---|---|
| Dr Asset cost | $19,000 |
| Dr Accumulated depreciation | $4,000 |
| Cr Revaluation surplus | $23,000 |

The depreciation must now be recalculated on the revalued amount for the remaining life of 46 years.

Depreciation is $1,500 pa ($69,000/46)

After 4 years (31/12/Y0) the carrying amount will be $63,000 ($69,000 – $6,000)

The asset cost increases by $15,000, $69,000 to $84,000.

This assets carrying amount increases in value from $63,000 to $84,000. The increase of $21,000 is credited to revaluation surplus.

| | |
|---|---|
| Dr Asset cost | $15,000 |
| Dr Accumulated depreciation | $6,000 |
| Cr Revaluation surplus | $21,000 |

The depreciation must now be recalculated on the revalued amount for the remaining life of 42 years.

Depreciation is $2,000 pa ($84,000/42)

**The carrying amount at 31/12/Y1 will be:**

**$84,000 – $2,000 = $82,000**

### Asset B

The asset initially cost increases by $8,000, ($100,000 to $108,000).

Depreciation is $2,500 pa ($100,000/40). Therefore, accumulated depreciation at 31/12/X6 is $10,000.

After 4 years (31/12/X6) the CV will be $90,000 ($100,000 – $10,000)

This asset's carrying value increases from $90,000 to $108,000. The increase of $18,000 is credited to the revaluation surplus.

| | |
|---|---|
| Dr Asset cost | $8,000 |
| Dr Accumulated depreciation | $10,000 |
| Cr Revaluation surplus | $18,000 |

The depreciation must now be recalculated on the revalued amount for the remaining life of 36 years.

Depreciation is $3,000 pa ($108,000/36)

After 4 years (31/12/Y0) the carrying amount will be $96,000 ($108,000 – $12,000)

The asset cost decreases by $44,000, ($108,000 to $64,000).

This assets carrying amount decreases from $96,000 to $64,000. The decrease is charged to the revaluation surplus to reduce it to nil and the balance is charged against profits.

| | |
|---|---|
| Dr Revaluation surplus | $18,000 |
| Dr Statement of profit or loss | $14,000 |
| Dr Accumulated depreciation | $12,000 |
| Cr Asset | $44,000 |

**Note:** The revaluation surplus for building A cannot be used for the reduction in value of building B.

The depreciation must now be recalculated on the revalued amount for the remaining life of 32 years.

Depreciation is $2,000 pa ($64,000/32)

**The carrying amount at 31/12/Y1 will be:**

**$64,000 – $2,000 = $62,000**

Under IAS 16 we need to revalue with sufficient regularity to ensure that carrying amount and fair value are not materially different. It is assumed that by revaluing every 4 years in the question meets this criteria.

## Test your understanding 4 – PPE note

| Non-current asset note | (a) $000 | (b) $000 |
|---|---|---|
| Cost/Valuation | | |
| At 1 July 20X0 | 200 | 200 |
| Revaluation | 550 | 550 |
| At 30 June 20X1 | 750 | 750 |
| Acc Dep'n | | |
| At 1 July 20X0 (200 – 132) | 68 | 68 |
| Charge for year | 23 | 4 |
| Revaluation | (68) | (72) |
| At 30 June 20X1 | 23 | 0 |
| Carrying amount | | |
| At 1 July 20X0 | 132 | 132 |
| At 30 June 20X1 | 727 | 750 |
| Revaluation surplus | 618 | 622 |
| | (750 – 132) | (750 – 128) |

If the revaluation takes place at the beginning of the year, the current year's depreciation charge should be based on the revalued amount. The depreciation charge was based on 2% of cost, i.e. $4,000 pa. If the carrying amount b/fwd is $132,000, it must mean we have already utilised the asset for 17 years ($4,000 × 17 = $68,000 depreciation to date). When the asset is revalued we must now depreciate the revalued amount over the remaining life of 33 years (50 – 17). This will result in the current year's depreciation charge of $22,727 ($750,000/33), rounded to $23,000.

If the revaluation takes place at the end of the year, the current year's depreciation should be based on the original amount, i.e. $200,000 × 2%. The total depreciation to date will then be removed from the books and transferred to the revaluation surplus, i.e. $68,000 + $4,000.

## Test your understanding 5 – Impairment

|  | A | B | C |
|---|---|---|---|
| Recoverable amount | 250 | 175 | 180 |
| Carrying amount | 200 | 200 | 200 |
| Impairment | No | (25) | (20) |

**NB:** Recoverable amount is the higher of the net selling price and value in use.

## Test your understanding 6 – Practice questions

1   C

2   D

| | |
|---|---|
| Current value | 500,000 |
| CA at date of revaluation | |
| (100,000 – (100,000 × 2% × 15yrs)) | (70,000) |
| | ——— |
| Revaluation gain | 430,000 |

3   A

|  | **Building A** | **Building B** |
|---|---|---|
| Current value | 400,000 | 250,000 |
| Carrying amount | (170,000) | (330,000) |
| | ——— | ——— |
| Revaluation gain/loss | 230,000 | (80,000) |

The gain on Building A will be credited to the revaluation surplus.

The loss on Building B will be debited to the statement of profit or loss expenses because we do not have a balance on the revaluation surplus in respect of building B to net the loss off against.

We make an overall Dr to non-current assets is $230,000 – $80,000 = $150,000

4  A

| | Asset A $ | Asset B $ | Asset C $ |
|---|---|---|---|
| Carrying amount | 100 | 50 | 40 |
| Value in use | 80 | 60 | 35 |
| Fair value less cost to sell | 90 | 65 | 30 |
| **Valued at higher of value in use/fair value** | 90 | 65 | 35 |
| **Impairment** | 10 | Nil | 5 |

Total Impairment = $15

5  C

| | |
|---|---|
| Carrying amount at 1 April 20X0 | $246,000 |
| ($312,000 – $66,000) | |
| Carrying amount of disposal | ($11,200) |
| Carrying amount at 31 March 20X1 | $234,800 |
| Depreciation at 40% | $93,920 |

6  C – Direct costs relating to the asset can be included such as labour costs, interest on loans to acquire the asset and hire costs. The administration cost is not a direct cost.

7  A

8  B

9  The answer is $ 40,000

| | $ |
|---|---|
| Cost 1 April 20X6 | 50,000 |
| 20% depreciation | (10,000) |
| Carrying amount 31 March 20X7 | 40,000 |
| 20% depreciation | (8,000) |
| Carrying amount 31 March 20X8 | 32,000 |
| Disposal book value ($25,000 × 80% × 80%) | (16,000) |
| (Cost $25,000 – depreciation for 2 years $9,000) | |
| Carrying amount after disposal | 16,000 |
| Purchase | 34,000 |
| | 50,000 |
| 20% depreciation | (10,000) |
| Carrying amount at 31 March 20X9 | 40,000 |

10   The annual charge for depreciation was $440,000/50 years 5 $8,800.

The asset had been used and depreciated for 4 years (2007 to 2010).

The carrying amount of the asset at the date of valuation was therefore $404,800 (cost of $440,000 – accumulated depreciation of $35,200).

The revaluation surplus is calculated as the valuation amount of $520,000 less the carrying amount of the asset of $404,800. The surplus is therefore $115,200.

The revaluation at 1 January 20X9 will be recorded as:

|        |                                  | $      | $       |
|--------|----------------------------------|--------|---------|
| Debit  | Accumulated depreciation         | 35,200 |         |
| Debit  | Cost ($520,000 – $440,000)       | 80,000 |         |
| Credit | Revaluation surplus              |        | 115,200 |

The depreciation charge for 20X9 and beyond will be based on the asset's valuation over the remaining useful life of the property. The useful life has also been revised to 40 years, so the depreciation will now be $13,000, being value of $520,000 over 40 years.

# IFRS 5 Non-current Assets Held for Sale and Discontinued Operations

## Chapter learning objectives

| Lead | Component outcome |
|---|---|
| B2. Explain specific IFRS financial reporting standards | Explain the specific financial reporting standards related to:<br><br>a. Non-current assets<br><br>IFRS 5 (Non-current Assets Held for Sale and Discontinued Operations) |

## 1    Session content

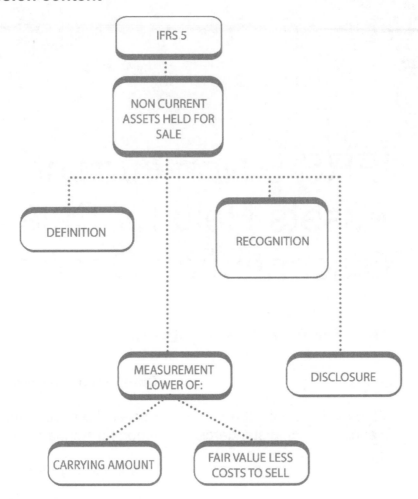

## 2    Introduction

The objective of IFRS 5 *Non-current Assets Held for Sale and Discontinued Operations* is to establish principles for reporting information about discontinued operations and non-current assets held for sale.

### Definition of discontinued operations

IFRS 5 Non-current Assets Held for Sale and Discontinued Operations defines a discontinued operation as **'a component of an entity that either has been disposed of or is classified as held for sale, and:**

- **that represents a separate major line of business or geographical area of operations**

- **that is part of a single co-ordinated plan to dispose of a separate major line of business or geographical area of operations, or**

- **that is a subsidiary acquired exclusively with a view to resale'.** (IFRS 5, para 32)

## 3    Non-current assets held for sale

In the previous chapter we considered disposals of non-current assets.

The disposal of an asset means the asset has been sold. It was removed from our records and a gain or loss on the sale is recorded.

At the date the financial statements are prepared, it is possible that parts of the business or separate assets may not have physically been disposed of but it is obvious that they are no longer going to be used by the entity e.g. an empty warehouse surplus to requirements which the entity is attempting to sell. The asset maybe classified as a **held for sale asset.**

An entity shall classify a non-current asset as held for sale if its carrying amount will be recovered principally through a sale transaction rather than through continuing use.

### Held for sale criteria

In accordance with IFRS 5 *Non-current Assets Held for Sale and Discontinued Operations,* assets will be treated as held for sale if all of the following criteria are met:

- it is available for immediate sale in its present condition

- the sale is highly probable

- management are committed to a plan to sell the asset

- an active programme to locate a buyer has been initiated

- the asset is being actively marketed at a reasonable price

- the sale is expected to complete within one year from the date of classification

- it is unlikely that the plan will change significantly or be withdrawn.

 All criteria must be met if the non-current asset is to be held for sale.

For example, for the sale to be highly probable the management must be committed to selling the asset and they must have an active programme to locate a buyer. The asset must also be available to sell immediately in its present condition, i.e. no major repairs are requirement on a building before it could be put on the market to sell.

The classification of an asset as held for sale has 2 implications to the financial statements:

- measurement

- classification.

## Measurement of non-current assets held for sale

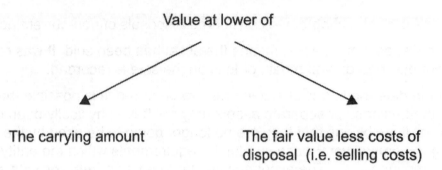

Value at lower of

The carrying amount

The fair value less costs of disposal (i.e. selling costs)

 Non-current assets 'held for sale' are not depreciated. Prior to classification as held for sale, the asset will be treated in line with the applicable accounting standard e.g. Property, plant and equipment should be depreciated as normal until date of classification as held for sale.

If the value of the asset held for sale is less than the carrying amount on the statement of financial position it should be written down and the impairment charged against profit.

## Presentation and disclosure

*   Held for sale assets will be classified as a separate category of current asset separately disclosed below the normal current asset section.

 **Illustration 1 – Assets held for sale**

On 1 January 20X8, an entity Mickey purchases a machine for $20,000. It has an expected useful life of 10 years and nil residual value. The entity uses the straight line method of depreciation.

On 31 December 20X9, the entity decides to sell the machine. Its current market value is $15,000 and the entity is confident they will find a buyer very quickly due to the short supply in the market for this type of machinery. It will cost the entity $500 to dismantle the machine.

**At what value should the machine be included in Mickey's statement of financial position at 31 December 20X9?**

## Solution

Current carrying amount = 8/10 × $20,000 = $16,000 (Mickey has had the machine for two years, hence charged two years' worth of depreciation against the asset).

Fair value less costs to sell = $15,000 − 500 = $14,500

The machine qualifies as an "asset held for sale" at 31 December 20X9 so should be valued at the lower of carrying amount or fair value less costs to sell, i.e. $14,500.

The carrying amount must be written down from $16,000 to $14,500. The impairment will be charged against profit for the year in the statement of profit or loss.

The machine is no longer depreciated.

## The revaluation model

Any assets valued under the revaluation model that meet the criteria of an asset held for sale should first be revalued as normal and then separately written down to the fair value less costs to sell.

For example, property plant and equipment measured using the revaluation model with a carrying amount of $10,000 met the criteria of an asset held for sale when the fair value of the asset was $12,000 and the costs to sell were $3,000.

The asset would first be revalued by $2,000 as per IAS 16 by debiting the asset cost account and crediting the revaluation reserve.

Dr PPE $2,000

Cr Revaluation reserve $2,000

Remove the PPE and show at lower of carrying amount or FV less cost to sell. The carrying amount is now $12,000, the FV less cost to sell is $9,000 ($12,000 − $3,000). The held for sale asset is recorded at $9,000.

Dr Held for sale asset $9.000

Dr Profit or loss $3,000

Cr PPE $12,000

This results in the costs to sell being recognised as an immediate impairment cost to the SPL.

The revaluation reserve will be transferred upon disposal to retained earnings.

**2015 CIMA Professional Qualification Syllabus, Operational Level Case Study Exam, May 2017 – Question**

You receive the following email from Aaron Jenkins, Senior Management Accountant

**From:**     Aaron Jenkins, Senior Management Accountant

**To:**     Finance Officer

**Subject:**     Transfer of production

As part of the ongoing integration of policies, procedures and systems throughout the group, it has been decided to transfer production of all Ashworth Lea's cars to the Naas production facility in Mayland. It is intended that production at the new facility will commence in July and we will vacate the existing factory at that time. The plant and equipment currently used will be transferred to their production facility.

We need to decide how we are going to account for the vacated factory premises. At the moment, we don't have a buyer but we are actively seeking one. We have had the premises valued by a specialist surveyor, who is confident that we should be able to find a buyer in the next 6 to 9 months.

Hannah Wilson is on holiday at the moment so the Finance Director has asked me to deal with this issue. We will need to review the provisions of IAS 16 Property, Plant and Equipment and IFRS 5 Non-current Assets Held for Sale and Discontinued Operations.

As part of the integration of the group's systems, we have also been asked to consider the implementation of an activity based costing system which is already being used in the Naas Group. In order to get an idea of how it might operate, I have looked at the operations in the paint shop and prepared a schedule (attached) explaining some of the different activities carried out in that area. At the moment we treat the paint shop as a cost centre and use direct labour hour absorption rate to produce product costings for our cars.

Prepare a draft report for me covering the following areas:

How the specific requirements under IAS 16 Property Plant and Equipment and IFRS 5 Non-current Assets Held for Sale and Discontinued Operations would apply in respect of the vacated factory premises.

How we could use the activity information, given in the schedule, to produce costings for our cars. Please also provide suggestions and explanations, for appropriate cost drivers for each of the activities in the schedule.

Regards

Aaron Jenkins

Senior Management Accountant Ashworth Lea

(note for the purpose of this illustration the cost drivers have not been discussed as they are not relevant to the F1 exam)

© Copyright CIMA – 2015 CIMA Professional Qualification Operational Level F1 Financial Reporting and Taxation Case Study Exam May 2017

 **Case Study Suggested Answer**

**2015 CIMA Professional Qualification Syllabus, Operational Level Case Study Exam, May 2017 – Suggested Answer**

**Note this is an extract from the suggested answer and focuses solely on the areas of the case study relevant to the F1 exam, the cost drivers are not discussed below.**

### REPORT ON VACATED FACTORY AND ABC

Accounting treatment of the vacated factory

The decision about how to treat the vacated factory will depend on whether we sell it between now and the financial year end on 31 December 2017. If we sell the factory before 31 December 2017, we will need to derecognise it as part of property, plant and equipment and recognise a profit or loss on disposal in the statement of profit or loss.

If we do not sell before 31 December 2017 we will still own the factory but we will no longer be using it for business purposes. IFRS 5 requires that it should be classified as an asset held for sale if its carrying amount will be recovered through a sale transaction rather than through continuing use. To be treated as an asset held for sale, it needs to meet certain criteria:

- It needs to be available for immediate sale in its present condition. We intend to sell the factory as soon as possible after it is vacated and it is likely to be in a saleable condition given that we would have been using the space up until July.

- The sale is highly probable. This is evidenced by the following:

  A reasonable price has been set. We have taken the advice of specialist surveyors regarding price.

  The sale is expected to complete within one year from the date of the classification. The surveyor has indicated that they should be able to find a buyer within the next 6-9 months.

  There is a firm commitment to sell and an active programme to find a buyer. Again the fact that we have engaged a specialist surveyor to act on our behalf is evidence of this.

The vacated factory therefore would meet all the criteria necessary to be recognised separately in the statement of financial position as 'assets held for sale'. Assets held for sale should be disclosed separately under the current asset section of the statement of financial position.

The value of the factory should be recognised at the lower of its carrying amount on the date it becomes held for sale and the fair value less the costs to sell. In order to determine the carrying amount we will need to depreciate the factory up until the date it becomes held for sale but no depreciation is required after that date.

© Copyright CIMA – 2015 CIMA Professional Qualification Operational Level F1 Financial Reporting and Taxation Case Study Exam May 2017

### Test your understanding 1 – Practice questions

1   According to IFRS 5 *Non-current Assets Held for Sale and Discontinued Operations* which of the following relate to the criteria for an asset held for sale?

(i)     Available for immediate sale in its present condition

(ii)    Sales is highly probable

(iii)   The sale is expected to be completed within the next month

(iv)   A reasonable price has been set

A     All of the above

B     i, ii and iii

C     i, ii and iv

D     ii, iii and iv

2   According to IFRS 5 *Non-current Assets Held for Sale and Discontinued Operations* how should non-current assets held for sale be valued?

A     Lower of the carrying amount or the fair value

B     Lower of the carrying amount or the fair value less costs of disposal

C     Higher of the carrying amount or the fair value

D     Higher of the carrying amount or the fair value less costs of disposal

3    At the reporting date an asset is identified as an asset held for sale after meeting the criteria according to IFRS 5 *Non-current Assets Held for Sale and Discontinued Operations*. At the reporting date the carrying amount of the asset was $150,000 (original cost $200,000 two years ago). The asset had an original 10 year useful life and the entity has a policy to depreciate assets using the straight-line method.

**What should the depreciation be for the year?**

A    $20,000

B    $15,000

C    None

D    $25,000

4    At the reporting date an asset is identified as an asset held for sale after meeting the criteria according to IFRS 5 Non-current Assets Held for Sale and Discontinued Operations.

**Where should the asset appear on the statement of financial position?**

A    Part of the property, plant and equipment under non-current assets

B    It is not shown on the statement of financial position

C    Separately below non-current assets

D    Separately below current assets

5    In order for an asset to be classified as held for sale under IFRS 5, certain conditions need to be met.

**Which of these is not one of the conditions?**

A    Management has committed itself to scrap the asset.

B    The asset is expected to be sold within 12 months following classification to held for sale.

C    It is unlikely that the plan will be changed significantly.

D    The sale is highly probable

6    Kat has a year-end of 31st December. On the 1st January 20X9, it classified one of its freehold properties as held for sale. At that date the property had a carrying amount of $667,000 and had been accounted for according to the revaluation model. Its fair value was estimated at $825,000 and the costs to sell at $3,000.

**In accordance with IFRS 5 (*Non-current Assets Held for Sale and Discontinued Operations*), what amounts should be recognised in the financial statements for the year to 31 December 20X9?**

A    Statement of profit or loss gain $155,000
Statement of profit or loss impairment loss $3,000
Revaluation gain nil

B    Statement of profit or loss gain $158,000
Statement of profit or loss impairment loss nil
Revaluation gain nil

C    Statement of profit or loss gain nil
Statement of profit or loss impairment loss nil
Revaluation gain $155,000

D    Statement of profit or loss gain nil
Statement of profit or loss impairment loss $3,000
Revaluation gain $158,000

7    **Which of the following statements are true in relation to assets held for sale under IFRS 5 *Assets Held for Sale And Discontinued Operations*?**

(i)    Assets held for sale are always separately disclosed within the statement of profit or loss.

(ii)    An asset with a carrying amount of £20,000 and a fair value less cost to sell of £18,000 would have suffered a £2,000 impairment.

A    Both.

B    (i) only

C    (ii) only

D    Neither

## 4   Summary diagram

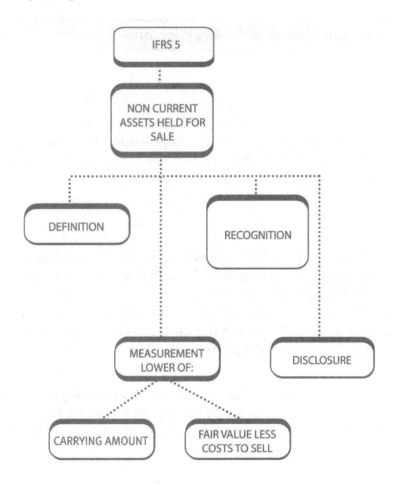

## Test your understanding answers

| **Test your understanding 1 – Practice questions** |
|---|

1   C

2   B

3   A – The asset does not meet the criteria of an asset held for sale until the reporting date, hence depreciate the asset as normal for the year. No further depreciation will occur on this asset after the reporting date.

4   D

5   A

6   D – The asset held for sale will be revalued to the fair value of $825,000 creating a gain of $158,000 to the revaluation reserve. The asset held for sale will then be reduced to the fair value less costs to sell value of $825,000 – $3,000, i.e. create an impairment cost of $3,000. There will not be a gain to the SPL until the asset is sold and the gain is realised.

7   C – The asset held for sale will be valued at the fair value less costs to sell, i.e. $18,000. This will reduce the carrying amount by $2,000 impairment. Item one is not correct as the asset held for sale appears on the SFP as a separate item and not on the SPL.

# IFRS 16 Leases

## Chapter learning objectives

**Lead outcome**

B2. Explain specific IFRS financial reporting standards

**Component outcome**

Explain the specific financial reporting standards related to:

b. Leases

# 1 Session content

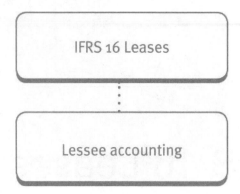

# 2 Introduction

An entity may need a particular asset for its operations but may not have the cash available to purchase the asset outright. As a result, the entity may enter a lease agreement whereby the entity gets to use the asset on a day to day basis but pays for the asset via periodic rental payments.

This is a common method of financing utilised by many businesses.

 **Definitions**

**'A lease is a contract, or part of a contract, that conveys the right to use an asset (the underlying asset) for a period of time in exchange for consideration.'**

The **lessor** is the **'entity that provides the right to use an underlying asset in exchange for consideration.'**

The **lessee** is the **'entity that obtains the right to use an underlying asset in exchange for consideration.'**

A **right-of-use asset 'represents the lessee's rights to use an underlying asset for the lease term.'** (IFRS 16, Appendix A).

 # 3 Lessee accounting

As defined above, the lessee is the entity using the asset on a day-to-day basis. It has the right-of-use of the asset. The lessee will be paying rentals.

### Basic principle

At the commencement of the lease, the lessee should recognise:

- a lease liability, and

- a right-of-use asset.

As ever, the accounting treatment considers the initial measurement and the subsequent treatment of a lease.

## Initial measurement

### Lease liability

Per IFRS 16 *Leases*, the lease liability is initially measured at the **present value** of the lease payments that have **not yet been paid.**

Lease payments should include the following:

*   Fixed payments over the lease term.

*   Amounts expected to be payable under residual value guarantees. A residual value guarantee is provided by the lessee and states that the underlying asset at the end of the lease term will not be worth less than a specified amount. This reduces the risk of damage and unauthorised usage of the asset.

*   Options to purchase the asset that are reasonably certain to be exercised.

*   Termination penalties, if the lease term reflects the expectation that these will be incurred.

The discount rate should be the rate **implicit in the lease**.

If the implicit rate of the lease cannot be determined, then the entity should use its incremental borrowing rate (the rate at which it could borrow funds to purchase a similar asset).

### The right-of-use asset

The right-of-use asset is initially recognised at **cost**.

Per IFRS 16 *Leases*, the initial cost of the right-of-use asset comprises:

*   The amount of the initial measurement of the lease liability (see above)

*   Lease payments made at or before the commencement date

*   Any initial direct costs

*   The estimated costs of removing or dismantling the underlying asset, as per the conditions of the lease.

### The lease term

The lease term is the length of time that the lessee has the right-of-use of an asset.

To calculate the initial value of the liability and right-of-use asset, the lessee must consider the length of the lease term. As per IFRS 16 *Leases*, the lease term comprises:

*   Non-cancellable periods

*   Periods covered by an option to extend the lease, if they are reasonably certain to be exercised

*   Periods covered by an option to terminate the lease, if these are reasonably certain not to be exercised.

### Illustration 1 – Initial recognition

Sadio leases a machine over a 5 year lease term from BH from 1 December 20X5. Rental payments of $75,000 are made in advance on 1 December each year and the first instalment has just been paid.

The useful life of the asset is 7 years. A lease arrangement fee of $1,500 was incurred by Sadio. The rate implicit on the lease cannot be readily determined but the rate of incremental borrowing for Sadio is 8%.

Ownership of the asset is retained by the lessor at the end of the lease term.

**Required:**

What would be the initial journal entry required to record the lease on 1 December 20X5?

**Solution**

The lessee must record a lease liability and a right-of-use asset.

The lease liability will be recorded at the present value of lease payments that have not been paid. The implicit rate of the lease is unknown therefore, the rate of incremental borrowing of 8% should be used as a discount factor.

The lease liability will be recorded at:

| Date of repayment | Lease payment $ | Discount factor at 8% | Present value $ |
|---|---|---|---|
| 1st Dec 20X6 – 20X9 | 75,000 | 3.312 | 248,400 |
| | | | 248,400 |

The right-of-use asset is recorded at the lease liability + lease payments already made + initial direct costs = 248,400 + 75,000 + 1,500 = $324,900

The journals required on 1st December 20X5 are:

| | |
|---|---|
| Dr Right-of-use asset | $324,900 |
| Cr Lease liability | $248,400 |
| Cr Cash | $76,500 |

### Test your understanding 1 – Dynamic

On 1 January 20X1, Dynamic entered into a two year lease for a lorry. The contract contains an option to extend the lease term for a further year. Dynamic believes that it is reasonably certain to exercise this option. Lorries have a useful life of ten years.

Lease payments are $10,000 per year for the initial term and $15,000 per year for the option period. All payments are due at the end of the year. To obtain the lease, Dynamic incurs initial direct costs of $3,000. The lessor reimburses $1,000 of these costs.

The interest rate for the lease is not readily determinable. Dynamic's incremental rate of borrowing is 5%.

**Required:**

Calculate the initial carrying amount of the lease liability and the right-of-use asset and provide the double entries needed to record these amounts in Dynamic's financial records.

### Subsequent measurement

### Lease liability

The carrying amount of the lease liability is increased by the interest charge. Interest is also recorded in the statement of profit or loss:

| | |
|---|---|
| Dr Finance costs (SPL) | X |
| Cr Lease liability (SFP) | X |

The carrying amount of the lease liability is reduced by cash repayments:

| | |
|---|---|
| Dr Lease liability | X |
| Cr Cash | X |

The layout of the lease table will depend on whether payments are made at the end of the year (in arrears) or at the start of the year (in advance).

### Lease liability tables

*Payments in arrears*

| Year | Balance b/f | Interest | Payment | Balance c/f |
|---|---|---|---|---|
| 1 | X | X | (X) | A |
| 2 | X | X | (X) | B |

*Payments in advance*

| Year | Balance b/f | Payment | Subtotal | Interest | Balance c/f |
|---|---|---|---|---|---|
| 1 | X | (X) | X | X | A |
| 2 | X | (X) | B | | |

The current liability element will be A – B

The non-current liability element will be figure B.

### The right-of-use asset

The right-of-use asset is measured using the cost model. This means that it is measured at its initial cost less accumulated depreciation and impairment losses.

Depreciation is calculated as follows:

- If ownership of the asset transfers to the lessee at the end of the lease term then depreciation should be charged over the asset's remaining useful life

- Otherwise, depreciation is charged over the shorter of the useful life and the lease term (as defined previously).

### Other measurement models

Note that IFRS 16 does allow other measurement models varying from the cost model to be applied to the right-of-use asset. For example, fair value methods or revaluation methods may be applied.

This is applicable if the right-of-use relates to an asset that would normally be accounted for using these models.

Examples include:

- Investment properties valued at fair value. The right-of-use asset can be revalued to fair value, gains or losses to profit or loss

- Items of property, plant and equipment using a policy of revaluation. The right-of-use asset may be revalued with gains or losses to revaluation reserves.

### Illustration 2 – Subsequent treatment

Using the details from illustration 1, prepare extracts to the financial statements for the year ended 30 November 20X6.

### Solution

Journals required on 1st December 20X5 (as noted previously in illustration 1):

Dr Right-of-use asset $324,900

Cr Lease liability $248,400

Cr Cash $76,500

The lease liability is increased by finance charges and decreased by the lease repayment each year. The interest is recorded using the 8% incremental borrowing rate.

| Period | Liability | Repayment | Sub-total | Interest 8% | c/f |
|---|---|---|---|---|---|
| | $ | $ | $ | $ | $ |
| 20X6 | 248,400 | (already made) | 248,400 | 19,872 | 268,272 |
| 20X7 | 268,272 | (75,000) | 193,272 | 15,462 | 208,734 |

Current liability = 268,272 – 193,272 = $75,000

Non-current liability = $193,272

Finance costs of $19,872 will be expensed to the statement of profit or loss.

The right-of-use asset uses the cost model as at the year end. As ownership is retained by the lessor at the end of the lease, the right-of-use asset is depreciated over the shorter of the lease term or the remaining useful life of the asset. In this case, this would be the lease term of 5 years.

Depreciation = $324,900/5 = $64,980

Dr Expense $64,980

Cr Right-of-use asset $64,980

**Extracts from the financial statements for the year ended 30 November 20X6**

| | $ |
|---|---|
| **Statement of profit or loss** | |
| Depreciation | 64,980 |
| Finance cost | 19,872 |
| | |
| **Statement of financial position** | |
| Non-current assets – Right-of-use asset | |
| (324,900 – 64,980) | 259,920 |
| Non-current liabilities – Lease liability | 193,272 |
| Current liabilities – Lease liability | 75,000 |

---

**Test your understanding 2 – Dynamic (continued)**

This question follows on from the previous TYU.

**Required:**

Prepare extracts from Dynamic's financial statements in respect of the lease agreement for the year ended 31 December 20X1.

## Test your understanding 3

GBT entered into a four year lease on 1 January 20X0 for a machine with a fair value of $2 million. The lease contract requires the annual payment of $600,000 for four years and the machine has a useful life of five years. The interest implicit in the lease is given below.

**Required:**

Prepare extracts from the statement of financial position and statement of profit or loss for the year ended 31 December 20X0, assuming that instalments are paid in:

(1)  arrears – first payment made on 31 December 20X0 (implicit rate of interest 8%)

(2)  advance – first payment made on 1 January 20X0 (implicit rate of interest 14%).

Prepare all answers to the nearest $000.

## Test your understanding 4

GTA entered into an agreement to lease an item of plant on 1 January 20X1. The lease requires the annual payment in arrears of $400,000 for six years and the machine has a useful life of seven years. The lease agreement transfers legal title to GTA at the end of the lease agreement. The present value of future lease payments was $1,700,000. No direct costs were incurred on setting up the lease. The interest implicit in the lease is 10.84%.

**Required:**

Complete the following extract from the statement of profit or loss for the year ended 31 December 20X1. Give your answers to the nearest $000.

$000

**Statement of profit or loss (extract)**

Depreciation charge

Finance cost

## Test your understanding 5

GTA entered into a second agreement to lease a further item of plant on 1 January 20X2. This lease requires the annual payment **in advance** of $400,000 for six years and the machine has a useful life of six years. The first repayment has been paid already. The present value of future lease payments was $1,300,000. The interest implicit in the lease is 16%. The present value of future repayments was $1,700,000.

### Required:

Calculate the carrying amount of the non-current lease liability at 31 December 20X2. Give your answer to the nearest $000.

## Short-life and low value assets

If the lease is short-term (less than 12 months at the inception date) or of a low value then a simplified treatment is allowed.

In these cases, the lessee can choose to recognise the lease payments in profit or loss on a straight line basis. No lease liability or right-of-use asset would be recognised.

## Low value assets

IFRS 16 *Leases* does not specify a particular monetary amount below which an asset would be considered 'low value'.

The standard gives the following examples of low value assets:

- tablets
- small personal computers
- telephones
- small items of furniture.

The assessment of whether an asset qualifies as having a 'low value' must be made based on its value when new. Therefore, a car would not qualify as a low value asset, even if it was very old at the commencement of the lease.

**Illustration 3 – Short term or low value lease**

Zoo Ltd entered into a four year lease of mobile phones for its sales force on 1 January 20X1. The initial deposit is $1,000 on 1 January 20X1 followed by four annual payments of $1,000 in arrears on 31 December each year. The annual payments commence on 31 December 20X1. The leases are deemed low value by Zoo Ltd.

**What is the charge to the statement of profit or loss and what amount would appear on the statement of financial position at the end of the first year of the lease?**

IFRS 16 *Leases* permits a simplified treatment for assets with a lease period of 12 months or less, or of low value.

The simplified treatment allows the lease payments to be charged as an expense over the lease period, applying the accruals concept.

$$\text{Annual lease rental expense} = \frac{\text{Total rentals payable}}{\text{Total lease period}}$$

Total payments = $5,000 (deposit plus (4 × $1,000) rentals)

Charge to profit or loss = 5,000/4 = $1,250

In year ended 31 December 20X1, the cash paid was $1,000 deposit plus $1,000 rental = $2,000.

A prepayment of $750 is shown on the statement of financial position.

**Statement of profit or loss (extract)**

| | $ |
|---|---|
| Lease expense ($5,000/4) | 1,250 |

**Statement of financial position (extract)**

| | $ |
|---|---|
| Current assets | |
| Prepayments (paid $2,000 – $1,250 to the P/L) | 750 |

**Test your understanding 6**

DJT hires laptops, which are considered by DJT to be low value items, under a lease for three years with payments to be made as follows:

| | |
|---|---|
| Year 1 | $5,000 |
| Year 2 | $10,000 |
| Year 3 | $6,000 |

**Prepare extracts from the statement of profit or loss and the statement of financial position for each of the three years.**

## Test your understanding 7

FGH entered into a four year lease on 1 April 20X2 for the use of an item of office equipment considered to be of low value. It paid a deposit of $600 and will make lease payments of $1,200 on 31 March 20X3, 20X4, 20X5 and 20X6.

In the year ended 31 March 20X3, FGH has recorded all payments related to the lease as an expense in the statement of profit or loss.

**Prepare the journal entry required to correct the accounting treatment.**

## Test your understanding 8

**Questions (1) to (3) below are based on the following scenario:**

Cuthbert Ltd has entered into a 5 year lease for the use of a machine on 1 January 20X1. The present value of the future repayments at the date of inception of the lease is $342,600. Direct costs relating to setting up the lease totalled $10,000. Under the terms of the lease five annual instalments of $120,000 are payable at the start of each year. The first rental has already been paid. The rate of interest implicit in the lease is 15%. The remaining useful life of the asset is 5 years.

(1) **Calculate the finance cost that would be recognised in the statement of profit or loss in the year ended 31 December 20X1 (to the nearest $).**

(2) **Calculate the non-current element of the finance lease liability shown in Cuthbert Ltd's statement of financial position as at 31 December 20X1 (to the nearest $).**

(3) **Calculate the carrying amount of the right-of-use asset at 31 December 20X2.**

(4) MB entered into a four year lease for some low value bluetooth headsets on 1 November 20X5 and was required to pay an initial deposit of $500, plus the first of four annual payments of $250 (payable in advance each year).

   **Complete the journal entry required to correctly recognise the lease for the year ended 31 October 20X6.**

   Dr

   Dr

   Cr

   Note: In the assessment, you would choose the headings for the Drs and Crs from a selection of choices.

(5) A company leases a computer with legal title of the asset passing after two years. The company usually depreciates computers over three years. The company also leases a machine for seven years but legal title does not pass to the lessee at the end of the agreement. The company usually depreciates machinery over ten years.

**Over what period of time should the computer and machine be depreciated?**

|   | Computers | Machine |
|---|---|---|
| A | 2 years | 7 years |
| B | 2 years | 10 years |
| C | 3 years | 7 years |
| D | 3 years | 10 years |

(6) A company leases a motor vehicle. The present value of minimum lease payments is $17,355 and the rate implicit in the lease is 10%. The terms of the lease require three annual instalments to be paid of $10,000 each at the start of each year and the first instalment was already paid.

**At the end of the first year of the lease what amount will be shown for the lease liability in the company's statement of financial position under the headings of non-current liabilities and current liabilities?**

|   | Current liabilities | Non-current liabilities |
|---|---|---|
| A | $9,091 | $10,000 |
| B | $10,000 | $10,900 |
| C | $10,900 | $10,000 |
| D | $10,000 | $9,091 |

(7) CS acquired a machine using a lease on 1 January 20X7. The lease was for a five-year term with rentals of $20,000 per year payable in arrears. The present value of the lease rentals was $80,000 and the implied interest rate was 7.93% per year.

**Calculate the non-current liability and current liability figures to be shown in CS's statement of financial position at 31 December 20X8.**

Non-current liability _____

**Current liability _____**

## 4    Chapter summary

**IFRS 16 Leases**

**Lessee accounting**

**Initial recognition**
- Lease liability – PV of future payments
- Right-of-use asset – lease liability plus previous payments and direct costs

**Subsequent treatment**
- Liability – amortised cost
- Right-of-use asset – depreciated over lower of UEL or lease term

## Test your understanding answers

### Test your understanding 1 – Dynamic

The lease term is three years. This is because the option to extend the lease is reasonably certain to be exercised.

The lease liability is calculated as the present value of future payments as follows:

| Date | Cash flow ($) | Discount factor (5%) | Present value ($) |
|---|---|---|---|
| 31/12/X1 | 10,000 | 0.952 | 9,520 |
| 31/12/X2 | 10,000 | 0.907 | 9,070 |
| 31/12/X3 | 15,000 | 0.864 | 12,960 |
| | | | 31,550 |

The initial cost of the right-of-use asset is calculated as the value of the liability plus any direct costs and other payments already incurred. The calculation is as follows:

| | $ |
|---|---|
| Initial liability value | 31,550 |
| Direct costs | 3,000 |
| Reimbursement | (1,000) |
| | 33,550 |

The reimbursement reduces the overall direct costs so is removed from the capitalised right-of-use asset.

The double entries to record are as follows:

| | |
|---|---|
| Dr Right-of-use asset | $31,550 |
| Cr Lease liability | $31,550 |

| | |
|---|---|
| Dr Right-of-use asset | $3,000 |
| Cr Cash | $3,000 |

| | |
|---|---|
| Dr Cash | $1,000 |
| Cr Right-of-use asset | $1,000 |

This can be summarised as:

| | |
|---|---|
| Dr Right-of-use asset | $33,550 |
| Cr Lease liability | $31,550 |
| Cr Cash | $2,000 |

## Test your understanding 2 – Dynamic (continued)

| Statement of profit or loss | $ |
|---|---|
| Depreciation **(W1)** | (11,183) |
| Finance costs **(W2)** | (1,578) |

| Statement of financial position | $ |
|---|---|
| Non-current assets | |
| Right-of-use asset (33,550 – 11,183) | 22,367 |
| Non-current liabilities | |
| Lease **(W2)** | 14,284 |
| Current liabilities | |
| Lease **(W2)** | 8,844 |

(W1) The right-of-use asset is depreciated over the three year lease term, because it is shorter than the useful life. This gives a charge of $11,183 ($33,550/3 years).

| | |
|---|---|
| Dr Depreciation (SOPL) | $11,183 |
| Cr Right-of-use asset (SFP) | $11,183 |

(W2) **Lease liability table**

| Year-ended | Opening $ | Interest (5%) $ | Payments $ | Closing $ |
|---|---|---|---|---|
| 31/12/X1 | 31,550 | 1,578 | (10,000) | 23,128 |
| 31/12/X2 | 23,128 | 1,156 | (10,000) | 14,284 |

The total lease liability at 31 December 20X1 is $23,128, of which $14,284 is non-current and $8,844 (23,128 – 14,284) is current.

## Test your understanding 3

|  | (1) **Arrears** $000 | (2) **Advance** $000 |
|---|---|---|
| **Statement of profit or loss (extract)** | | |
| Depreciation (1987/4)/(1,992/4) | 497 | 498 |
| Finance cost (see workings) | 159 | 195 |
| | | |
| **Statement of financial position (extract)** | | |
| Right-of-use asset (1,987 – 497)/ (1,992 – 498) | 1,490 | 1,494 |
| Non-current liabilities (see workings) | 1,070 | 987 |
| Current liabilities (see workings) | 476 | 600 |

**Workings**

**Arrears:**

The lease liability is calculated as the present value of future payments as follows:

| Date | Cash flow ($000) | Discount factor (8%) | Present value ($000) |
|---|---|---|---|
| 31/12/X0 | 600 | 0.926 | 556 |
| 31/12/X1 | 600 | 0.857 | 514 |
| 31/12/X2 | 600 | 0.794 | 476 |
| 31/12/X3 | 600 | 0.735 | 441 |
| | | | |
| | | Lease liability | 1,987 |

The initial cost of the right-of-use asset is calculated as the value of the liability plus any direct costs and other payments already incurred. In this case, the right-of-use asset is equal to the lease liability upon initial recognition.

As at the year end, the right-of-use asset is depreciated over the lower of the lease term or the useful lifetime. In this situation, this is the lease term of 4 years.

At the year end, the lease liability is shown at amortised cost split between non-current and current components as calculated below:

| Year | Opening $000 | Interest 8% $000 | Payment $000 | Closing $000 |
|---|---|---|---|---|
| 1 | 1,987 | 159 | (600) | 1,546 |
| 2 | 1,546 | 124 | (600) | 1,070 |

Non-current liability at the end of year 1 = $1,070,000

Current liability at the end of year 1 = 1,546k – 1,070k = $476,000

**Advance:**

The lease liability is calculated as the present value of future payments as follows:

| Date | Cash flow ($000) | Discount factor (14%) | Present value ($000) |
|---|---|---|---|
| 1/1/X1 | 600 | 0.877 | 526 |
| 1/1/X2 | 600 | 0.769 | 461 |
| 1/1/X3 | 600 | 0.675 | 405 |
| | | Lease liability | 1,392 |

The initial cost of the right-of-use asset is calculated as the value of the liability plus any direct costs and other payments already incurred. In this case, the right-of-use asset is equal to the lease liability upon initial recognition plus the advance payment. The right-of-use asset equals $1,392k + $600k = $1,932k.

As at the year end, the right-of-use asset is depreciated over the lower of the lease term or the useful lifetime. In this situation, this is the lease term of 4 years.

At the year end, the lease liability is shown at amortised cost split between non-current and current components as calculated below:

| Year | Opening | Payment | Revised total | Interest 14% | Closing |
|---|---|---|---|---|---|
| | $000 | $000 | $000 | $000 | $000 |
| 1 | 1,392 | (–) | 1,392 | 195 | 1,587 |
| 2 | 1,587 | (600) | 987 | 138 | 1,125 |

Non-current liability at the end of year 1 = $987,000

Current liability at the end of year 1 = 1,587k – 987k = $600,000

NB Please note that using formulas rather than discount factors may create rounding errors when compared with the above answers.

**Test your understanding 4**

| | $000 |
|---|---|
| **Statement of profit or loss (extract)** | |
| Depreciation (1,700/7) | 243 |
| Finance cost (1,700 × 10.84%) | 184 |

**Tutorial note re depreciation**

Depreciation is typically charged on a right-of-use asset over the shorter of the lease term and the asset's useful life which, in this case, would be 6 years. However, as legal title transfers to GTA at the end of the lease term, it is appropriate to depreciate the right-of-use asset over 7 years (as GTA will still have the use of the asset after the lease term finishes).

### Test your understanding 5

**Non-current portion of lease liability at 31 December 20X2 = $1,108,000**

**Lease liability working**

| Year | Opening | Payment | Revised total | Interest 16% | Closing |
|---|---|---|---|---|---|
| | $000 | $000 | $000 | $000 | $000 |
| 1 | 1,300 | – | 1,300 | 208 | 1,508 |
| 2 | 1,508 | (400) | **1,108** | | |

### Test your understanding 6

Total lease payments = $5,000 + $10,000 + $6,000 = $21,000.

Length of lease = three years

Annual charge to statement of profit or loss = $21,000/3 = $7,000

**Statement of profit or loss (extract)**

| | 1 | 2 | 3 |
|---|---|---|---|
| Lease expense | 7,000 | 7,000 | 7,000 |

**Statement of financial position (extract)**

| | 1 | 2 | 3 |
|---|---|---|---|
| Prepayments | | 1,000 | nil |
| Accruals | 2,000 | | |

**Workings**

By the end of year one, a total of $7,000 has been charged to the statement of profit or loss but only $5,000 has been paid. An accrued expense is required in the statement of financial position of $2,000.

By the end of year two, a total of $14,000 has been charged to the statement of profit or loss and $15,000 has been paid. A prepayment is required in the statement of financial position of $1,000.

### Test your understanding 7

Total lease payments = 600 + (4 × 1,200) = $5,400

Length of lease = four years

Annual charge to statement of profit or loss = $5,400/4 = $1,350.

Expense erroneously charged to statement of profit or loss in year ended 31 March 20X3 = 600 + 1,200 = $1,800.

A prepayment of $450 is required.

Therefore, the journal entry required to correct the current accounting treatment is:

| | |
|---|---|
| Dr Prepayments | $450 |
| Cr Statement of profit or loss | $450 |

### Test your understanding 8

(1) **Finance cost = $51,390**

342,600 × 15% = $51,390

or see below for lease table.

(2) **Non-current lease liability at end of year 1 = $273,990**

| Year | Opening | Payment | Total | Interest 15% | Closing |
|---|---|---|---|---|---|
| | $ | $ | $ | $ | $ |
| 1 | 342,600 | (–) | 342,600 | 51,390 | 393,990 |
| 2 | 393,990 | (120,000) | **273,990** | 41,099 | 315,089 |

The non-current liability at the end of the year is the amount outstanding immediately after next year's payment.

(3) **Carrying amount of the right-of-use asset = $283,560**

The right-of-use asset would be initially recorded at the value of the lease liability plus payments already made + direct costs = 342,600 + 120,000 + 10,000 = $472,600

The right-of-use asset is depreciated over the lower of the useful life and the lease term. The lease term and useful lifetime are both 5 years. Depreciation per annum is 472,600/5 = $94,520.

The carrying amount in the 2nd year of the lease will be 472,600 – (94,520 × 2) = $283,560

(4) **Dr Prepayments $375**

**Dr Profit or loss $375**

**Cr Cash $750**

Total payments = 500 + (4 × 250) = $1,500

Lease term = 4 years

Therefore, rental expense each year = 1,500/4 = $375

Amount prepaid = 750 – 375 = $375

(5) **C** – Assets should usually be depreciated over the lease term. However, the ownership of the computer transfers at the end of the lease, so the computer will be depreciated over its useful life of 3 years.

(6) **D**

| Year | Opening | Payment | Sub-total | Interest 10% | Closing |
|------|---------|---------|-----------|--------------|---------|
| 1 | 17,355 | (–) | 17,355 | 1,736 | 19,091 |
| 2 | 19,091 | (10,000) | 9,091 | 909 | 10,000 |

(7) Non-current liability – **$35,697**

Current liability – **$15,908**

**Working:**

| Year | Opening | Interest @ 7.93% | Payment | Closing |
|------|---------|------------------|---------|---------|
| 20X7 | 80,000 | 6,344 | (20,000) | 66,344 |
| 20X8 | 66,344 | 5,261 | (20,000) | 51,605 |
| 20X9 | 51,605 | 4,092 | (20,000) | 35,697 |

The total liability at the end of 20X8 = $51,605

The non-current liability = $35,697 (amount still owing in one year's time)

The current liability = $15,908 ($51,605 – $35,697)

# IAS 2 Inventories and IAS 10 Events after the reporting period

## Chapter learning objectives

**Lead outcome**

B2. Explain specific IFRS financial reporting standards

**Component outcome**

Explain the specific financial reporting standards related to:

d. Inventory

e. Events after the reporting period

## 1 Session content

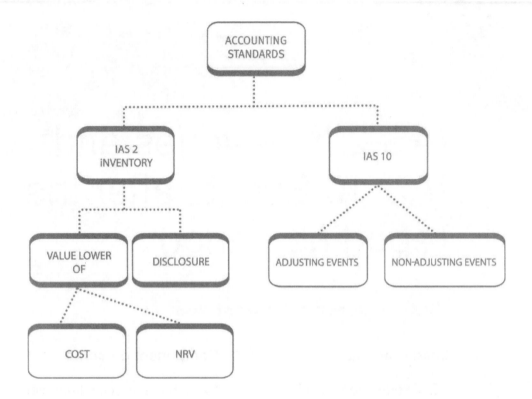

## 2 IAS 2 Inventories

Inventories are assets that are:

- held for sale
- in the process of production
- materials that will be used in the production process

**Measurement of inventories**

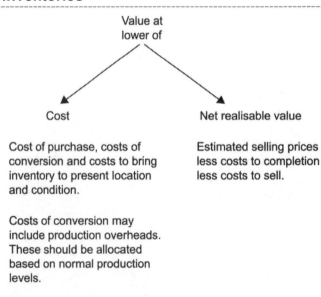

## Costs not included in inventory

Examples of costs that should not be included in inventory are:

- abnormal amounts of wasted materials, labour, or other production costs

- storage costs

- administration costs that do not contribute to bringing the inventories to their present location and condition

- selling and distribution costs

These costs should be treated as expenses against profit in the period that they arise.

## Determining cost

**Costs of purchase** include the purchase price, import duties, handling costs and other costs directly connected with the acquisition of the goods.

**Costs of conversion** include costs directly related to the units being produced, e.g. direct labour costs, allocation of fixed and variable overhead costs incurred in production.

**Variable production overheads** are those indirect costs of production that vary directly with the volume produced, e.g. heat, light and power.

**Fixed production overheads** are those indirect costs of production that do not vary directly with the volume produced and remain constant regardless of the number of units produced, e.g. depreciation of machinery, factory administration costs.

## Allocation of overheads

The allocation of fixed production overheads should be based on the normal capacity of the business. Any excess overheads due to inefficiencies or production problems should be treated as an expense in the period that they occur.

**Illustration 1 – Calculation of the cost of inventory**

The following costs relate to a unit of inventory:

| | |
|---|---|
| Cost of raw materials | $1.00 |
| Direct labour | $0.50 |

During the year $60,000 of fixed production overheads were incurred.

8,000 units were produced during the year which is lower than the normal level of 10,000 units. This was as a result of a fault with some machinery which resulted in 2,000 units having to be scrapped.

At the year-end, 700 units are in closing inventory.

**Required:**

What is the cost of closing inventory?

 **Solution**

Production overheads should be allocated based on the normal level of production, i.e. 10,000 units.

$60,000/10,000 units = $6.00 per unit.

Cost per unit:

| | $ |
|---|---|
| Raw materials | 1.00 |
| Direct labour | 0.50 |
| Production overheads | 6.00 |
| | ___ |
| Total cost per unit | 7.50 |

Cost of 700 units in closing inventory = 700 × $7.50 = $5,250.

 **Calculation of costs**

If inventory should be valued at cost (when cost is lower than net realisable value) either the actual cost of an item (unit cost) or a reasonable approximation to actual cost should be used.

A reasonable approximation would be used if the determination of an items actual cost is impractical e.g. there are a large number of items in a particular line of inventory or it is impossible to identify the actual costs.

The most common approximations are:

1   First in, first out (FIFO). The closing inventory is assumed to consist of the latest purchases, i.e. oldest inventory is sold first. This means the closing inventory will be valued at the most recent purchase prices.

    This method of cost valuation would be appropriate for inventory lines like bananas in supermarkets. They would be purposely stacked on shelves so that the older ones would sell first.

2   Average cost (AVCO). The weighted average cost is calculated by taking the total purchase price of all units purchased in the period divided by the total number of units purchased in the period. This can be calculated using periodic or a continuous method – see illustration 2 for more detail.

    This method of cost valuation would be appropriate for inventory lines like oil in an oil refinery. Inventory would be stored together, cost prices would fluctuate and it would be impossible to distinguish between the different cost lines.

### Illustration 2 – Calculation of the cost of inventory

**Calculation of the cost of inventory using FIFO and average cost**

The following purchases and sales took place in Tyrone during the first four days of June:

Day 1 Opening inventory nil

Day 1 Purchase 200 units at $15 per unit

Day 2 Purchase 100 units at $18 per unit

Day 3 Sales of 250 units at $30 per unit

Day 4 Purchase 150 units at $20 per unit

**Required:**

Calculate the cost of inventory at the end of day 4 for Tyrone using:

(a)   The FIFO method;

(b)   the average cost method.

**Solution**

(a) **FIFO method**

Total purchases = 200 + 100 + 150 = 450 units

Sales = 250 units

Closing inventory = 450 – 250 = 200 units

FIFO method assumes the oldest inventory is sold first, therefore the 200 units remaining must be from the most recent purchases on day 4 (150 units) and the balance from the day 2 purchases (50 units).

Cost:

| | |
|---|---|
| 50 × $18 = | $900 |
| 150 × $20 = | $3,000 |
| | $3,900 |

**Total cost of closing inventory = $3,900**

(b) **Average cost method**

Total purchases = 200 + 100 + 150 = 450 units

Total cost of purchases =

| | |
|---|---|
| 200 × $15 = | $3,000 |
| 100 × $18 = | $1,800 |
| 150 × $20 = | $3,000 |
| | $7,800 |

Weighted average cost = $7,800/450 units = $17.33 per unit

**Total cost of closing inventory = 200 units × $17.33 = $3,467**

**Note** An alternative approach could be to calculate the average cost after each transaction,

After day 2 total purchases:

| Units | Price | |
|---|---|---|
| 200 | $15 | $3,000 |
| 100 | $18 | $1,800 |
| 300 | | $4,800 |

| Average cost | $4,800/300 | $16 per unit |
|---|---|---|

**Day 3**
(250) sales

| | AVCO | |
|---|---|---|
| 50 | $16 | $800 |

**Day 4**

| | Price | |
|---|---|---|
| 150 purchases | $20 | $3,000 |
| 200 | | $3,800 |
| Average cost | $3,800/200 | $19 per unit |

This would result in a higher closing inventory value of $3,800.

**Illustration 3 – Inventory valuation**

**Value the following items of inventory.**

(a) Materials costing $12,000 bought for processing and assembly for a profitable special order. Since buying these items, the cost price has fallen to $10,000.

(b) Equipment constructed for a customer for an agreed price of $18,000. This has recently been completed at a cost of $16,800. It has now been discovered that, in order to meet certain regulations, further work with an extra cost of $4,200 will be required. The customer has accepted partial responsibility and agreed to meet half of the extra cost.

### Solution

(a)   Value at $12,000. IAS 2 states value at lower of cost and NRV. The order is profitable and therefore NRV must be higher than cost. $10,000 is irrelevant as this is the replacement cost.

(b)   Value at NRV, i.e. $15,900 as below cost,

NRV = contract price of $18,000 – the entity's share of costs to complete $2,100 = $15,900.

Original cost = $16,800.

## Disclosure

The main disclosure requirements of IAS 2 *Inventories* are:

- Accounting policy adopted, including the cost formula used.

- Total carrying amount, classified as follows:

|                    | $ |
|--------------------|---|
| Raw materials      | X |
| Work in progress   | X |
| Finished goods     | X |
|                    | — |
|                    | X |

This would be disclosed in a note to the financial statements. The total amount of closing inventory will be shown as a current asset on the statement of financial position and a reduction to the cost of sales in the statement of profit or loss.

- Amount of inventories carried at NRV.

- Amount of inventories recognised as an expense during the period.

- Details of circumstances that have led to the write-down of inventories to their NRV.

## 3   IAS 10 Events after the Reporting Period

The purpose of IAS 10 *Events after the Reporting Period*, is to define to what extent events that occur after the reporting period should be recognised in the financial statements.

IAS 10 *Events after the Reporting Period*, defines an event after the end of the reporting period as '**those events, favourable and unfavourable, that occur between the end of the reporting period and the date when the financial statements are authorised for issue**' (IAS 10, para 3).

IAS 10 identifies two main types of events after the reporting period: adjusting events and non-adjusting events.

**Adjusting events**

'Those events which provide evidence of conditions that existed at the reporting date'

FS should be adjusted to reflect the adjusting event

**Non-adjusting events**

'Those that are indicative of conditions that arose after the reporting date'

FS should not be adjusted to reflect non-adjusting events

Non-adjusting events should be disclosed if they affect users' understanding of the FS

---

 **Examples of adjusting and non-adjusting events**

**Adjusting events** are event that gives evidence of conditions that existed at the reporting date.

Examples of adjusting events would be:

- Selling inventory post year-end for lower than cost price (This is evidence that inventory is incorrectly valued at the year-end).

- Evidence that a customer has gone into liquidation.

- Discovery of fraud or error that existed prior to the year-end.

- Completion of a court case entered into before the reporting date.

- Completion of an insurance claim relating to an event that occurred prior to the year-end.

- Determination after year end, of the sale or purchase price of assets sold or purchased before year end.

**Non-adjusting events** show conditions that have arisen since the reporting date, then no adjustment would be made.

Examples of non-adjusting events would be:

- Acquisition or disposal of a subsidiary after the year end.

- Announcements of a plan to discontinue an operation.

- Destruction of an asset by a fire or flood after the reporting date.

- Announcements of a plan to restructure.

- Share capital transactions after the reporting date.

- Changes in taxation or exchange rates after the reporting date.

- Strikes or other labour disputes

- Equity dividends declared after the reporting period but before the financial statements are authorised for issue

## Going concern

If an event after the reporting date indicates that the entity is no longer a going concern, the financial statements for the current period should not be prepared on the going concern basis.

## Disclosure

A non-adjusting event after the reporting date should be disclosed (by note) where the event has a material effect on the financial statements.

The note should disclose

- The nature of the event.

- An estimate of the financial effect, or a statement that it is not practicable to make such an estimate. The estimate should be made before taking account of taxation, with an explanation of the taxation implications where necessary for a proper understanding of the financial position.

- The date the directors approve financial statements. The date on which the financial statements are authorised for issue should be disclosed.

### Illustration 4 – Events after the reporting period

Shortly after the reporting date, 31/12/X0, a major credit customer of an entity went into liquidation and it is expected that none of a $12,000 debt will be recoverable. $10,000 of the debt relates to sales made before the year end.

In the 20X0 financial statements the whole of the debt has been written off but one of the directors has pointed out that, as the liquidation is an event after the reporting date, the debt should not have been written off but disclosure made by a note.

**Advise whether the director is correct.**

### Solution

The liquidation of the customer is treated as an adjusting event. Only $10,000 debt existed at the reporting date.

Under IAS 10 only the existing debt should be written off in the 20X0 financial statements. The remaining $2,000 did not exist at the reporting date and should be written off in the 20X1 financial statements.

## Test your understanding 1 – Events after the reporting period

Classify each of the following events, which all occurred after the reporting period, as adjusting or non-adjusting.

| | Adjusting event | Non-adjusting event |
|---|---|---|
| Insolvency of a major customer | | |
| Decline in market value of investments | | |
| Loss of non-current assets/inventory due to fire or flood | | |
| Discovery of fraud/error showing that the FS were incorrect | | |
| Announcement of plan to discontinue certain operations | | |
| Evidence concerning the net realisable value of inventory being less than cost | | |
| Resolution of a court case after the reporting date | | |

## Test your understanding 2 – Practice questions

1   Tracey's business sells three products – A, B and C. The following information was available at the year-end:

| | A | B | C |
|---|---|---|---|
| | $ per unit | $ per unit | $ per unit |
| Original cost | 7 | 10 | 19 |
| Estimated selling price | 15 | 13 | 20 |
| Selling and distribution costs | 2 | 5 | 6 |
| Units of inventory | 20 | 25 | 15 |

**The value of inventory at the year-end should be:**

A   $675

B   $670

C   $795

D   $550

2    Item XYZ has 150 items in inventory as at 31 March 20X1. The following alternative valuations have been found.

**Which value should be used in the accounts at 31 March 20X1?**

A    Net realisable value $4,750

B    Original cost $5,500

C    Selling price $7,000

D    Replacement cost $6,500

3    Jackson's year end is 31 December 20X0. In February 20X1, a major customer went into liquidation and the directors' believe that they will not be able to recover the $450,000 owed to them.

**How should this item be treated in the financial statements of Jackson for the year ended 31 December 20X0?**

A    The irrecoverable debt should be disclosed by note

B    The financial statements are not affected

C    The debt should be provided against

D    The financial statements should be adjusted to write off the irrecoverable debt

4    **Which of the following items are non-adjusting items per IAS 10 *Events after the Reporting Period*?**

(i)    Changes in the rates of foreign exchange after the year-end.

(ii)    Destruction of machinery by fire after the year-end.

(iii)    Information regarding the post year-end selling price of year-end inventory.

(iv)    Plans for mergers and acquisitions.

(v)    Insolvency of a customer who had a receivable balance at the year-end.

A    (i), (ii) and (iv)

B    (iii) and (v)

C    (i), (iii) and (v)

D    (ii), (iii) and (v)

5   **Which of the following could be classified as an adjusting event occurring after the end of the reporting period:**

A   A serious fire, occurring 1 month after the year-end, that damaged the sole production facility, causing production to cease for 3 months.

B   One month after the year-end, a notification was received advising that a large receivables balance would not be paid as the customer was being wound up. No payments are expected from the customer.

C   A large quantity of parts for a discontinued production line was discovered at the back of the warehouse during the year-end inventory count. The parts have no value except a nominal scrap value and need to be written off.

D   The entity took delivery of a new machine from the USA in the last week of the financial year. It was discovered almost immediately afterwards that the entity supplying the machine had filed for bankruptcy and would not be able to honour the warranties and repair contract on the new machine. Because the machine was so advanced, it was unlikely that any local entity could provide maintenance cover.

6   The following material events took place after entity X's reporting date of 31 October 20X1 but before the accounts were authorised:

–   Ordinary dividends were approved by the shareholders in relation to the year ended 31 October X1.

–   The discovery of an error in relation to the year-end inventory valuation.

**Please state the correct accounting treatment:**

A   Dividends: Provide for dividend.
    Error: Adjust accounts.

B   Dividends: Disclose dividend.
    Error: Adjust accounts.

C   Dividends: Provide for dividend.
    Error: Disclose error.

D   Dividends: Disclose dividend.
    Error: Disclose error.

7    Bond Ltd has a 31 August year end and on 10 September the company received notification that one of their customers had gone into liquidation owing $30,000, $5,000 of which was from September sales.

Additionally on 10 October the company received $100,000 in insurance following a fire to their premises which occurred on 28th August.

**What amounts will be included in Bond Ltd's accounts as at the year-end under IAS 10 *Events after the Reporting Period*?**

A    Liquidation receivable: $30,000.
Insurance receivable: $Nil.

B    Liquidation receivable: $30,000.
Insurance receivable: $100,000.

C    Liquidation receivable: $25,000.
Insurance receivable: $Nil.

D    Liquidation receivable: $Nil
Insurance receivable: $100,000.

# 4    Summary diagram

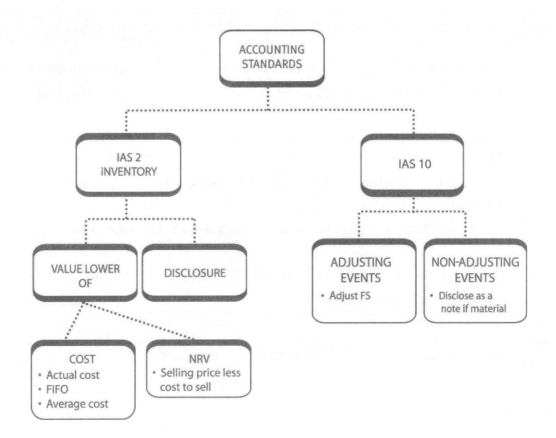

# Test your understanding answers

**Test your understanding 1 – Events after the reporting period**

| | |
|---|---|
| Insolvency of a major customer | Adjusting event |
| Decline in market value of investments | Non-adjusting event |
| Loss of non-current assets/inventories due to fire/flood | Non-adjusting event |
| Discovery of fraud/error showing that the FS were incorrect | Adjusting event |
| Announcement of a plan to discontinue operations | Non-adjusting event |
| Evidence concerning the NRV of inventories | Adjusting event |
| Resolution of a court case | Adjusting event |

**Test your understanding 2 – Practice questions**

1   D

| | A | B | C |
|---|---|---|---|
| Cost | 7 | 10 | 19 |
| NRV | 13 | 8 | 14 |
| Valuation | 20 × 7 = 140 | 25 × 8 = 200 | 15 × 14 = 210 |

Total Valuation = 140 + 200 + 210 = 550

2   A – IAS 2 states that inventory should be valued at the lower of cost or net realisable value.

3   D – This is an example of an adjusting event as per IAS 10.

4   A

5   B

6   B – Dividends are only provided for when they are paid or declared at the reporting date, however, disclosure will be made if discovered prior to authorisation of the financial statements

7   D – The liquidation and the insurance are both adjusting events. As a result, the receivable from the liquidated customer will be written off for the amount recoverable at the year-end, i.e. $25,000 leaving a balance of nil. The insurance receivable would be recorded at the full amount outstanding as at the year end.

# IAS 7 Statement of Cash flows

## Chapter learning objectives

**Lead outcome**

B3.Apply financial reporting standards to prepare basic financial statements

**Component outcome**

Apply financial reporting standards to prepare:

d. Statement of cash flows

## 1    Session content

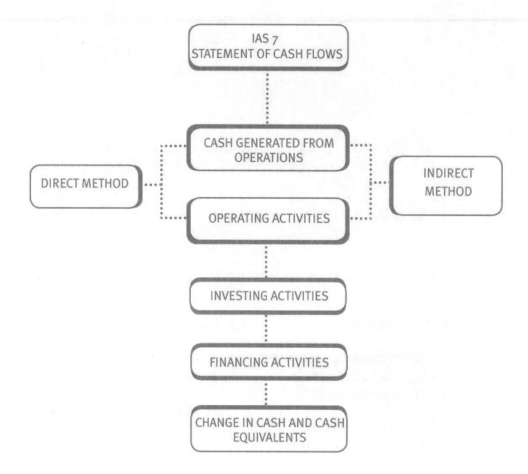

## 2    The importance of statements of cash flows

The statement of cash flows is an important part of the financial statements because:

- It helps users to assess liquidity and solvency – an adequate cash position is essential in the short term both to ensure the survival of the business and to enable debts and dividends to be paid.

- It helps users to assess financial adaptability – will the entity be able to take effective action to alter its cash flows in response to any unexpected events?

- It helps the users assess future cash flows – an adequate cash position in the longer term is essential to enable asset replacement, repayment of debt and to fund further expansion. Users will use current cash flow information to help them assess future cash flows.

- It helps to highlight where cash is being generated – the cash flow statement will clearly detail cash that is being generated from the core activities of the business and other non-operating activities.

- Cash flows are objective – a cash flow is a matter of fact whereas the calculation of profit is subjective.

- It can help to indicate problems early on.

## 3 Definitions in IAS 7

The following definitions are from IAS 7 *Statement of Cash flows*:

### Cash

Cash '**comprises cash on hand and at bank including overdrafts and demand deposits**' (IAS 7, para 6)

### Cash equivalents

Cash equivalents are '**short-term, highly liquid investments that are readily convertible to known amounts of cash and which are subject to an insignificant risk of changes in value, e.g. short-dated treasury bill**' (IAS 7, para 6).

### Operating activities

Operating activities are '**the principal revenue-producing activities of the enterprise and other activities that are not investing or financing activities**' (IAS 7, para 6).

### Investing activities

Investing activities are '**the acquisition and disposal of long-term assets and other investments not included in cash equivalents**' (IAS 7, para 6).

### Financing activities

Financing activities are '**activities that result in changes in the size and composition of the contributed equity and borrowings of the entity**' (IAS 7, para 6).

**Pro-forma statement of cash flows the year ended 31 December 20X9**

|  | $ | $ |
|---|---|---|
| Cash flows from operating activities |  |  |
| Profit before taxation | X |  |
| Adjustments for: |  |  |
| Depreciation | X |  |
| (Profit)/loss on disposal | (X)/X |  |
| Interest receivable/investment income | (X) |  |
| Finance costs | X |  |
|  | ——— |  |
| Operating profit before working capital changes | X |  |
| (Increase)/decrease in inventories | (X)/X |  |
| (Increase)/decrease in trade and other receivables | (X)/X |  |
| Increase/(decrease) in trade and other payables | X/(X) |  |
|  | ——— |  |
| Cash generated from operations | X |  |
| Interest paid | (X) |  |
| Tax paid | (X) |  |
|  | ——— |  |
| Net cash from operating activities |  | X |
| **Cash flows from investing activities** |  |  |
| Purchase of property, plant and equipment | (X) |  |
| Purchase of investments | (X) |  |
| Proceeds from sale of property, plant and equipment | X |  |
| Proceeds from sale of investments | X |  |
| Interest received | X |  |
| Dividends received | X |  |
|  | ——— |  |
| Net cash from investing activities |  | (X) |
| **Cash flows from financing activities** |  |  |
| Proceeds from issue of ordinary shares | X |  |
| Proceeds from issue of preference shares | X |  |
| Proceeds from long-term borrowings | X |  |
| Redemption of long-term borrowings | (X) |  |
| Dividends paid | (X) |  |
|  | ——— |  |
| Net cash from financing activities |  | (X) |
|  |  | ——— |
| Net increase/(decrease) in cash and cash equivalents |  | X/(X) |
| Cash and cash equivalents at beginning of period |  | X/(X) |
|  |  | ——— |
| Cash and cash equivalents at end of period |  | X/(X) |
|  |  | ——— |

## 4 Cash flows from operating activities

The first main heading in the standard statement of cash flows pro-forma is 'cash flows from operating activities.

This can be broken down into 'cash generated from operations', tax paid and interest paid.

### Cash generated from operations

There are two ways the cash generated from operations can be calculated. The direct method and the indirect method.

The indirect method is the most likely to be examined in F1.

### Indirect method

This method involves a reconciliation from profit before tax to cash generated from operations.

The working starts with profit before taxation from the statement of profit or loss, adjusting it for non-cash items and converting the income and expenses figure from the accruals basis to the cash basis, so that just the cash flows generated from operating activities remain.

|  | $ |
|---|---|
| Profit before taxation | X |
| Adjustments for: | |
| **(i) Non-cash items** | |
| Depreciation/amortisation/impairments | X |
| (Profit)/loss on disposal | (X)/X |
| **(ii) Non-operating items** | |
| Interest receivable/investment income | (X) |
| Finance costs | X |
| | |
| Operating profit before working capital changes | X |
| **(iii) Working capital movements** | |
| (Increase)/decrease in inventories | (X)/X |
| (Increase)/decrease in trade and other receivables | (X)/X |
| Increase/(decrease) in trade and other payables | X/(X) |
| | |
| Cash generated from operations | X |

## Adjustments using the indirect method

### Depreciation/amortisation

Depreciation is not a cash flow.

- Capital expenditure purchases/disposals will be recorded under "investing activities" at the time of the cash outflow/inflow.

- Depreciation is the writing off of the capital expenditure over its useful life and simply an 'accounting entry'. It should be added back to profit because it was a non-cash expense deducted from the profit.

### Profit/loss on disposal

When a non-current asset is disposed of:

- the cash inflow from the sale (the proceeds) is recorded under 'investing activities'

- a profit/loss on disposal is calculated by comparing carrying amount and proceeds which is recorded in the statement of profit or loss. This does not equal the cash flow and should be removed from the reconciliation for cash generated from operations.

- a loss on disposal should be added back because it is a non-cash expense deducted from the profit

- a profit on disposal should be deducted because it is a non-cash reduction to expenses added to the profit.

### Interest receivable/investment income

Interest received and investment income are not considered part of day to day operations and will be adjusted within the reconciliation for cash generated from operations.

The amount from the statement of profit or loss should be deducted from the profit because this is not necessarily the amount that has been received (statement of profit or loss is prepared on the accruals basis).

### Finance costs

Finance costs are not considered part of day to day operations and will be adjusted within the reconciliation for cash generated from operations.

The expense from the statement of profit or loss should be added to the profit because this is not necessarily the amount that has been paid.

### Change in receivables

- An increase in receivables is a reduction to cash (the more the customers owe, the less cash in the bank) and

- a decrease in receivable is an increase to cash.

**Change in inventory**

- An increase in inventory is a reduction to cash (the more inventory we buy, the less cash in the bank) and

- a decrease in inventory is an increase to cash.

**Change in payables**

- An increase in payables is an increase to cash (the more the suppliers are owed, the more cash we have in the bank) and

- a decrease in payables is a reduction to cash.

## Direct method

This method involves simply adding cash inflows and deducting cash outflows in respect of operating activities.

|                                              | $    |
| -------------------------------------------- | ---- |
| Cash receipts from customers                 | X    |
| Cash receipts from other operational sources | X    |
| Cash payments to suppliers                   | (X)  |
| Cash payments to employees                   | (X)  |
| Cash payments for expenses                   | (X)  |
|                                              | —    |
| Cash generated from operations               | X    |

## Comparison of the methods

IAS 7 encourages, but does not require, the use of the direct method.

- Indirect method

  - The reconciliation highlights the fact that profit and cash are not equal.

  - Does not show significant elements of trading cash flows.

  - Low cost in preparing the information.

- Direct method

  - Discloses information not shown elsewhere in the financial statements.

  - Shows the cash flows from trading.

  - Gives the users more information in estimating future cash flows.

Illustration 1 – Indirect method

The following information is available for an entity Splatter for the year ended 30 September 20X1:

**Statement of profit or loss**

|  | $000 |
|---|---|
| Revenue | 444 |
| Cost of sales | (269) |
| Gross profit | 175 |
| Distribution costs | (35) |
| Administrative expenses | (8) |
| Profit from operations | 132 |
| Finance costs | (18) |
| Profit before tax | 114 |
| Income tax expense | (42) |
| Profit for the year | 72 |

The total expenses, i.e. cost of sales $269 + distribution costs $35 + administrative expenses $8, can be analysed as follows:

|  | $000 |
|---|---|
| Wages | 72 |
| Auditors' remuneration | 12 |
| Depreciation | 84 |
| Cost of materials used | 222 |
| Profit on disposal of non-current assets | (60) |
| Rental income | (18) |
|  | 312 |

The following information is also available:

|  | 30/09/X1 $000 | 30/09/X0 $000 |
|---|---|---|
| Inventories | 42 | 24 |
| Receivables | 48 | 42 |
| Payables | (30) | (18) |

**Required:**

Produce the section of the statement of cash flows for cash generated from operations using the indirect method for the year ended 30 September 20X1 in compliance with IAS 7 *Statement of Cash Flows.*

**Solution**

**Splatter Statement of cash flows for the year ended 30 September 20X1**

|  | $000 |
|---|---|
| **Cash flows from operating activities** | |
| Profit before tax | 114 |
| Depreciation | 84 |
| Profit on disposal of non-current assets | (60) |
| Finance costs | 18 |
| | ___ |
| Operating profit before working capital changes | 156 |
| Increase in inventories (42 – 24) | (18) |
| Increase in trade receivables (48 – 42) | (6) |
| Increase in trade payables (30 – 18) | 12 |
| | ___ |
| Cash generated from operations | 144 |

Both inventory and receivable balances are increasing, hence a reduction in cash, i.e. the more money tied up in inventory or the more money owed by receivables the less cash we have available in the bank. Therefore, this is shown as a decrease in the statement.

Payables also increase but this means we have an increase in cash, i.e. the more money we owe suppliers, the longer we are keeping the cash in the bank.

**Illustration 2 – Direct method**

**Required:**

Using the information for Splatter in the previous illustration, produce the section of the statement of cash flows for cash generated from operations using the direct method for the year ended 30 September 20X1 in compliance with IAS 7 *Statement of Cash Flows*.

**Solution**

**Splatter Statement of cash flows for the year ended 30 September 20X1**

|  | $000 |
|---|---|
| Cash flows from operating activities | |
| Cash receipts from customers (W1) | 438 |
| Rental income | 18 |
| Cash payments to suppliers (W2) | (228) |
| Cash payments to employees | (72) |
| Cash payments for expenses | (12) |
| | ——— |
| Cash generated from operations | 144 |

**(W1)**

Cash receipts from customers

|  | $000 |
|---|---|
| Opening receivables | 42 |
| Sales revenue | 444 |
| Closing receivables | (48) |
| | ——— |
| Cash received from customers | 438 |

**(W2)**

Cash payments to suppliers

|  | $000 |
|---|---|
| Opening inventories | 24 |
| Purchases (ß) | 240 |
| Closing | (42) |
| | ——— |
| Cost of materials used | 222 |

|  | $000 |
|---|---|
| Opening payables | 18 |
| Purchases (above) | 240 |
| Closing payables | (30) |
| | ——— |
| Payments to suppliers | 228 |

## Test your understanding 1 – Cash generated from operations

Yog's statement of profit or loss for the year ended 31 December 20X1 and statements of financial position as at 31 December 20X0 and 31 December 20X1 were as follows:

**Statement of profit or loss for the year ended 31 December 20X1**

|  | $000 | $000 |
|---|---|---|
| Sales |  | 360 |
| Raw materials consumed | 35 |  |
| Staff costs | 47 |  |
| Depreciation | 59 |  |
| Loss on disposal | 9 |  |
|  |  | (150) |
| Profit from operations |  | 210 |
| Finance costs |  | (14) |
| Profit before tax |  | 196 |
| Income tax expense |  | (62) |
| Profit for the period |  | 134 |

**Statements of financial position as at**

|  | 31 Dec 20X1 | | 31 Dec 20X0 | |
|---|---|---|---|---|
|  | $000 | $000 | $000 | $000 |
| **Assets** |  |  |  |  |
| **Non-current assets** |  |  |  |  |
| Cost |  | 798 |  | 780 |
| Depreciation |  | (159) |  | (112) |
|  |  | 639 |  | 668 |
| **Current assets** |  |  |  |  |
| Inventories | 12 |  | 10 |  |
| Trade receivables | 34 |  | 26 |  |
| Cash and cash equivalents | 24 |  | 28 |  |
|  | —— | 70 | —— | 64 |
| **Total assets** |  | 709 |  | 732 |

**Equity and liabilities**

**Capital reserves**

| | | | |
|---|---|---|---|
| Share capital | | 180 | 170 |
| Share premium | | 18 | 12 |
| Retained earnings | | 343 | 245 |
| | | 541 | 427 |
| **Non-current liabilities** | | | |
| Long-term loans | | 100 | 250 |
| **Current liabilities** | | | |
| Trade payables | 21 | | 15 |
| Interest payable | 7 | | 5 |
| Income tax | 40 | | 35 |
| | | 68 | 55 |
| **Total equity and liabilities** | | 709 | 732 |

During the year, the entity paid $45,000 for a new piece of equipment and a dividend was paid amounting to $36,000.

**Required:**

Calculate the cash generated from operations using the indirect method.

## Test your understanding 2 – Direct method

**Required:**

Using the information for Yog in the previous TYU, produce the section of the statement of cash flows for cash generated from operations using the direct method for the year ended 31 December 20X1 in compliance with IAS 7 *Statement of Cash Flows*.

## Other cash flows from operating activities

Other cash flows that will be considered cash flows from operating activities may include:

- interest paid, and
- income tax paid.

Income tax paid is included here for completeness purposes. However, the CIMA F1 syllabus does not include the accounting for taxation. No questions will ever require tax paid to be calculated. As a result, the following example focusses on the calculation of interest paid.

The cash flow should be calculated using the following pro-forma:

### Interest payable

| | | | | |
|---|---|---|---|---|
| Bank (ß) | X | Bal b/d (SOFP) | | X |
| Bal c/d (SOFP) | X | Profit or loss | | X |
| | ___ | | | ___ |
| | X | | | X |
| | ___ | | | ___ |
| | | Bal b/d | | X |

 **Test your understanding 3 – Operating activities**

Using the information in TYU 1, calculate the interest paid by Yog.

## 5    Cash flows from investing activities

Cash inflows from investing activities may include:

- interest received
- dividends received and
- proceeds from the sale of non-current assets.

Cash outflows from investing activities may include:

- purchases of non-current assets.

### Interest/Dividends received

The cash flow for interest and dividends received should be calculated using the following pro-forma:

### Interest/Dividends received

| | | | | |
|---|---|---|---|---|
| Bal b/d (SOFP) | X | Bank (ß) | | X |
| Profit or loss | X | Bal c/d (SOFP) | | X |
| | ___ | | | ___ |
| | X | | | X |
| | ___ | | | ___ |
| Bal b/d | X | | | |

### Cash paid to acquire non-current assets

The cash flow for non-current assets should be calculated using the following pro-forma:

**Non-current assets – Carrying amount**

| | | | |
|---|---|---|---|
| Bal b/d (SOFP) | X | Disposal (Carrying amount) | X |
| Additions (cash) | X | Depreciation for the year | X |
| Revaluation gain for the year | X | Bal c/d (SOFP) | X |
| | ─── | | ─── |
| | X | | X |
| | ─── | | ─── |
| Bal b/d | X | | |

### Cash received on disposal of non-current assets

The proceeds on disposal of a non-current asset may need to be calculated. The proceeds can be determined by using the profit or loss on disposal as follows:

**Non-current assets – Disposal account**

| | | | |
|---|---|---|---|
| Cost | X | Accumulated depreciation | X |
| Profit on disposal (SPL) | X | Loss on disposal (SPL) | X |
| Bank (ß) | X | | |
| | ─── | | ─── |
| | X | | X |
| | ─── | | ─── |

**Test your understanding 4 – Investing activities**

Using the information in TYU 1 prepare the investing activities section of the statement of cash flow.

## 6 Cash flow from financing activities

Cash inflows from financing activities may include:

- proceeds from the issue of shares, and

- proceeds from the issue of loans/debentures.

Cash outflows from financing activities may include:

- repayments of loans/debentures, and

- dividends paid.

## Proceeds from new share issues

The proceeds from share issues will be calculated by looking at the movement on the share capital and share premium accounts extracted from the statement of financial position. A pro-forma can be used as follows:

**Share capital and share premium**

|  |  | Bal b/d share capital (SOFP) | X |
|---|---|---|---|
| Bal c/d share capital | X | Bal b/d share premium | X |
| Bal c/d share premium (SOFP) | X | Proceeds from new shares issued (ß) | X |
|  | ___ |  | ___ |
|  | X |  | X |
|  | ___ |  | ___ |
|  |  | Bal b/d | X |

## Proceeds/repayments from loan and debentures

The proceeds/repayment of loans/debentures will be calculated by looking at the movement on the loan/debenture accounts extracted from the statement of financial position.

**Loans**

| Repayment of loans (ß) | X | Bal b/d (SOFP) | X |
|---|---|---|---|
| Bal c/d share premium (SOFP) | X | Proceeds from loans (ß) | X |
|  | ___ |  | ___ |
|  | X |  | X |
|  | ___ |  | ___ |
|  |  | Bal b/d | X |

## Dividends paid

The dividend payment can either be found in the statement of changes in equity or by looking at the movement on the retained earnings account as follows:

**Retained earnings**

| Dividend paid (ß) | X | Bal b/d (SOFP) | X |
|---|---|---|---|
| Bal c/d (SOFP) | X | Profit or loss for the year | X |
|  | ___ |  | ___ |
|  | X |  | X |
|  | ___ |  | ___ |
|  |  | Bal b/d | X |

### Test your understanding 5 – Financing activities

Using the information in TYU 1 produce the financing activities section of the statement of cash flows.

### Test your understanding 6 – Statement of cash flows

Using all of you answers from TYU 1 and TYU 3-5 to produce the final statement of cash flows for Yog.

### Illustration 3 – Statement of cash flows

Below are extracts from the financial statements of an entity Pincer:

**Statement of profit or loss and other comprehensive income for the year ended 31 March 20X1**

| | $m |
|---|---|
| Sales revenue | 1,162 |
| Cost of sales | (866) |
| | ——— |
| Gross profit | 296 |
| Distribution costs | (47) |
| Administrative expenses | (103) |
| | ——— |
| Profit from operations | 146 |
| Interest receivable | 79 |
| Finance costs | (55) |
| | ——— |
| Profit before tax | 170 |
| Income tax expense | (24) |
| | ——— |
| Profit for the year | 146 |
| **Other comprehensive income** | |
| Gain on revaluation | 251 |
| | ——— |
| **Total comprehensive income for the year** | 397 |

**Statement of financial position as at 31 March 20X1:**

|  | 31 March 20X1 | | 31 March 20X0 | |
|---|---|---|---|---|
|  | $m | $m | $m | $m |
| **Assets** | | | | |
| **Non-current assets** | | | | |
| Property, plant and equipment | 1,023 | | 600 | |
| Investments | 69 | | 68 | |
|  | | 1,092 | | 668 |
| **Current assets** | | | | |
| Inventories | 246 | | 128 | |
| Trade and other receivables | 460 | | 373 | |
| Cash and cash equivalents | 527 | | 358 | |
|  | | 1,233 | | 859 |
| Total Assets | | 2,325 | | 1,527 |
| **Equity and liabilities** | | | | |
| **Capital and reserves** | | | | |
| Share capital | 29 | | 24 | |
| Share premium | 447 | | 377 | |
| Revaluation reserve | 251 | | – | |
| Retained profit | 116 | | 26 | |
|  | | 843 | | 427 |
| **Non-current liabilities** | | | | |
| Loan | 755 | | 555 | |
|  | | 755 | | 555 |
| **Current liabilities** | | | | |
| Trade and other payables | 244 | | 311 | |
| Overdrafts | 437 | | 207 | |
| Taxation | 46 | | 27 | |
|  | | 727 | | 545 |
| Total equity and liabilities | | 2,325 | | 1,527 |

**Additional information:**

- Profit from operations includes depreciation on the property, plant and equipment of $22 million. The revaluation reserve relates wholly to property, plant and equipment.

- During the year ended 31 March 20X1, plant and machinery costing $1,464 million, which had a carrying amount of $424 million, was sold for $250 million.

- During the year ended 31 March 20X1, 25 million 20c shares were issued at a premium of $2.80.

- Dividends paid during the year were $56 million.

**Required:**

Produce a statement of cash flows for Pincer for the year ended 31 March 20X1 in compliance with IAS 7 *Statement of Cash Flows* using the indirect method.

## Solution

**Pincer Statement of cash flows for the year ended 31 March 20X1**

|  | $m | $m |
|---|---|---|
| **Cash flows from operating activities** | | |
| Profit before tax | 170 | |
| Depreciation | 22 | |
| Loss on disposal of non-current assets (250 – 424) | 174 | |
| Interest receivable | (79) | |
| Finance costs | 55 | |
|  | ——— | |
| Operating profit before working capital changes | 342 | |
| Increase in inventories (246 – 128) | (118) | |
| Increase in trade receivables (460 – 373) | (87) | |
| Decrease in trade payables (244 – 311) | (67) | |
|  | ——— | |
| Cash generated from operations | 70 | |
| Interest paid | (55) | |
| Income tax paid (W1) | (5) | |
|  | ——— | |
| Net cash from operating activities | | 10 |

**Cash flows from investing activities**

| | | |
|---|---:|---:|
| Purchases of property, plant and equipment (W2) | (618) | |
| Purchase of investments (69 – 68) | (1) | |
| Proceeds of property, plant and equipment | 250 | |
| Interest received | 79 | |
| | ——— | |
| Net cash from investing activities | | (290) |

**Cash flow from financing activities**

| | | |
|---|---:|---:|
| Proceeds from issue of shares (W3) | 75 | |
| Proceeds from long-term borrowing (755 – 555) | 200 | |
| Dividends paid | (56) | |
| | ——— | |
| Net cash from financing activities | | 219 |
| | | ——— |
| Net decrease in cash and cash equivalents | | (61) |
| Cash and cash equivalents at beginning of period (358 – 207) | | 151 |
| | | ——— |
| Cash and cash equivalents at end of period (527 – 437) | | 90 |
| | | ——— |

**Workings**

(W1)

**Tax**

| | | | |
|---|---:|---|---:|
| Bank (ß) | 5 | Bal b/d (current) | 27 |
| Bal c/d (current) | 46 | SPL | 24 |
| | —— | | —— |
| | 51 | | 51 |
| | —— | | —— |
| | | Bal b/d (current) | 46 |

(W2)

**Property, plant and equipment**

| | | | |
|---|---:|---|---:|
| Bal b/d | 600 | Dep'n | 22 |
| Reval'n | 251 | Disposal | 424 |
| Bank (ß) | 618 | Bal c/d | 1,023 |
| | ——— | | ——— |
| | 1,469 | | 1,469 |
| | ——— | | ——— |
| Bal b/d | 1,023 | | |

(W3) Proceeds from share issue = **25 million × ($2.80 + 0.20) = $75 million**

Please note, the following two TYUs are for illustrative purposes and do not reflect exam standard requirements. Candidates will never be asked in the exam to produce a full statement of cash flows. Candidates are likely to be tested on extracts from the statement or to determine specific cash flows shown within the statement of cash flows

**Test your understanding 7 – Practice question**

Below are extracts from the financial statements of an entity Poochie:

**Statement of profit or loss for the year ended 31 March 20X1**

|  | $ |
|---|---|
| Revenue | 30,650 |
| Cost of sales | (26,000) |
|  |  |
| Gross profit | 4,650 |
| Distribution costs | (900) |
| Administrative expenses | (500) |
|  |  |
| Profit from operations | 3,250 |
| Investment income | 680 |
| Finance costs | (400) |
|  |  |
| Profit before tax | 3,530 |
| Income tax expense | (300) |
|  |  |
| Profit for the period | 3,230 |

## Statements of financial position as at 31 March 20X1

| | 20X1 | | 20X0 | |
|---|---|---|---|---|
| | $ | $ | $ | $ |
| **Assets** | | | | |
| **Non-current assets** | | | | |
| Property, plant and equipment | 2,280 | | 850 | |
| Investments | 2,500 | | 2,500 | |
| | | 4,780 | | 3,350 |
| **Current assets** | | | | |
| Inventories | 1,000 | | 1,950 | |
| Trade and other receivables | 1,900 | | 1,200 | |
| Cash and cash equivalents | 410 | | 160 | |
| | | 3,310 | | 3,310 |
| **Total Assets** | | 8,090 | | 6,660 |
| **Equity and liabilities** | | | | |
| **Capital and reserves** | | | | |
| Share capital | 1,000 | | 900 | |
| Share premium | 500 | | 350 | |
| Retained earnings | 3,410 | | 1,380 | |
| | | 4,910 | | 2,630 |
| **Non-current liabilities** | | | | |
| Long term borrowings | 2,300 | | 1,040 | |
| | | 2,300 | | 1,040 |
| **Current liabilities** | | | | |
| Trade and other payables | 250 | | 1,890 | |
| Interest payable | 230 | | 100 | |
| Taxation | 400 | | 1,000 | |
| | | 880 | | 2,990 |
| **Total equity and liabilities** | | 8,090 | | 6,660 |

**Additional information:**

- Profit from operations is after charging depreciation on the property, plant and equipment of $450.

- During the year ended 31 March 20X1, plant and machinery costing $80 and with accumulated depreciation of $60, was sold for $20.

- The receivables at the end of 20X1 includes $100 of interest receivable. There was no balance at the beginning of the year.

- Investment income of $680 is made up of $300 interest receivable and $380 dividends received.

- Dividends paid during the year were $1,200.

**Required:**

Produce a statement of cash flows for Poochie for the year ended 31 March 20X1 in compliance with IAS 7 *Statement of Cash Flows* using the indirect method.

### Test your understanding 8 – Practice question

Below are extracts from the financial statements of an entity Yam Yam:

**Statement of profit or loss and other comprehensive income for the year ended 30 September 20X1**

|  | $000 |
|---|---|
| Revenue | 2,900 |
| Cost of sales | (1,734) |
| Gross profit | 1,166 |
| Distribution costs | (520) |
| Administrative expenses | (342) |
| Profit from operations | 304 |
| Investment income | 5 |
| Finance costs | (19) |
| Profit before tax | 290 |
| Income tax expense | (104) |
| Profit for the period | 186 |
| **Other comprehensive income** | |
| Gain on revaluation | 50 |
| **Total comprehensive income for the year** | 236 |

**Statements of financial position as at 30 September 20X1**

|  | 30 September 20X1 | | 30 September 20X0 | |
| --- | --- | --- | --- | --- |
|  | $000 | $000 | $000 | $000 |
| **Assets** | | | | |
| **Non-current assets** | | | | |
| Property, plant and equipment | 634 | | 510 | |
|  | | 634 | | 510 |
| **Current assets** | | | | |
| Inventories | 420 | | 460 | |
| Trade receivables | 390 | | 320 | |
| Interest receivable | 4 | | 9 | |
| Investments | 50 | | 0 | |
| Cash at bank | 75 | | 0 | |
| Cash at hand | 7 | | 5 | |
|  | | 946 | | 794 |
| **Total Assets** | | 1,580 | | 1,304 |
| **Equity and liabilities** | | | | |
| **Capital and reserves** | | | | |
| Share capital $0.50 each | 363 | | 300 | |
| Share premium | 89 | | 92 | |
| Revaluation reserve | 50 | | 0 | |
| Retained earnings | 63 | | (70) | |
|  | | 565 | | 322 |
| **Non-current liabilities** | | | | |
| 10% Loan notes | 0 | | 40 | |
| 5% Loan notes | 329 | | 349 | |
|  | | 329 | | 389 |
| **Current liabilities** | | | | |
| Trade and other payables | 550 | | 400 | |
| Bank overdraft | 0 | | 70 | |
| Accruals | 36 | | 33 | |
| Taxation | 100 | | 90 | |
|  | | 686 | | 593 |
| **Total equity and liabilities** | | 1,580 | | 1,304 |

**Additional information:**

- On 1 October 20X0, Yam Yam issued 60,000 $0.50 shares at a premium of 100%. The proceeds were used to finance the purchase and cancellation of all of its 10% loan notes and some of its 5% loan notes, both at par. A bonus issue of one for ten shares held was made at 1 November 20X0; all shares in issue qualified for the bonus.

- The current asset investment was a 30 day government bond.

- Non-current assets included certain properties that were revalued during the year.

- Non-current assets disposed of during the year had a carrying amount of $75,000; cash received on disposal was $98,000.

- Depreciation charged for the year was $87,000.

- The accruals balance includes interest payable of $33,000 at 30 September 20X0 and $6,000 at 30 September 20X1.

- Interim dividends paid during the year were $53,000.

**Required:**

Produce a statement of cash flows for Yam Yam the year ended 30 September 20X1 in compliance with IAS 7 *Statement of Cash Flows* using the indirect method.

---

## Test your understanding 9 – Practice questions

1   Barlow uses the 'indirect method' for the purpose of calculating cash generated from operations in the statement of cash flows.

The following information is provided for the year ended 31 December 20X0:

|  | $ |
|---|---|
| Profit before tax | 5,600 |
| Depreciation | 956 |
| Profit on sale of equipment | 62 |
| Increase in inventories | 268 |
| Increase in receivables | 101 |
| Increase in payables | 322 |

**What is the cash generated from operations?**

A   $6,571

B   $6,541

C   $6,447

D   $5,803

2    Evans had the following balances in its statement of financial position as at 30 June 20X0 and 20X1:

|  | 20X1 | 20X0 |
|---|---|---|
| 10% Loan | $130,000 | $150,000 |
| Share Capital | $120,000 | $100,000 |
| Share Premium | $45,000 | $35,000 |

**How much will appear in the statement of cash flows for the year ended 30 June 20X1 as the total for 'cash flows from financing activities'?**

A    $10,000 outflow

B    $10,000 inflow

C    $50,000 inflow

D    $50,000 outflow

3    At 1 January 20X0 Casey had non-current assets with a carrying amount of $250,000. In the year ended 31 December 20X0, the entity disposed of assets with a carrying amount of $45,000 for $50,000. The entity revalued a building from $75,000 to $100,000. Casey charged depreciation for the year of $20,000. At the end of the year, the carrying amount of non-current assets was $270,000.

**How much will be reported in the statement of cash flows for the year ended 31 December 20X0 as the total for 'cash flows from investing activities'?**

A    $10,000 outflow

B    $10,000 inflow

C    $35,000 outflow

D    $50,000 inflow

**The following information relates to Questions 4 and 5:**

IAS 7 requires cash flows to be analysed under three headings – cash flows from operating activities, investing activities and financing activities. Several items that may appear in a cash flow statement are listed below:

(i)    Cash paid for the purchase of non-current assets

(ii)   Dividends received

(iii)  Interest paid

(iv)   Repayment of borrowings

(v)    Tax paid

4   **Which of the above items would appear under the heading 'cash flows from investing activities'?**

   A   i only

   B   i and ii

   C   i, ii, iii and iv

   D   ii, iii and iv

5   **Which of the above items would appear under the heading 'cash flows from operating activities'?**

   A   i only

   B   iii and v

   C   iii, iv and v

   D   ii, iii and v

6   **How much interest was paid in the year?**

|                                                  | $000 |
|--------------------------------------------------|------|
| Interest accrued b/fwd                           | 600  |
| Interest charged to the statement of profit or loss | 700  |
| Interest accrued c/fwd                           | 500  |

   A   $600,000

   B   $700,000

   C   $800,000

   D   $1,300,000

7   At 1 October 20X0, BK had the following balance:

   Accrued interest payable $12,000 credit.

   During the year ended 30 September 20X1, BK charged interest payable of $41,000 to its statement of profit or loss. The closing balance on accrued interest payable account at 30 September 20X1 was $15,000 credit.

   **How much interest paid should BK show on its statement of cash flows for the year ended 30 September 20X1?**

   A   $38,000

   B   $41,000

   C   $44,000

   D   $53,000

8   Interest payable balance at 31 March 20X0 $1,120,000.

Interest payable balance at 31 March 20X1 $1,140,000.

Interest charged to the statement of profit or loss for the year to 31 March 20X1 $850,000.

**How much should be included in the statement of cash flows for interest paid in the year?**

A   $800,000

B   $830,000

C   $850,000

D   $880,000

9   During the year to 31st July, Smartypants made a profit of $37,500 after accounting for depreciation of $2,500.

During the year non-current assets were purchased for $16,000, receivables increased by $2,000, inventories decreased by $3,600 and trade payables increased by $700.

**What was the increase in cash and bank balances during the year?**

A   $21,300

B   $21,700

C   $24,900

D   $26,300

10  Which of the following lists consists of items that would be added to profit before taxation in the calculation of net cash from operating activities according to IAS 7?

A   Decrease in trade receivables, increase in trade payables, profit on sale of non-current assets.

B   Loss on sale of non-current assets, depreciation, increase in trade receivables.

C   Decrease in inventories, depreciation, profit on sale of non-current assets.

D   Decrease in trade receivables, increase in trade payables, loss on sale of non-current assets.

## 7 Summary diagram

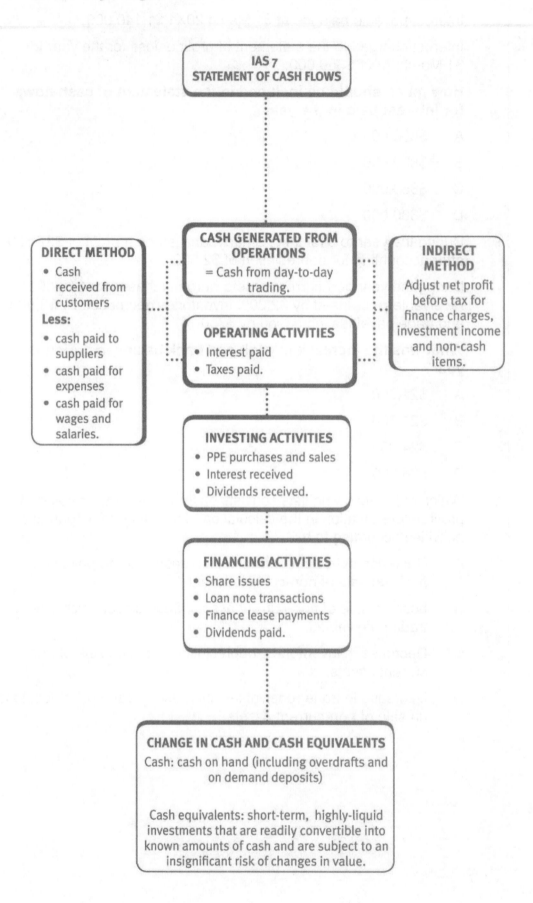

# Test your understanding answers

## Test your understanding 1 – Cash generated from operations

**Yog statement of cash flows for the year ended 31 December 20X1**

| | $000 |
|---|---|
| Cash flows from operating activities | |
| Profit before taxation | 196 |
| Adjustments for: | |
| Depreciation | 59 |
| Loss on disposal | 9 |
| Finance costs | 14 |
| | ——— |
| Operating profit before working capital changes | 278 |
| Increase in inventories (12 – 10) | (2) |
| Increase in trade receivables (34 – 26) | (8) |
| Increase in trade payables (21 – 15) | 6 |
| | ——— |
| Cash generated from operations | 274 |

## Test your understanding 2 – Direct method

**Yog statement of cash flows for the year ended 31 December 20X1**

| | $000 |
|---|---|
| **Cash flows from operating activities** | |
| Cash receipts from customers (W1) | 352 |
| Cash payments to suppliers (W2) | (31) |
| Cash payments to employees | (47) |
| | ——— |
| Cash generated from operations | 274 |

(W1)

Cash receipts from customers

| | $000 |
|---|---|
| Opening receivables | 26 |
| Sales revenue | 360 |
| Closing receivables | (34) |
| | ——— |
| Cash received from customers | 352 |

(W2)

Cash payments to suppliers

|  | $000 |
|---|---|
| Opening inventories | 10 |
| Purchases (ß) | 37 |
| Closing | (12) |
| Cost of materials used | 35 |

|  | $000 |
|---|---|
| Opening payables | 15 |
| Purchases (above) | 37 |
| Closing payables | (21) |
| Payments to suppliers | 31 |

### Test your understanding 3 – Operating activities

| Interest paid (W1) | (12) |
|---|---|

**Workings**

(W1)

**Interest payable**

| Bank (ß) | 12 | Bal b/d | 5 |
|---|---|---|---|
| Bal c/d | 7 | Profit or loss | 14 |
|  | 19 |  | 19 |
|  |  | Bal b/d | 7 |

## Test your understanding 4 – Investing activities

**Cash flows from investing activities**

| | |
|---|---|
| Purchase of non-current assets | (45) |
| Proceeds from sale of non-current assets ($15 (W1) – loss on sale of $9 = $6) | 6 |
| | —— |
| Net cash from investing activities | (39) |

(W1)

**Non-current assets – CV**

| | | | |
|---|---|---|---|
| Bal b/d | 668 | Disposal (ß) | 15 |
| | | Depreciation for the year | 59 |
| Additions | 45 | Bal c/d | 639 |
| | —— | | —— |
| | 713 | | 713 |
| | —— | | —— |
| Bal b/d | 639 | | |

## Test your understanding 5 – Financing activities

**Cash flows from financing activities**

| | |
|---|---|
| Proceeds from issues of ordinary shares (W1) | 16 |
| Repayment of loans (100 – 250) | (150) |
| Dividends paid | (36) |
| | —— |
| Net cash from financing activities | (170) |

(W1) Share issue = (180 + 18) – (170 + 12 ) = $16

**Test your understanding 6 – Statement of cash flows**

**Yog statement of cash flows for the year ended 31 December 20X1**

|  | $000 | $000 |
|---|---|---|
| Cash flows from operating activities |  |  |
| Profit before taxation | 196 |  |
| Adjustments for: |  |  |
| Depreciation | 59 |  |
| Loss on disposal | 9 |  |
| Finance costs | 14 |  |
|  | —— |  |
| Operating profit before working capital changes | 278 |  |
| Increase in inventories (12 – 10) | (2) |  |
| Increase in trade receivables (34 – 26) | (8) |  |
| Increase in trade payables (21 – 15) | 6 |  |
|  | —— |  |
| Cash generated from operations (TYU 1) | 274 |  |
| Interest paid (TYU 3) | (12) |  |
| Income tax paid (TYU 3) | (57) |  |
|  | —— |  |
| Net cash from operating activities |  | 205 |
| Cash flows from investing activities |  |  |
| Purchase of non-current assets | (45) |  |
| Proceeds from sale of non-current assets (TYU 4) | 6 |  |
|  | —— |  |
| Net cash from investing activities |  | (39) |
| Cash flows from financing activities |  |  |
| Proceeds from issues of ordinary shares (TYU 5) | 16 |  |
| Repayment of loans (100 – 250) | (150) |  |
| Dividends paid | (36) |  |
|  | —— |  |
| Net cash from financing activities |  | (170) |
|  |  | —— |
| Net decrease in cash and cash equivalents |  | (4) |
| Cash and cash equivalents at beginning of period |  | 28 |
|  |  | —— |
| Cash and cash equivalents at end of period |  | 24 |
|  |  | —— |

## Test your understanding 7 – Practice question

### Poochie Statement of cash flows for the year ended 31 March 20X1

|  | $ | $ |
|---|---|---|
| **Cash flows from operating activities** | | |
| Profit before tax | 3,530 | |
| Depreciation | 450 | |
| Investment income | (680) | |
| Finance costs | 400 | |
| | ——— | |
| Operating profit before working capital changes | 3,700 | |
| Decrease in inventories (1,950 – 1,000) | 950 | |
| Increase in trade receivables (W4) | (600) | |
| Decrease in trade payables (1,890 – 250) | (1,640) | |
| | ——— | |
| Cash generated from operations | 2,410 | |
| Interest paid (W2) | (270) | |
| Income tax paid (W1) | (900) | |
| | ——— | |
| Net cash from operating activities | | 1,240 |
| **Cash flows from investing activities** | | |
| Purchase of property, plant and equipment (W3) | (1,900) | |
| Proceeds from sale of property, plant and equipment | 20 | |
| Interest received (W4) | 200 | |
| Dividends received | 380 | |
| | ——— | |
| Net cash from investing activities | | (1,300) |
| **Cash flow from financing activities** | | |
| Proceeds from issue of shares (W5) | 250 | |
| Proceeds from long-term borrowing (2,300 – 1,040) | 1,260 | |
| Dividends paid | (1,200) | |
| | ——— | |
| **Cash flows from operating activities** | | |
| Net cash from financing activities | 310 | |
| | ——— | |
| Net increase in cash and cash equivalents | | 250 |
| Cash and cash equivalents at beginning of period | | 160 |
| | | ——— |
| Cash and cash equivalents at end of period | | 410 |
| | | ——— |

**Workings**

(W1)

### Tax

| Bank (ß) | 900 | Bal b/d | 1,000 |
|---|---|---|---|
| Bal c/d | 400 | Profit or loss | 300 |
| | 1,300 | | 1,300 |
| | | Bal b/d | 400 |

(W2)

### Interest payable

| Bank (ß) | 270 | Bal b/d | 100 |
|---|---|---|---|
| Bal c/d | 230 | Profit or loss | 400 |
| | 500 | | 500 |
| | | Bal b/d | 230 |

(W3)

### Property, plant and equipment

| Bal b/d | 850 | Dep'n | 450 |
|---|---|---|---|
| | | Disposal (80 – 60) | 20 |
| Bank (ß) | 1,900 | Bal c/d | 2,280 |
| | 2,750 | | 2,750 |
| Bal b/d | 2,280 | | |

(W4)

### Interest receivable

| Bal b/d | 0 | Bank (ß) | 200 |
|---|---|---|---|
| Profit or loss | 300 | Bal c/d | 100 |
| | 300 | | 300 |
| Bal b/d | 100 | | |

Receivable B/d = $1,200

Receivables C/d = $1,800 ($1,900 – $100 interest receivable)
Increase in receivables = $600

(W5)

Share issue = ($1,000 + $500) – ($900 + $350) = $250

## Test your understanding 8 – Practice question

**Yam Yam Statement of cash flows for the year ended 30 September 20X1**

| | $000 | $000 |
|---|---:|---:|
| **Cash flows from operating activities** | | |
| Profit before tax | 290 | |
| Depreciation | 87 | |
| Profit on disposal of non-current asset (98 – 75) | (23) | |
| Investment income | (5) | |
| Finance costs | 19 | |
| | —— | |
| Operating profit before working capital changes | 368 | |
| Decrease in inventories (420 – 460) | 40 | |
| Increase in trade receivables (390 – 320) | (70) | |
| Increase in trade payables (550 – 400) | 150 | |
| Increase in sundry accruals (W5) | 30 | |
| | —— | |
| Cash generated from operations | 518 | |
| Interest paid (W2) | (46) | |
| Income tax paid (W1) | (94) | |
| | —— | |
| Net cash from operating activities | | 378 |

| | $000 | $000 |
|---|---:|---:|
| **Cash flows from investing activities** | | |
| Purchase of property, plant and equipment (W3) | (236) | |
| Proceeds from sale of property, plant and equipment | 98 | |
| Interest received (W4) | 10 | |
| | —— | |
| Net cash from investing activities | | (128) |

**Cash flow from financing activities**

| | | |
|---|---|---|
| Proceeds from issue of shares (60 × $1) | 60 | |
| Redemption of 10% loan notes (0 – 40) | (40) | |
| Redemption of 5% loan notes (329 – 349) | (20) | |
| Dividends paid | (53) | |
| | ——— | |
| Net cash from financing activities | | (53) |
| | | ——— |
| Net increase in cash and cash equivalents | | 197 |
| Cash and cash equivalents at beginning of period (5 – 70) | | (65) |
| | | ——— |
| Cash and cash equivalents at end of period | | 132 |
| (50 + 75 + 7 + 0) | | ——— |

**Working**

(W1)

**Tax**

| | | | | |
|---|---|---|---|---|
| Bank (ß) | 94 | Bal b/d | | 90 |
| Bal c/d | 100 | Profit or loss | | 104 |
| | ——— | | | ——— |
| | 194 | | | 194 |
| | ——— | | | ——— |
| | | Bal b/d | | 100 |

(W2)

**Interest payable**

| | | | | |
|---|---|---|---|---|
| Bank (ß) | 46 | Bal b/d | | 33 |
| Bal c/d | 6 | Profit or loss | | 19 |
| | ——— | | | ——— |
| | 52 | | | 52 |
| | ——— | | | ——— |
| | | Bal b/d | | 6 |

(W3)

**Property, plant and equipment**

| | | | | |
|---|---|---|---|---|
| Bal b/d | 510 | Dep'n | | 87 |
| Revaluation | 50 | Disposal | | 75 |
| Bank (ß) | 236 | Bal c/d | | 634 |
| | ——— | | | ——— |
| | 796 | | | 796 |
| | ——— | | | ——— |
| Bal b/d | 634 | | | |

(W4)

**Interest receivable**

| Interest Receivable | | | |
|---|---|---|---|
| Bal b/d | 9 | Bank (ß) | 10 |
| Profit or loss | 5 | Bal c/d | 4 |
| | 14 | | 14 |
| Bal b/d | 4 | | |

(W5)

Accruals b/d (excluding interest) = $33 – 33 = 0

Accruals c/d (excluding interest) = $36 – 6 = 30

Increase in accruals = 30

## Test your understanding 9 – Practice questions

1    C

| Cash flows from operating activities | $ |
|---|---|
| Profit before tax | 5,600 |
| Adjustments for: | |
| Depreciation | 956 |
| (Profit)/loss on disposal | (62) |
| (Increase)/decrease in inventories | (268) |
| (Increase)/decrease in trade and other receivables | (101) |
| (Decrease)/increase in trade and other payables | 322 |
| Cash generated from operations | 6,447 |

2    B

| | $ |
|---|---|
| Repayment of loans (150,000 – 130,000) | (20,000) |
| Issue of shares ((120,000 – 100,000) + (45,000 – 35,000)) | 30,000 |
| Net inflow | 10,000 |

**3    A**

### Non-current assets

|  | $ |  | $ |
|---|---|---|---|
| Bal b/d | 250,000 | Disposals | 45,000 |
| Revaluation | 25,000 | Depreciation | 20,000 |
| Additions (ß) | 60,000 |  |  |
|  |  | Bal c/d | 270,000 |
|  | _____ |  | _____ |
|  | 335,000 |  | 335,000 |
|  | _____ |  | _____ |
| Bal b/d | 270,000 |  |  |

| Purchase of non-current assets | (60,000) |
|---|---|
| Proceeds from sale of non-current assets | 50,000 |
|  | _____ |
| Net outflow | (10,000) |
|  | _____ |

**4    B**

**5    B**

**6    C**

### Interest payable

|  | $000 |  | $000 |
|---|---|---|---|
| Bank (ß) | 800 | Bal b/d (SOFP) | 600 |
| Bal c/d (SOFP) | 500 | Profit or loss | 700 |
|  | _____ |  | _____ |
|  | 1,300 |  | 1,300 |
|  | _____ |  | _____ |
|  |  | Bal b/d | 500 |

**7    A**

### Interest payable

|  | $ |  | $ |
|---|---|---|---|
| Bank (ß) | 38,000 | Bal b/d (SOFP) | 12,000 |
| Bal c/d (SOFP) | 15,000 | Profit or loss | 41,000 |
|  | _____ |  | _____ |
|  | 53,000 |  | 53,000 |
|  | _____ |  | _____ |
|  |  | Bal b/d | 15,000 |

8    B

### Interest payable

|  | $000 |  | $000 |
|---|---|---|---|
| Bank (ß) | 830 | Bal b/d (SOFP) | 1,120 |
| Bal c/d (SOFP) | 1,140 | Profit or loss | 850 |
|  | ——— |  | ——— |
|  | 1,970 |  | 1,970 |
|  | ——— |  | ——— |
|  |  | Bal b/d | 1,140 |

9    D

$37,500 + $2,500 – $16,000 – $2,000 + $3,600 + $700 = $26,300

10    D

# Short-term Finance and Investments

## Chapter learning objectives

| **Lead outcome** | **Component outcome** |
| --- | --- |
| D1. Distinguish between the types and sources of short term finance | Distinguish between: <br><br> a. Types of short term finance <br><br> b. Financial institutions |
| D3. Apply different techniques used to manage working capital | |

## 1    Session content

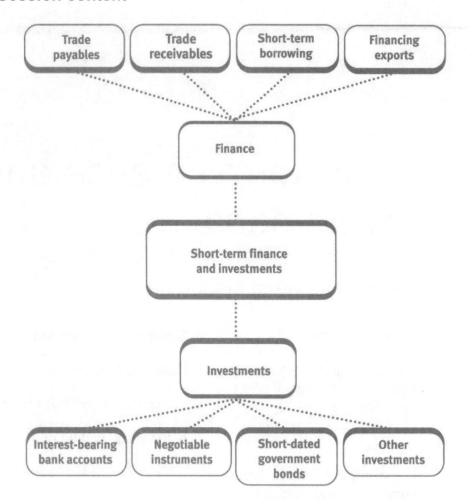

## 2    Short-term finance and financial institutions

Current liabilities should not be allowed to increase to a level where the cash position and liquidity of the company are at risk. This requires careful management of short-term finance.

### Financial institutions

Short term finance can be obtained by an entity from a variety of institutions such as:

*   Commercial and corporate banks

*   Non-banking financial institutions e.g. other companies who provide short terms loans with their cash surpluses

*   Trading partners – trading partners are the entities which a business buy from or sell to. Finance can be obtained from an entity's trading partners through normal business practices (e.g. through trade payables) or via specifically organised financing transactions (e.g. bills of exchange).

## Commercial and Corporate banks

Commercial and corporate banks are financial institutions who provide financial products for customers (whether individuals or businesses) with the aim of making a profit. They accept deposits from customers into savings, current or investment accounts and will also provide loans and overdrafts as required. Typical high street banks are examples of commercial banks.

## Non- financial institutions

Short term financing could be sourced from entities whose main operating activities are not necessarily to provide finance. Other companies, from any industry, with surplus cash may decide to invest its surpluses in shares or debentures of other entities. These investments may mature in the short term.

## Trading partners

Trading partners will often enter into formal **trade agreements**. Trade agreements are legally defined arrangements setting out specific, and often exclusive, terms and conditions of trade between those involved in the agreement.

Trade agreements are particularly common between exporters and importers and are a topical issue within the UK due to the possible implications of Brexit. Will the UK be able to negotiate trade agreements within the EU or will they have to agree trade deals with the US, Canada or further afield?

## 3 Types of short term financing

The main types of short-term finance are:

- trade payables
- factoring or invoice discounting of trade receivables
- bank overdrafts and short-term loans
- financing exports

## Trade payables

Payables may be used as a source of short-term finance by delaying payment to suppliers.

By paying on credit the entity is able to 'fund' its inventory of material through its suppliers. To maximize this benefit, the entity should aim to pay as late as possible without damaging its trading relationship with its suppliers.

If a cash discount is offered, the entity must weigh the saving from the discount against the additional cost of borrowing the funds needed to finance the early payment. The entity must also be aware of whether the funds are available to take up the discount.

| Benefits of paying suppliers late | Potential problems when paying suppliers late |
|---|---|
| • alleviates cash flow difficulties | • loss of any settlement discount |
| • cash can earn a return whilst still in the paying entity's account | • could obtain a poor credit rating |
| | • supplier may stop further supplies |
| | • supplier may increase future selling prices to compensate |
| | • could face legal action from the supplier |

## Trade payables as a source of short-term funds

Suppliers are a source of short-term finance because they provide goods (inventory) on credit. In some cases, suppliers might not be paid until after the goods they have supplied have been re-sold. This occurs, for example, in supermarkets. A supermarket might re-sell the goods provided by a supplier many days before the supplier is eventually paid.

It is a well-established business practice that trade credit should be agreed, which means that suppliers finance the business of their customers to some extent.

The amount of trade credit varies from one industry to another, and can also vary with changes in economic conditions. However, if normal credit terms are 30 days (1 month), and a company purchases, say, $1,200,000 of goods on credit each year, it is normally financed by $100,000 of trade credit on average (1/12 of the total annual purchases).

A huge attraction of trade credit is that it has no interest cost. Unlike banks, trade suppliers do not charge interest on debts unless payment occurs after the due date, in which case suppliers might charge interest.

## Trade receivables

Receivables may be used as a source of short-term finance by:

• Factoring

• Invoice discounting

### Factoring

The debts of the entity are effectively sold to a factoring company (normally owned by a bank). The factor may take on the responsibility to collect the debt for a fee. The factor offers three services:

1   **Debt collection** – The credit control function. This is outsourcing of the credit control department to the factoring entity.

2　**Financing** – Funds may be advanced to the company prior to the debt being collected. This may provide the financing element of the arrangement.

3　**Credit insurance** – The factor may take the responsibility for irrecoverable debt. For this to be the case the factor would dictate to whom the entity was able to offer credit. This is called 'without recourse' factoring.

The factor is often more successful at enforcing credit terms, leading to a lower level of debts outstanding. Factoring is therefore not only a source of short-term finance but also an external means of controlling or reducing the level of receivables.

### Invoice discounting

This is a service also provided by a factoring entity. Selected invoices are used as security against which the entity may borrow funds. This is a temporary source of finance, repayable when the debt is cleared. The key advantage of invoice discounting is that it is a confidential service and the customer need not know about it.

One use for invoice discounting is as a key financing tool for new businesses such as management buyouts (MBOs). The creditworthiness of their customers is probably higher than their own and is utilised to borrow funds.

### Short-term borrowing

Short-term cash requirements can also be funded by borrowing from the bank. There are two main sources of bank lending:

* bank overdraft
* bank loans

### Bank overdrafts

Short term, flexible financing linked to company bank accounts that are in deficit. Bank overdrafts are mainly provided by the clearing banks and are an important source of finance for an entity.

| Advantages | Disadvantages |
|---|---|
| • Flexibility | • Repayable on demand |
| • Only pay for what is used, so generally cheaper | • May require security |
| | • Variable finance costs |

### Bank loans

Bank loans are a contractual agreement for a specific sum, loaned for a fixed period, at an agreed rate of interest. They are less flexible than overdrafts, can be more expensive but provide greater security.

### Financing exports

Entities exporting goods to other countries often have much greater problems with credit and finance than entities selling goods and services to domestic markets.

Several methods are available for dealing with the problems of financing exports and controlling the credit risk. These include:

- documentary credits
- bills of exchange
- export factoring
- forfaiting

### Documentary credits (irrevocable letters of credit)

Trading between other countries, can be complex, particularly when it will take a considerable time to ship the goods from the exporter's country to the importer. The exporter might want payment as soon as possible, but the importer needs to be satisfied that the exporter has complied with the terms of the sale agreement before paying.

The problem of guaranteeing payment can be overcome by using an irrevocable letter of credit, also called an irrevocable documentary credit. A letter of credit is an undertaking given by its issuer that payment will be guaranteed for the exporter, provided that the exporter complies with certain specific requirements within a specified time limit.

A letter of credit is a document, issued by a bank on behalf of a customer, authorising a person to draw money to a specified amount from its branches or correspondents, usually in another country, when the conditions set out in the document have been met.

### A bill of exchange

A bill of exchange is used primarily in international trade and binds one party to pay a fixed sum of money to another party on demand or at a predetermined date. They are similar to post-dated cheques.

For example, a supplier of goods (the drawer) can draw a bill of exchange on a customer (the drawee). The customer, by signing the bill of exchange, acknowledges the debt exists and commits to paying it.

There are two types of bill of exchange:

(i)   a sight draft/bill – which is payable immediately

(ii)  a time draft/bill – which is payable  at a predetermined future date (can be described as term bills)

The holder of a bill of exchange can use an accepted time draft to pay a debt to a separate third party (one not involved in the bill of exchange so transferring the customers debt) , or can discount it to raise cash (sell it on to a third party for a lump sum lower than the outstanding amount).

The drawer and the payee are often the same person.

A significant characteristic of bills of exchange is that:

- the drawee is given a period of credit before having to pay a term bill, but

- the drawer or payee can obtain payment earlier than the bill's maturity date, by means of discounting the bill.

When a bill is discounted, it is sold in the financial markets at a discount to face value. The size of the discount reflects the rate of interest that the buyer of the bill requires from holding the bill to maturity.

Bills of exchange can also be known as 'acceptance credit'.

### Export factoring

Export factoring is similar to ordinary factoring, with the exception that the factoring organisation agrees to factor the client's export trade receivables (overseas trading).

The factor's services include administration of the receivables ledger and collecting payment, and providing factor finance. The export factor buys the sellers overseas receivables for a lump sum which is often lower than the outstanding debt owed.

In view of the problems that can arise with collecting payments from customers in other countries, the expertise of an export factor can be very helpful, particularly for small and medium-sized businesses with little experience in collecting foreign payments.

### Forfaiting

Forfaiting is the same as export factoring except that the seller (exporter) will receive 100% of the receivable as a lump sum from the forfaiter.

The exporter will draw a bill of exchange from an importer (the buyer). This bill of exchange is purchased by a forfaiting company (typically banks) without recourse to the exporter.

The exporter receives the total amount owed, the forfaiter chases the debt and the importer settles direct to the forfaiter.

The exporter has obtained payment for the goods, without any risk of having to return the money if the importer fails to meet its payment obligations.

The key features of forfaiting are that:

- The importer obtains medium-term finance for much of the purchase cost of the goods.

- The exporter receives immediate payment.

- The credit risk is accepted by the forfaiting bank, although this risk is reduced by the guarantee of the promissory notes (another name for a bill of exchange).

## 4    Short-term investments

A business might have surplus cash for a period of time. Surplus cash is usually temporary and available for several weeks or months. Eventually it will be used to pay suppliers or settle other liabilities, invest in new non-current assets or pay a dividend.

Money in an operational bank account earns no income, because banks do not pay interest to businesses for cash in their day-to-day accounts. If a business wishes to maximise its profits, it should consider using the cash to earn some return in the time when it is temporarily surplus to requirements.

Cash surpluses can be invested in a range of short-term interest-earning investments such as:

- Interest-bearing bank accounts
- Negotiable instruments
- Short-dated government bonds
- Other short-term investments

### Investment criteria

When a business has surplus cash to invest temporarily, it has to decide which investments to select from the different choices available. There are several criteria that should be considered when making these choices:

- maturity
- return
- risk
- liquidity
- diversification

### More details

**Future commitments**

Before investing surplus cash, an entity must consider its future plans. Is the cash really surplus to requirements or will it be needed in the future? Proper planning through forecasts (see chapter 18) will be utilised to determine how much cash is surplus and can be invested in the short term investments. The business does not want to miss out on opportunities through cash being tied into short term investments at the point that the cash is needed.

## Maturity

A short-term investment might involve investing an amount of money for a specific period of time, and receiving interest and the payment of a principal amount at a specified future date (the 'maturity' of the investment). If the investment is cashed in or sold before maturity, there could be a risk of some loss of market value or some loss of interest.

The maturity of a short-term investment should ideally be no longer than the duration of the cash surplus. If the cash is needed before the investment reaches maturity, the investment will have to be 'cashed in' early, with some risk of loss of capital value or interest.

## Return

With short-term investments, return is the interest yield on the investment. Some investments offer a higher yield than others. If the investment is 'redeemable' (i.e. where a capital amount will be repaid to the investor) then the capital repayment will also form part of the return.

## Risk

Some investments are more risky than others. Risk refers to the possibility that the investment might fall in value, or that there might be some doubt about the eventual payment of interest or repayment of investment principal. As a general rule, higher-risk investments have to offer a higher return in order to attract investors.

For example, suppose that two banks offer high-interest savings accounts to businesses, for which there is a minimum notice period of two weeks for withdrawal of funds. Bank A might be a major bank with a 'triple-A' credit rating, and Bank B might be a regional bank in a developing country. To attract investors, Bank B would have to offer a higher interest rate on its savings accounts than Bank A, because the perceived risk for investors in an investment in Bank B would be higher.

Investing in equities (shares) is high risk. The value of equities depends on the profitability and future prospects of the company, and share prices also rise or fall more generally in line with broader movements in the stock market. Since share prices can fall by a large amount in a short period of time, equities are generally regarded as an unsuitable form of short-term investment.

Short-term investments should usually be preferred to longer-dated investments, because the risk of a fall in market value is less. Prudent entities should also avoid high-risk investments such as equities, and should look for short-term investments that will keep the value of the investment secure.

## Liquidity

Liquidity refers to the ease with which an investment can be 'cashed in' quickly, without any significant loss of value or interest. All short-term investments are less liquid than cash in an operational bank account, but some are more liquid than others. For example, many savings accounts or deposit accounts are reasonably liquid, and a depositor can often withdraw cash immediately losing only several days' interest.

In contrast, works of art such as paintings might be a profitable long-term investment, but they are very illiquid as short-term investments. Paintings cannot be sold quickly without a significant risk of having to sell at below true market value.

## Diversification

There is a general rule that investors should not 'put all their eggs in one basket'. They should perhaps diversify by investing in a range of different investments. In this way, if some investments perform badly, the investor is not exposed to significant losses, because the other investments in the portfolio should perform better.

However, diversification is less essential for investing short-term cash surpluses than for investing long-term in equities and bonds.

## Interest-bearing accounts

These can fall into two categories:

- bank deposit accounts
- money market deposits

### Deposit accounts

- Some deposit accounts are 'instant access' accounts, which allow the investor to withdraw the money without notice and without loss of interest. The interest rate is usually low on these accounts, and they are used when the investor wants to earn some interest on surplus cash, but places great importance on instant liquidity.

- Some deposit accounts or savings accounts allow the investor to withdraw funds without notice, but the investor will suffer some loss of interest. For example, a deposit account might require a notice of withdrawal of at least seven days, but the investor might be permitted to withdraw the funds without notice with a penalty of seven days' lost interest.

- In some cases, an investor might be unable to withdraw funds from the account without giving a minimum notice period.

## Money market deposits

Money market deposits are amounts of money deposited through a bank in the money markets. These are the financial markets for short-term borrowing and lending. The money markets are used largely by banks and other financial institutions, for depositing and lending funds. Banks can deposit short-term funds with other banks, or borrow short-term from other banks in the inter-bank market.

Interest yields in the inter-bank market are often reasonably attractive, and it is now quite common for entities with large temporary cash surpluses to arrange with their bank to have the money deposited in the money markets (inter-bank market) or at money market interest rates.

Money invested in a money market deposit cannot be withdrawn until the deposit matures. It is therefore important that money should not be invested for a period longer than the investor's expected cash surplus. Money market deposits can be for very short periods of time, as little as one day, or for as long as several months (and even up to one year). However, very short-term deposits should be large amounts of money, so that the interest earned justifies the effort of making the deposits.

### Interest earned

If you are required to calculate the amount of interest earned on a deposit or savings account within a particular period of time, calculation is simply:

$$\left(\text{Amount deposited} \times \text{annualized interest rate} \times \frac{\text{Number of days interest earned}}{\text{Annual day count}}\right.$$

The annual day count is the number of days in the year, for interest calculation purposes. Since a year has either 365 or 366 days (for leap years), you may expect this to always be those numbers. However, in the financial markets, there are special conventions for the number of days in a year. Whereas interest on sterling is calculated on the assumption of a 365-day year, interest on the US dollar in the money markets is calculated on the assumption of 360 days in the year.

### Negotiable instruments

Negotiable instruments are financial instruments that may be obtained as investments. A key feature of negotiable instruments is that title passes when the instrument is handed from one person to another. They are 'bearer instruments', and ownership does not have to be recorded in a register of owners. This means that a negotiable instrument can easily be sold by one person to another or one entity to another.

Examples of negotiable instruments are:

- bank notes
- bearer bonds
- Certificates of Deposit

- Bills of exchange

- Treasury bills

The most important negotiable instruments as short-term investments are Certificates of Deposit and Treasury bills, and bills of exchange (particularly bank bills of high quality banks).

 **More details**

### Certificate of Deposit

A Certificate of Deposit or CD is a negotiable instrument that provides evidence of a short-term deposit with a bank for a fixed term and earning a specified amount of interest. The maturity of the deposit is usually 90 days or less, but can be longer. The amount deposited is at least US$100,000 (or its equivalent in other currencies), but usually larger.

The holder of the CD at maturity has the right to take the deposit with interest. The CD holder presents the CD at maturity to a recognised bank, which will then present the instrument to the bank holding the deposit, and arrange for the withdrawal of the deposit with interest.

Until maturity, the money is 'locked up' with the bank, and cannot be withdrawn.

When an organisation has a temporary cash surplus, it might arrange with its bank to place the money in a fixed term deposit account, and for the bank to issue a CD. The CD will state the identity of the bank, the amount deposited, the maturity date of the deposit and the interest that will accumulate.

- The organisation can hold the CD until maturity and then claim the money.

- Alternatively, if it needs cash before the deposit matures, it can sell the CD. There is an active secondary market in Certificates of Deposit, and a company can arrange for its bank to sell a CD on its behalf.

Another company with a short-term cash surplus could either arrange its own Certificate of Deposit or purchase an existing CD in the secondary market.

### Investment yield on CDs

Since Certificates of Deposit are negotiable instruments, they are more attractive investments than money market deposits from the point of view of liquidity. A CD holder can sell the CD to obtain funds quickly, whereas a money market deposit cannot be withdrawn until maturity. Yields on CDs are therefore slightly lower than interest yields on money market deposits.

## Bills of exchange

Bills of exchange have been described earlier in the chapter, in the context of export finance, although they have a broader use and are not restricted to export finance arrangements.

The significance of bills of exchange as a short-term investment is that they are negotiable instruments. There is an active money market for bills of exchange (which is called the discount market) and investors can buy bills. The market is particularly active in bills of exchange that are payable by top-quality banks: in the UK these are sometimes called 'eligible bank bills'.

The buyer of a bill of exchange obtains the right to receive payment by the issuer of the bill when it matures. A bill of exchange is usually an undertaking to pay a fixed sum of money at maturity, with no interest. An investor in a bill will therefore buy the bill at a discount to face value (and hence the right to receive the payment). Bills of exchange are therefore examples of discount paper.

Although it is possible to buy bills of exchange that have been accepted (and so are payable) by trading entities, investors place more value in bank bills. These are bills of exchange that have been accepted by a bank, and are payable by the bank. If the bank has a high credit status, the risk of investing in its bills is very low.

Yields on bills vary according to the credit risk associated with the bill, and an investor will be prepared to pay more for a top-quality bank bill than for a trade bill with much higher credit risk.

## Treasury bills

Treasury bills are negotiable instruments issued by the government, with a maturity of less than one year. In practice, most Treasury bills have a maturity of three months (91 days). Treasury bills are used by a government to finance short-term cash requirements, and in countries such as the US and the UK, Treasury bills are issued at regular intervals when investors are invited to apply to buy bills in the new issue.

Since Treasury bills are debts of the government, they have a high credit quality, risk is low, and yields for investors are also lower than for many other short-term investments. Treasury bills issued by a government and denominated in the domestic currency should be risk-free. For example, US Treasury bills are risk-free investments, because there is no doubt that the US government will redeem the debt at maturity.

Treasury bills are redeemable at face value. For example, the US government will redeem a 91-day $1,000 Treasury bill for $1,000 91 days after its issue. Since the bills are redeemable at par, investors pay less than face value to buy them. Like bills of exchange, Treasury bills are examples of discount paper.

Although yields on Treasury bills are relatively low, they can be attractive short-term investments because of their risk-free nature and their liquidity. There is a large and active secondary market in Treasury bills, such as US Treasury bills in the US and UK government Treasury bills in the UK.

### Short-dated government bonds

Entities can invest temporary surplus cash in government bonds. If they do:

- they will receive interest on the due payment dates

- they can liquidate their investment at any time by selling the bonds in the secondary market

- if the bonds are short-dated when purchased, they can hold the bonds to maturity and have them redeemed at par.

However, there is some price risk with bonds, particularly longer-dated bonds. If interest rates change in the market, the market value of bonds will rise or fall. Bond prices rise when interest rates fall, but prices fall when interest rates go up. The movement in price is greater for longer-dated bonds.

### Other short-term investments

This chapter has described the short-term investments that are most commonly purchased or used by entities. There are other short-term investments such as:

- corporate bonds, and

- commercial paper (CP).

These are more likely to be purchased by investment institutions rather than by entities with a short-term cash surplus.

### More details

#### Corporate bonds

Corporate bonds are bonds issued by an entity. They are long-term investments, and so unsuitable for investing a short-term cash surplus, and they can also be a high risk investment. Bond prices fluctuate with movements in the general level of interest rates, and corporate bond values are also affected by the perceived credit risk of the entity issuing the bonds.

#### Commercial paper (CP)

Commercial paper consists of short-dated negotiable debt instruments issued by an entity, and sold by a bank managing the entity's commercial paper programme. In practice, although CP is negotiable, it is generally purchased by large investment institutions and held to maturity. It is not normally regarded as a suitable type of short-term investment of cash surpluses by a trading entity.

## Test your understanding 1

1   On 1 April 20X4, an entity placed $5 million on deposit at an interest rate of 6.25%. The deposit has a maturity date of 30 June 20X4 (91 days later).

**Calculate the amount of cash that the entity will receive on maturity of the deposit.**

(There are 360 days in a year for interest purposes.)

2   **Which of the following would not normally be used to deal with the credit risk associated with exporting:**

A   Documentary credits

B   Forfaiting

C   Bills of exchange

D   Treasury bills

3   **Which of the following factors would not normally be considered when choosing between different sources of investment:**

A   Risk

B   Liquidity

C   Currency

D   Maturity

## 5 Summary

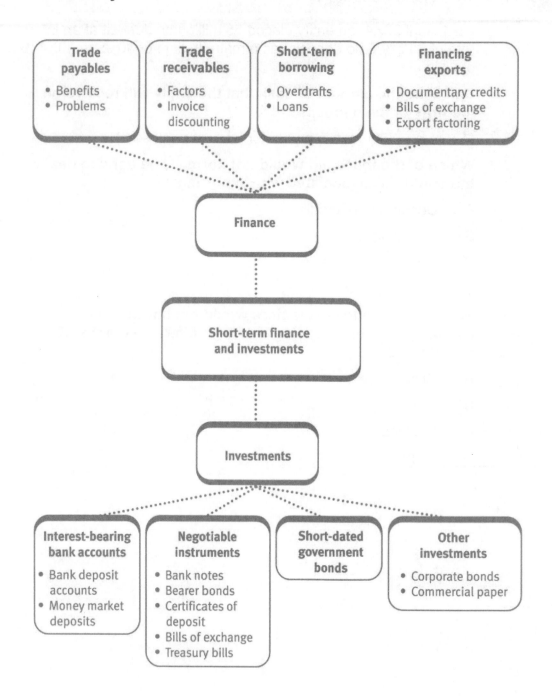

## Test your understanding answers

| Test your understanding 1 |
| --- |

1    The interest on the deposit will be $5 million × 6.25% × 91/360 = $78,993.

The interest will be added to the face value of the deposit on maturity.

At maturity the deposit will be $5 million + $78,993 = $5,078,993.

2    The correct answer is D.

Treasury bills are used as a source of investment rather than a way for reducing export risks.

3    The correct answer is C.

Currency may influence areas such as risk and liquidity of the investment, but the currency itself would largely be irrelevant as long as the investment was within acceptable risk limits and sufficiently liquid.

# Working Capital Management

## Chapter learning objectives

| Lead outcome | Component outcome |
|---|---|
| D2. Explain and calculate operating and cash cycles | Explain and calculate:<br><br>a. Operating cycle<br><br>b. Cash flow cycle |
| D3. Apply different techniques used to manage working capital | a. Apply policies relating to elements of operating and cash cycle<br><br>c. Explain risks relating to working capital |

# 1 Session Content

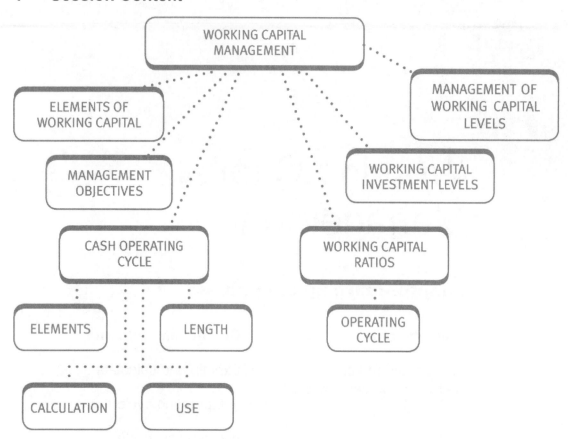

# 2 The elements of working capital

 Working capital is the capital available for conducting the day-to-day operations of an organisation. This is normally the excess of current assets over current liabilities.

Working capital management is the management of all aspects of both current assets and current liabilities, to minimise the risk of insolvency while maximising the return on assets.

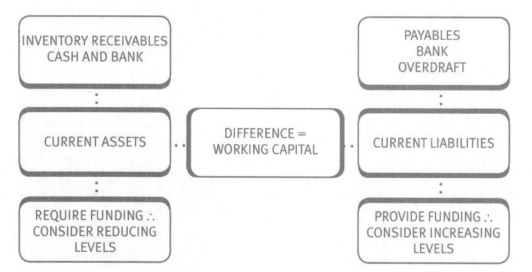

Investing in working capital has a cost, which can be expressed either as:

- the cost of funding it, or

- the opportunity cost of lost investment opportunities because cash is tied up and unavailable for other uses.

## 3 The objectives of working capital management

The main objective of working capital management is to get the balance of current assets and current liabilities right.

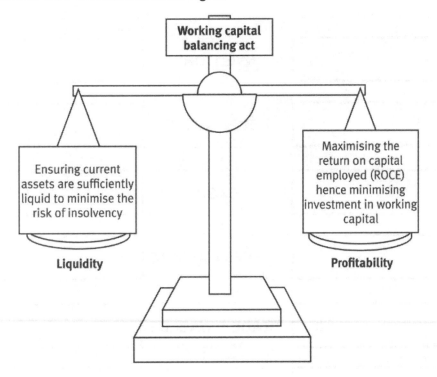

This can also be seen as the trade-off between cash flow versus profits.

Current assets are a major item on the statement of financial position and are especially significant to smaller firms. Mismanagement of working capital is therefore a common cause of business failure.

Consequences of poor working capital management include:

- inability to meet bills as they fall due

- demands on cash during periods of growth being too great (overtrading)

- over-stocking or stock-outs

The trade-off between liquidity and profitability and its role in determining a business' overall investment in working capital is fundamental to your understanding of working capital management for the examination.

## Test your understanding 1 – Liquidity v profitability

Fill in the blanks in the table to identify the advantages of having more or less working capital.

| Advantages of keeping it high | | Advantages of keeping it low |
|---|---|---|
| | INVENTORY | |
| | + | |
| | RECEIVABLES | |
| | + | |
| | CASH | |
| | = | |
| | CURRENT ASSETS | |
| | – | |
| | TRADE PAYABLES | |
| | = | |
| | WORKING CAPITAL | |

## Profitability v liquidity

The decision regarding the level of overall investment in working capital is a cost/benefit trade-off – liquidity versus profitability, or cash flow versus profits.

### Cash flow versus profit

Cash flow is as important as profit. Unprofitable entities can survive if they have cash. Profitable entities can fail if they run out of cash to pay their liabilities (wages, amounts due to suppliers, overdraft interest, etc.).

Some examples of transactions that have this 'trade-off' effect between cash flows and profits are as follows:

(a) Purchase of non-current assets for cash. The cash is often paid in full to the supplier when the asset is delivered, however, profits will be reduced over the life of the asset as a result of the depreciation charged.

(b) Sale of goods on credit. Profits will be credited in full once the sale has been confirmed, however the cash may not be received for some considerable period afterwards.

(c) With some payments such as tax, there may be a significant timing difference between the impact on reported profit and the cash flow.

Clearly, cash balances and cash flows need to be monitored just as closely as trading profits.

### Profitability versus liquidity

Liquidity in the context of working capital management means having enough cash (or ready access to cash) to meet all payment obligations when these fall due. The main sources of liquidity are usually:

- cash in the bank

- short-term investments that can be cashed in easily and quickly

- cash inflows from normal trading operations (cash sales and payments by receivables for credit sales)

- an overdraft facility or other ready source of extra borrowing.

The basis of the trade-off is where an entity is able to improve its profitability but at the expense of tying up cash.

For example,

- receiving a bulk purchase discount (improved profitability) for buying more inventory than is currently required (reduced liquidity), or

- offering credit to customers (attracts more customers so improves profitability but reduces liquidity).

Sometimes, the opposite situation can be seen where an entity can improve its liquidity position but at the expense of profitability. For example, offering an early settlement discount to customers.

## 4    The working capital cycle

### The elements of the working capital cycle

 The working capital cycle is the length of time between the entity's outlay on raw materials, wages and other expenditures and the inflow of cash from the sale of goods.

The working capital cycle is easily summarised as:

Inventory days + trade receivable days – trade payable days = Working capital cycle.

This is also commonly known as the cash operating cycle.

The faster a firm can 'push' items around the cycle the lower its investment in working capital will be.

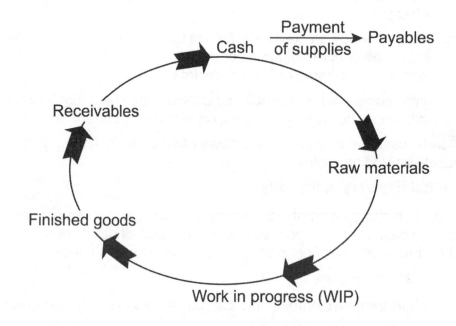

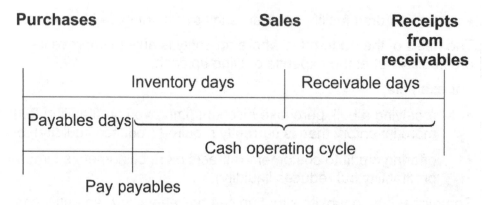

## The working capital cycle

The working capital cycle reflects a firm's investment in working capital as it moves through the production process towards sales. The investment in working capital gradually increases, first being only in raw materials, but then in labour and overheads as production progresses. This investment must be maintained throughout the production process, the holding period for finished goods and up to the final collection of cash from trade receivables.

(**Note:** The net investment can be reduced by taking trade credit from suppliers.)

Factors affecting the length of the working capital cycle

The length of the cycle depends on:

- liquidity versus profitability decisions

- management efficiency

- industry norms, e.g. retail versus construction.

The optimum level of working capital is the amount that results in no idle cash or unused inventory, but does not put a strain on liquid resources.

## The length of the cycle

The length of the cycle depends on how the balancing act between liquidity and profitability is resolved, the efficiency of management and the nature of the industry.

Trying to shorten the cash cycle may have detrimental effects elsewhere, with the organisation lacking the cash to meet its commitments and losing sales, since customers will generally prefer to buy from suppliers who are prepared to extend trade credit, and who have items available when required.

Additionally, any assessment of the acceptability or otherwise of the length of the cycle must take into account the nature of the business involved.

A supermarket chain will tend to have a very low or negative cycle as they have very few, if any, credit customers, they have a high inventory turnover and they can negotiate quite long credit periods with their suppliers.

A construction entity will have a long cycle as their projects tend to be long-term, often extending over more than a year, and whilst progress payments may be made by the customer (if there is one), the bulk of the cash will be received towards the end of the project.

The amount of cash required to fund the working capital cycle will increase as either:

- the cycle gets longer
- the level of activity/sales increases.

This can be summed up as follows:

| Activity/sales | Length of cycle | Funds needed increase proportionate to: |
|---|---|---|
| Stays constant = | Increases ↑ | Days in cycle |
| Increase ↑ | Stays constant = | Sales |

Where level of activity (sales) is constant and the number of days of the working capital cycle increase, the amount of funds required for working capital will increase in approximate proportion to the number of days.

Where the cycle remains constant but activity (sales) increase, the funds required for working capital will increase in approximate proportion to sales.

It may be a key target for management to reduce the operating cycle to improve the efficiency of the business.

## 5 The investment in working capital

All entities require working capital, but there is no standard fixed amount required.

The amount required will depend on many factors, such as:

- **the industry within which the firm operates** – in some industries, customers expect long payment periods (impacting receivables) whereas in other industries cash payments are the norm (low receivables).

  For example, a retail company will usually have very low receivables (because most sales are for cash) but high levels of inventories.

  In contrast, a manufacturing company will tend to have high levels of receivables (long credit terms offered to attract customers) and high levels of work in progress (inventories).

- **the type of products sold** – a business selling perishable products will have to keep a lower level of inventory

- **whether products are manufactured or bought in** – a manufacturing company will have high levels of raw material and work in progress inventory as well as finished goods

- **the level of sales** – if sales are high, it is likely that receivables will be high too

- **Policies towards working capital management** – different entities can have different approaches or strategies towards working capital management

It is essential that an appropriate amount of working capital is budgeted to meet anticipated future needs.

In conditions of uncertainty, entities must hold some minimal level of cash and inventories based on expected revenue, plus an additional safety buffer.

### Working capital investment levels

The level of working capital investment required is affected by the following factors

1    The nature of the business, e.g. manufacturing entities need more inventory than service entities.

2    Uncertainty in supplier deliveries. Uncertainty would mean that extra inventory needs to be carried in order to cover fluctuations.

3    The overall level of activity of the business. As output increases, receivables, inventory, etc. all tend to increase.

4    The entity's credit policy. The tighter the entity's policy, the lower the level of receivables.

5    The length of the working capital cycle. The longer it takes to convert material into finished goods into cash, the greater the investment in working capital

6    The credit policy of suppliers. The less credit the entity is allowed to take, the lower the level of payables and the higher the net investment in working capital.

### Test your understanding 2 – Working capital investment levels

XY has the following expectations for the forthcoming period.

|  | $m |
| --- | --- |
| Sales revenue | 10 |
| Cost of sales | (6) |
| Non-production costs | (2) |
| Net profit | 2 |

The following working capital ratios are expected to apply.

| | |
| --- | --- |
| Finished goods inventory days | 30 days |
| Receivables days | 60 days |
| Payables days | 40 days |

**Required:**

Calculate the working capital requirement.

## 6 Working capital management policies

 **Aggressive, moderate and conservative working capital policies**

The choice of working capital management policy is a matter for managerial judgement, and depends to an extent on the cost vs risk trade-off.

Three possible policies exist to manage working capital:

(1) **Aggressive policy** – This approach attempts to reduce costs by holding the lowest levels of cash, inventory and receivables as possible. This produces a short operating cycle. This policy carries the greatest risk of illiquidity, as well as the greatest returns. Financing of the variable and a portion of the fixed working capital is typically sourced through short term financing.

(2) **Conservative policy** – This approach attempts to reduce risks by holding high levels of cash, inventory and receivables. This produces a long operating cycle. Risks such as stock-outs or liquidity problems are low, but, resultantly, costs are increased.

(3) **Moderate policy** – This adopts a middle ground between aggressive and conservative approaches.

 **More detail on aggressive, moderate and conservative policies**

A company could pursue a more aggressive approach towards the management of working capital or a more conservative (relaxed) approach.

**Benefits of a more aggressive approach:**

1 Lower levels of current assets therefore lower financing costs.

2 The lower financing costs should result in better profitability.

3 Quicker cash turnover may allow more reinvestment and hence allow the business to expand more quickly.

**Benefits of a more conservative approach:**

1 Lower liquidity risk i.e. less risk of the company running out of cash or going into liquidation.

2 Greater ability to meet a sudden surge in sales demand.

3 More relaxed credit policy for receivables may improve sales.

**Note:**

Generally the more conservative the approach, the lower the risk, but the higher the cost in terms of money tied up in working capital.

## The traditional approach to working capital funding

Traditionally current assets were seen as fluctuating, originally with a seasonal pattern. Current assets would then be financed out of short-term credit, which could be paid off when not required, whilst non-current assets would be financed by long-term funds (debt or equity).

This analysis is rather simplistic. In most businesses, a proportion of the current assets are actually fixed over time, being thus expressed as 'permanent'.

For example, certain base levels of inventory are always carried, or a certain level of trade credit is always extended.

Given the permanent nature of a large proportion of current assets, it is generally felt prudent to fund a proportion of net current assets with long-term finance.

Short-term financing is generally cheaper than long-term finance, since short-term interest rates are generally lower than long-term rates. However, the price paid for reduced cost is increased risk for the borrower, because of:

- **Renewal problems** – short-term finance may need to be continually renegotiated as various facilities expire and renewal may not always be guaranteed.

- **Stability of interest rates** – if the company is constantly having to renew its funding arrangements it will be at the mercy of fluctuations in short-term interest rates.

An aggressive policy of working capital management would expect to finance the variable and a portion of the fixed working capital through short term financing.

A conservative approach would use long-term funding to finance all of the permanent assets (both non-current and current) as well as part of the fluctuating current assets. Short-term financing is used only for part of the fluctuating current assets.

Moderate policies matches the short-term finance to the fluctuating current assets, and the long-term finance to the permanent part of current assets plus non-current assets.

## 7    Overtrading

### Overtrading

Healthy trading growth typically leads to:

- increased profitability and

- the need to increase investment in non-current assets and working capital.

If the business does not have access to sufficient capital to fund the increase, it is said to be "overtrading". This can cause serious trouble for the business if it is unable to pay its business payables.

## Test your understanding 3 – Overtrading

**Over-trading is best described by which of the following statements?**

A   It occurs when an entity tries to grow too rapidly, backed by too small a capital base

B   It occurs when an entity tries to operate its equipment too far above its designed capacity

C   It occurs when sales grow rapidly, fuelled by extending longer credit periods

D   It occurs when an entity uses short-term finance in preference to long-term finance

## Typical indicators of overtrading

- A rapid increase in turnover

- A rapid increase in the volume of current assets

- Most of the increase in assets being financed by credit

- A dramatic drop in the liquidity ratios (see next section)

## Solutions to overtrading

Overtrading can be a very serious risk, especially if there is a possibility that the bank will withdraw its overdraft facility. Potential solutions to the problem include:

- raising more long-term capital, in the form of new shares or loans

- slowing down growth to reduce the increases in working capital requirements until sufficient cash has been built up to finance it

- improving working capital management, so that there is a reduction in the inventory holding period or a reduction in the average time for customers to pay

## 8   Working capital ratios

The periods used to determine the working capital cycle are calculated by using a series of working capital ratios.

The ratios for the individual components (inventory, receivables and payables) are normally expressed as the number of days/weeks/months of the relevant statement of profit or loss figure they represent.

## Calculation of the working capital cycle

For a manufacturing business, the working capital cycle is calculated as:

| | |
|---|---:|
| Raw materials holding period | X |
| Less: payables' payment period | (x) |
| WIP holding period | X |
| Finished goods holding period | X |
| Receivables' collection period | X |
| | ___ |
| | X |
| | ___ |

For a wholesale or retail business, there will be no raw materials or WIP holding periods, and the cycle simplifies to:

| | |
|---|---:|
| Inventory holding period | X |
| Less: payables' payment period | (x) |
| Receivables' collection period | X |
| | ___ |
| | X |
| | ___ |

The cycle may be measured in days, weeks or months and it is advisable, when answering a question, to use the measure used in the question (although typically it will be days).

**Test your understanding 4 – Working capital cycle**

An entity has provided the following information.

| | |
|---|---|
| Receivables collection period | 56 days |
| Raw material inventory holding period | 21 days |
| Production period (WIP) | 14 days |
| Suppliers' payment period | 42 days |
| Finished goods holding period | 28 days |

**Calculate the length of the working capital cycle**

### Raw material inventory holding period

This is the length of time raw materials are held between purchase and being used in production.

Calculated as:

$$= \frac{\text{Average raw material inventory held}}{\text{Material usage}} \times 365$$

$$= \frac{(\text{Opening inventory} + \text{closing inventory}) \div 2}{\text{Material usage}} \times 365$$

**NB.** Where usage cannot be calculated, purchases give a good approximation.

### Illustration 1 – Working capital ratios

XYZ has the following figures from its most recent accounts.

|  | $m |
|---|---|
| Average trade receivables | 4 |
| Average trade payables | 2 |
| Average raw material inventory | 1 |
| Average WIP inventory | 1.3 |
| Average finished goods inventory | 2 |
| Sales (80% on credit) | 30 |
| Materials usage | 20 |
| Materials purchases (all on credit) | 18 |
| Production cost | 23 |
| Cost of sales | 25 |

**Required:**

Calculate the raw materials holding period. Round your answer to the nearest day.

### Solution

$$\frac{\$1m}{\$20m} \times 365 = 18 \text{ days}$$

**WIP holding period**

This is the length of time goods spend in production.

Calculated as:

$$= \frac{\text{Average WIP}}{\text{Production cost}} \times 365$$

**NB.** Where production cost cannot be calculated, cost of goods sold gives a good approximation.

 **Illustration 2 – WIP holding period**

Using the information from illustration 1 calculate the WIP holding period. Round your answer to the nearest day.

 **Solution**

$$\frac{\$1.3m}{\$23m} \times 365 = 21 \text{ days}$$

 **Finished goods inventory holding period**

This is the length of time finished goods are held between purchase/completion and sale.

Calculated as:

$$= \frac{\text{Average finished goods inventory held}}{\text{Cost of goods sold}} \times 365$$

For all inventory period ratios, a low ratio is usually seen as a sign of good working capital management. It is very expensive to hold inventory and thus minimum inventory holding usually points to good practice.

 **Illustration 3 – Finished goods inventory holding period**

Using the information from illustration 1, calculate the finished goods inventory holding period. Round your answer to the nearest day.

 **Solution**

$$\frac{\$2m}{\$25m} \times 365 = 29 \text{ days}$$

## Inventory turnover

**For each ratio, the corresponding turnover ratio can be calculated as**

Inventory turnover (no of times) = $\dfrac{\text{Cost of goods sold}}{\text{Average inventory held}}$

Generally this is less useful.

Using finished goods information from illustration 1:

Inventory turnover = $\dfrac{\$25m}{\$2m}$ = 12.5 times

Thus finished goods inventory turns round/is turned into sales 12.5 times in the year.

## Interpreting inventory periods

If inventory days are relatively high, This may indicate a deliberately conservative policy of holding large amount of inventory (as management are worried about running out of inventory, or are stock-piling for a new product launch). However, this results in additional finance tied up in inventory which could be used more effectively elsewhere.

If cash is paid out when the inventories are purchased, but the cash does not come back in until the inventory is sold to a customer, then this temporary negative cash flow will have to be financed by the company. Moreover, if the inventory is sold on credit terms and the customer does not pay for, say 1 month, then the delay in getting the cash back in is even longer.

If the inventory is too low, this may show an overzealous application of the 'just in time' concept and consequential risks of running out of inventory. It may also indicate a company meeting a cash flow crisis by running down inventory levels. It may be considered that the management are adopting an overly aggressive working capital financing policy.

Inventory days needs to be compared to other companies and compared to previous years in the same company. Increasing inventory days may be investigated further by separately analysing raw materials (RM), work in progress (WIP) and finished goods (FG) to cost of goods sold. An increase in RM days may indicate mismanagement in the buying department; an increase in WIP may indicate production delays. If FG days increase, this may be a sign of decline in demand for the product and an increase in obsolete items.

Inventory levels are very much a balancing act between the risk of stock-outs and the cost associated with high levels of inventory.

**Trade receivables days**

This is the length of time credit is extended to customers.

Calculated as:

$$\frac{\text{Average receivables}}{\text{Credit sales}} \times 365$$

Generally shorter credit periods are seen as financially prudent but the length will also depend upon the nature of the business.

 **Illustration 4 – Receivable days**

Using the information from illustration 1 calculate the trade receivable days. Round your answer to the nearest day.

 **Solution**

$$\frac{\$4m}{\$30m \times 80\%} \times 365 = 61 \text{ days}$$

 **Interpreting trade receivables collection periods**

Businesses which sell goods on credit terms specify a credit period. Failure to send out invoices on time or to follow up late payers will have an adverse effect on the cash flow of the business. The receivables collection period measures the average period of credit allowed to customers.

In general, the shorter the collection period the better because receivables are effectively 'borrowing' from the entity. Remember, however, that the level of receivables reflects not only the ability of the credit controllers but also the sales and marketing strategy adopted, and the nature of the business. Any change in the level of receivables must therefore be assessed in the light of the level of sales.

 **Trade payables days**

This is the average period of credit extended by suppliers.

Calculated as:

$$= \frac{\text{Average payables}}{\text{Credit purchases}} \times 365$$

## Illustration 5 – Payable days

Using the information from illustration 1 calculate the trade payable days. Round your answer to the nearest day.

## Solution

$$\frac{\$2m}{\$18m} \times 365 = 41 \text{ days}$$

## Complications in calculations

There are differences in the way that the ratio might be calculated:

- Total purchases for the year should be used where possible. If the figure for purchases is not available, the cost of sales in the year should be used instead.

- The figure for purchases excludes any sales tax recoverable, whereas the carrying amount for payables includes sales tax. To make a like-for-like comparison, it might be appropriate to add recoverable sales tax back into purchases, or remove the sales tax element from trade payables. However, this is not usually done.

- Where available, the average trade payables during the year should be used, normally calculated as the average of the trade payables at the beginning and the end of the year. However, if you wish to compare the average payment period in the most recent year and the previous year, and you only have figures for the two years, it will be necessary to use the end-of-year trade payables rather than an average value for the year. The same issue will arise when making receivables calculations.

## Expandable Text

The result of this ratio can also be compared with the receivables days. An entity does not normally want to offer its customers more time to pay than it gets from its own suppliers, otherwise this could affect cash flow.

Generally, the longer the payables payment period, the better, as the entity holds on to its cash for longer, but care must be taken not to upset suppliers by delaying payment, which could result in the loss of discounts and reliability.

Generally, increasing payables days suggests advantage is being taken of available credit but there are risks:

- losing supplier goodwill

- losing prompt payment discounts

- suppliers increasing the price to compensate.

It is important to recognise when using these ratios that it is the trend of ratios that is important, not the individual values. Payment periods are longer in some types of entity than in others.

## The working capital cycle

The ratios can then be brought together to produce the working capital cycle.

|  | Days |
|---|---|
| Raw material inventory days | 18 |
| Trade payables days | (41) |
| WIP period | 21 |
| Finished goods inventory days | 29 |
| Receivables days | 61 |
| | ——— |
| Length of working capital cycle | 88 |
| | ——— |

The working capital cycle indicates that it takes the entity 88 days between paying for material purchases and receiving cash back from customers.

As always this must then be compared with prior periods or industry average for meaningful analysis.

**Case Study Question**

**2015 CIMA Professional Qualification Syllabus, Operational Level Case Study Exam, February 2017 – Question**

On 15 March 2017 you receive the following email from Pene Lopez, Finance Director:

**From:**  Pene Lopez

**To:**  Finance Officer

**Subject:**  Performance of the foundation business

We will be having a directors' meeting next week to discuss the performance of the business over the last financial year. I have also been tasked with writing a report to cover all aspects of performance. Cormac has already prepared the numerical information and narrative for the hive business. He has also prepared the numerical information for the foundation business, for which I would like you to draft some of the narrative.

The first section I'd like you to draft relates to production overhead variances for foundation production. I've attached to this email Cormac's schedule of the variances and what I need is an explanation of what these variances mean in terms of the performance of the foundation production cost centre. I have had a quick look and I know Thomas is going to be surprised that the total variance is adverse. We produced 54,000 more foundations than the 346,000 we had budgeted to produce for the year to 28 February 2017 and therefore I know how would have expected this increased production to have led to a favourable variance overall. Also the expenditure variance looks quite alarming, although I do know that our energy costs were higher than budgeted. In your analysis of the variances in Cormac's schedule please also address these points.

The second section I'd like you to draft relates to the working capital position for the foundation business. I've attached Cormac's schedule of working capital days. The report needs to explain what is likely to have caused the movements compared to the budget and any risk implications of these movements to our business.

Many thanks

*Pene Lopez*

Finance Director

*Mavis Venderby*

Working capital ratios for the foundation business attachment:

| Ratio | Actual balances at year- end 28 February 2017 | Budgeted balances at the year-end 28 February 2017 |
|---|---|---|
| Raw materials inventory days | 52 | 20 |
| Finished goods inventory days | 10 | 22 |
| Receivables days (for credit sales) | 45 | 25 |
| Payables days | 49 | 30 |

**(note – for the purpose of this illustration the variances have not been discussed as they are not relevant to the F1 exam)**

**Case Study Suggested Answer**

**2015 CIMA Professional Qualification Syllabus, Operational Level Case Study Exam, February 2017 – Suggested Answer**

**Note this is an extract from the suggested answer and focuses solely on the areas of the case study relevant to the F1 exam, the variances are not discussed below.**

## ANALYSIS OF WORKING CAPITAL RATIOS

### Raw materials inventory days

There has been a significant increase in raw materials inventory days, meaning that at 28 February 2017 the balance is significantly higher than we had budgeted. It could be that a significant order of wax and / or wire was received just before the year end, especially given the low level of finished goods inventory. Possibly a discount for bulk purchase was available and wax and wire are being stock-piled ahead of production expansion.

**There is no significant risk arising from this increase in raw material inventory, especially if it will be used in an expanded production facility shortly. Wax and wire have a long shelf life and are unlikely to deteriorate unless they are not stored correctly.**

### Finished goods inventory days

Finished goods inventory is lower than budgeted. This could be because production has not been able to keep up with the volume of sales, given the expanding market and selling to customers in other countries. We know that we produced 54,000 more foundation during the year than we expected and given the reduction in inventory days for finished goods it's probable that the increase in sales was even more than this.

Given that currently we only sell one foundation product, having a low level of finished goods inventory is not necessarily a risky issue as long as there are no production problems that limit what we could produce.

### Receivable days

Receivable days have increased from a budgeted 25 days to 45 days. This is likely the result of selling to customers located in other countries, which we had not budgeted for. Possibly we have offered them extended credit terms to match the credit terms available in their home markets. Alternatively, these customers are not as quick to pay as our Tucland customers, who we expected to pay on average just a little under the standard credit terms of 30 days.

The increase is slightly worrying as it could be an indication that the risk of us not receiving payment from our customers has increased. This could potentially lead to financial loss and we need to review the aged receivables report in detail to identify the specific customers that have caused this increase.

**Payable days**

Payable days have increased from a budget of 30 to 49. This could be linked to the increase in raw material inventory at the year end. If a significant order was received at the end of February, then we will not have paid for it yet. However, we need to be careful that we do not over-stretch our credit terms with our wax and wire suppliers, as this could damage our relationships with them.

**Test your understanding 5 – Raw material holding period**

| Statement of profit or loss account extract | $ | $ |
|---|---|---|
| Revenue | | 350,000 |
| Cost of sales | | 264,400 |
| Gross profit | | 85,600 |

| Statement of financial position extract | $ | $ |
|---|---|---|
| Current assets | | |
| Inventory | | |
| Raw materials | 25,000 | |
| Work in progress | 33,500 | |
| Finished goods | 46,500 | 105,000 |
| Trade receivables | | 35,200 |
| | | 140,200 |
| | | |
| Current liabilities | | |
| Trade payables | | 55,200 |

**Required:**

**Calculate the raw materials holding period.** Round your answer to the nearest day.

**Test your understanding 6 – WIP holding period**

**Using the information from TYU 5 calculate the WIP holding period.** Round your answer to the nearest day.

**Test your understanding 7 – Finished goods inventory holding**

**Using the information from TYU 5 calculate the finished goods inventory holding period.** Round your answer to the nearest day.

 **Test your understanding 8 – Receivable days**

**Using the information from TYU 5 calculate the receivable days.** Round your answer to the nearest day.

 **Test your understanding 9 – Payable days**

**Using the information from TYU 5 calculate the payable days.** Round your answer to the nearest day.

 **Test your understanding 10 – Working capital cycle**

**Using the information from TYU's 5 to 8 calculate the working capital cycle.**

### Additional points for calculating ratios

The ratios may be needed to provide analysis of an entity's performance or simply to calculate the length of the working capital cycle.

 There are a few simple points to remember which will be of great use in the examination.

- Where the period is required in days, the multiple in the ratios is 365, for months the multiple is 12, or 52 for weeks.

- If you are required to compare ratios between two statements of financial position, it is acceptable to base each holding period on closing figures on the statement of financial position each year, rather than an average, in order to see whether the ratio has increased or decreased.

- For each ratio calculated above, the corresponding turnover ratio can be calculated by inverting the ratio given and removing the multiple.

- When using the ratios to appraise performance, it is essential to compare the figure with others in the industry or identify the trend over a number of periods.

- Ratios have their limitations and care must be taken because:
    - the statement of financial position values at a particular time may not be typical
    - balances used for a seasonal business may not represent average levels, e.g. a fireworks manufacturer
    - ratios can be subject to window dressing/manipulation – ratios concern the past (historic) not the future
    - figures may be distorted by inflation and/or rapid growth.

### Shortening the working capital cycle

A number of steps can be taken to shorten the working capital cycle:

- Reduce raw materials inventory holding. This may be done by reviewing slow-moving lines, reorder levels and reorder quantities. Inventory control models may be considered, if not already in use. More efficient links with suppliers could also help. Reducing inventory may involve loss of discounts for bulk purchases, loss of cost savings from price rises, or could lead to production delays due to inventory shortages.

- Obtain more finance from suppliers by delaying payments, preferably through negotiation. This could result in a deterioration in commercial relationships or even loss of reliable sources of supply. Discounts may be lost by this policy.

- Reduce work in progress by improving production techniques and efficiency (with the human and practical problems of achieving such change).

- Reduce finished goods inventory perhaps by reorganising the production schedule and distribution methods. This may affect the efficiency with which customer demand can be satisfied and result ultimately in a reduction of sales.

- Reduce credit given to customers by invoicing and following up outstanding amounts more quickly, or possibly offering discount incentives. The main disadvantages would be the potential loss of customers as a result of chasing too hard and a loss of revenue as a result of discounts.

- Debt factoring, generating immediate cash flow by the sale of receivables to a third party on immediate cash terms. The main disadvantages would be that this may be costly to the entity to pay a factor.

The working capital cycle is the time span between incurring production costs and receiving cash returns. It says nothing in itself about the amount of working capital that will be needed over this period.

## Test your understanding 11 – Practice questions

1   **Calculate the length of the working capital cycle from the following information:**

| | |
|---|---|
| Raw materials holding period | 10 days |
| Receivables collection period | 60 days |
| Average time to pay suppliers | 45 days |
| Finished goods inventory holding period | 20 days |
| Production period (WIP) | 5 days |

2   Marlboro estimates the following figures for the coming year.

| | |
|---|---|
| Sales – all on credit | $3,600,000 |
| Average receivables | $306,000 |
| Gross profit margin * | 25% on sales |
| Finished goods | $200,000 |
| Work in progress | $350,000 |
| Raw materials (balance held) | $150,000 |
| Trade payables | $130,000 |

Inventory levels are constant.

* Raw materials are 80% of cost of sales – all on credit.

**Required:**

**Calculate the raw materials holding period.** Round your answer to the nearest day.

3   **Using the information from question 3, calculate the WIP holding period.** Round your answer to the nearest day.

4   **Using the information from question 3, calculate the finished goods inventory holding period.** Round your answer to the nearest day.

5   **Using the information from question 3, calculate the receivable days.** Round your answer to the nearest day.

6   **Using the information from question 3, calculate the payable days.** Round your answer to the nearest day.

7   **Using the information from questions 3 to 7, calculate the working capital cycle.**

8   **Identify which of the following transactions will result in an increase in working capital:**

A   Writing off a debt as uncollectable

B   Paying the invoice of a trade supplier

C   Selling goods on credit at a profit

D   Buying inventory for cash

## 9 Summary Diagram

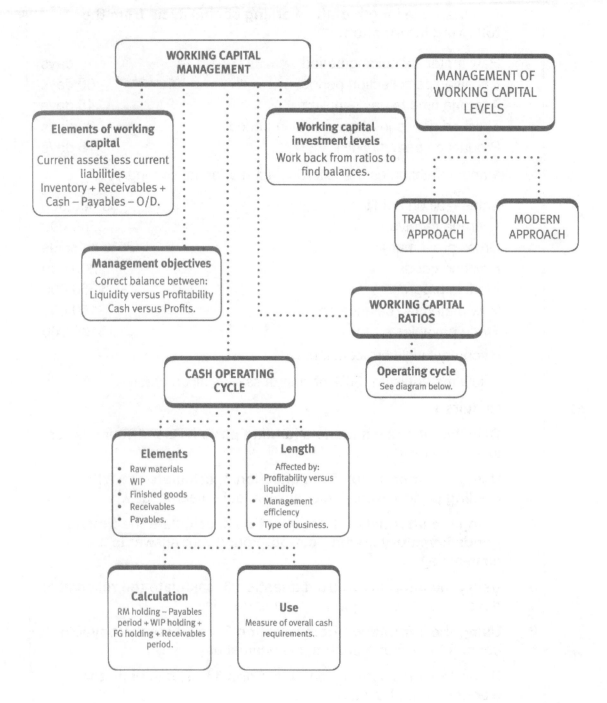

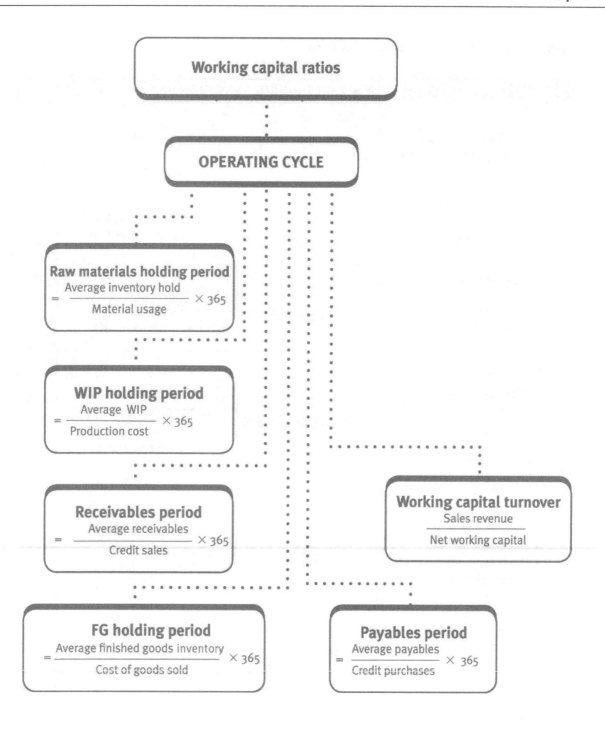

# Test your understanding answers

 **Test your understanding 1 – Liquidity v profitability**

| Advantages of keeping it high | | Advantages of keeping it low |
|---|---|---|
| Few stockouts<br><br>Bulk purchase discounts<br>Reduced ordering costs | **INVENTORY** | Less cash tied up in inventory<br>Lower storage costs |
| | **+** | |
| Customers like credit –<br>∴ profitable as attracts more sales | **RECEIVABLES** | Less cash tied up<br>Less chance of irrecoverable debts<br>Reduced costs of credit control |
| | **+** | |
| Able to pay bills on time<br>Take advantage of unexpected opportunities<br>Avoid high borrowing costs | **CASH** | Can invest surplus to earn high returns<br>Less vulnerable to takeover |
| | **=** | |
| | **CURRENT ASSETS** | |
| | **–** | |
| Preserves own cash – cheap source of finance | **TRADE PAYABLES** | Lose prompt payment discounts<br>Loss of credit status<br>Less favourable supplier treatment |
| | **=** | |
| | **WORKING CAPITAL** | |

## Test your understanding 2 – Working capital investment levels

We need to use the ratios to calculate statement of financial position values in order to construct the projected working capital position.

|  |  |  |  |  | $m |
|---|---|---|---|---|---|
| Inventory | = | 30 ÷ 365 × $6m | = | | 0.49 |
| Receivables | = | 60 ÷ 365 × $10m | | | 1.64 |
| Trade payables | = | 40 ÷ 365 × $6m | = | | (0.66) |
|  |  |  |  |  | ‾‾‾‾‾ |
| Working capital required |  |  |  |  | 1.47 |

## Test your understanding 3 – Overtrading

**A**

## Test your understanding 4 – Working capital cycle

|  | Days |
|---|---|
| Raw materials inventory holding period | 21 |
| Less: suppliers' payment period | (42) |
| WIP holding period | 14 |
| Finished goods holding period | 28 |
| Receivables' collection period | 56 |
|  | ‾‾‾‾ |
| Operating cycle (days) | 77 |
|  | ‾‾‾‾ |

## Test your understanding 5 – Raw material holding period

$$\frac{25,000}{264,400} \times 365 = 35 \text{ days}$$

## Test your understanding 6 – WIP holding period

$$\frac{33,500}{264,400} \times 365 = 46 \text{ days}$$

## Test your understanding 7 – Finished goods inventory holding

$$\frac{46,500}{264,400} \times 365 = 64 \text{ days}$$

## Test your understanding 8 – Receivable days

$$\frac{35,200}{350,000} \times 365 = 37 \text{ days}$$

## Test your understanding 9 – Payable days

$$\frac{55,200}{264,400} \times 365 = 76 \text{ days}$$

## Test your understanding 10 – Working capital cycle

The answer is 106 days.

See summary below:

| | | Days |
|---|---|---|
| Inventory days | | |
| Raw materials | $\frac{25,000}{264,400} \times 365 =$ | 35 |
| Work-in-progress | $\frac{33,500}{264,400} \times 365 =$ | 46 |
| Finished goods | $\frac{46,500}{264,400} \times 365 =$ | 64 |
| Receivable days | $\frac{35,200}{350,000} \times 365 =$ | 37 |
| Less Payable days | $\frac{55,200}{264,400} \times 365 =$ | (76) |
| Total | | 106 |

## Test your understanding 11 – Practice questions

1

|  | Days |
|---|---|
| Raw materials holding period | 10 |
| Production period (WIP) | 5 |
| Finished goods inventory holding period | 20 |
| Receivables collection period | 60 |
|  | 95 |
| Average time to pay suppliers | (45) |
|  | 50 |
| Working capital cycle | 50 |

2 **Statement of profit or loss**

|  | $ | $ |
|---|---|---|
| Turnover |  | 3,600,000 |
| Cost of sales |  |  |
| Materials – 80% (given) | 2,160,000 |  |
| Other (balancing figure) | 540,000 |  |
|  |  | 2,700,000 |
| Gross profit – 25% (given) |  | 900,000 |

**Raw materials holding period**

$$\frac{\$150,000}{\$2,160,000} \times 365 = 25 \text{ days}$$

3 **WIP holding days**

$$\frac{\$350,000}{\$2,700.000} \times 365 = 47 \text{ days}$$

4 **Finished goods holding period**

$$\frac{\$200,000}{\$2,700.000} \times 365 \qquad = 27 \text{ days}$$

5 **Receivables collection period**

$$\frac{\$306,000}{\$3,600,000} \times 365 \qquad = 31 \text{ days}$$

6    **Trade payables days**

$$\frac{\$130,000}{\$2,160,000} \times 365 \qquad\qquad = 22 \text{ days}$$

7    **The working capital cycle is 108 days**

Raw materials holding period

$$\frac{\$150,000}{\$2,160,000} \times 365 \qquad\qquad = 25 \text{ days}$$

Trade payable days

$$\frac{\$130,000}{\$2,160,000} \times 365 \qquad\qquad = (22) \text{ days}$$

WIP holding days

$$\frac{\$350,000}{\$2,700,000} \times 365 \qquad\qquad = 47 \text{ days}$$

Finished goods holding period

$$\frac{\$200,000}{\$2,700,000} \times 365 \qquad\qquad = 27 \text{ days}$$

Receivables collection period

$$\frac{\$306,000}{\$3,600,000} \times 365 \qquad\qquad = 31 \text{ days}$$

$$\overline{\qquad\qquad}$$

108 days

8    The correct answer is C

Items B and D result in no change in working capital. Item B results in an equal reduction in both cash and trade payables. Item D results in an increase in inventory but an equal decrease in cash. Writing off a receivable (item A) reduces working capital, because there is a reduction in receivables but no reduction in current liabilities. Selling goods on credit reduces inventory but increases receivables by a larger amount (= the gross profit on the sale); therefore total working capital increases by the amount of the gross profit.

# Working Capital Management – Accounts Receivable and Payable

## Chapter learning objectives

| Lead outcome | Component outcome |
| --- | --- |
| D3. Apply different techniques used to manage working capital | a. Apply policies relating to elements of operating and cash cycle |
| | c. Explain risks relating to working capital |

# 1    Session content

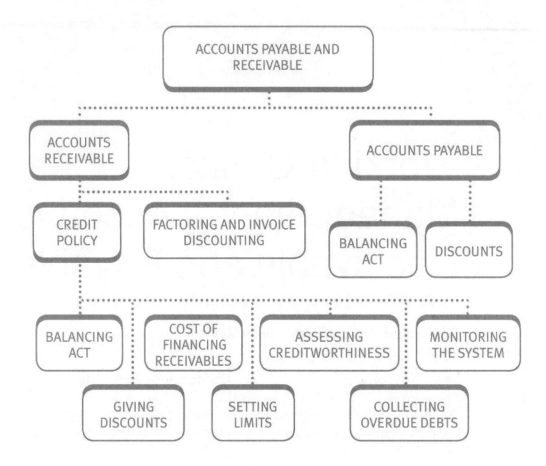

# 2    Accounts receivable – establishing a credit policy

## The balancing act

When businesses sell to customers, they would like to do it for cash to earn profits and stay liquid. However, in certain industries, the expectation is that sales are made on a 'buy now, pay later' basis. This is called selling on credit. On a credit sale, a receivable is created which sits as an asset in the statement of financial position of the entity. In a lot of industries, if you do not sell on credit, customers will go elsewhere.

The problem with selling on credit is that businesses have to wait for their cash. To manage liquidity appropriately, management must establish a credit policy when offering credit to customers. A credit policy outlines the businesses terms & conditions and internal procedures in relation to offering credit to their customers.

The optimum level of trade credit extended to customers represents a balance between two factors:

- profit improvement from sales obtained by allowing credit

- the cost of credit allowed.

## Why have a credit policy?

A firm must establish a policy for credit terms given to its customers. Ideally the firm would want to obtain cash with each order delivered, but that is impossible unless substantial settlement (or cash) discounts are offered as an inducement. It must be recognised that credit terms are part of the firm's marketing policy. If the trade or industry has adopted a common practice, then it is probably wise to keep in step with it.

A lenient credit policy may well attract additional customers, but at a disproportionate increase in cost.

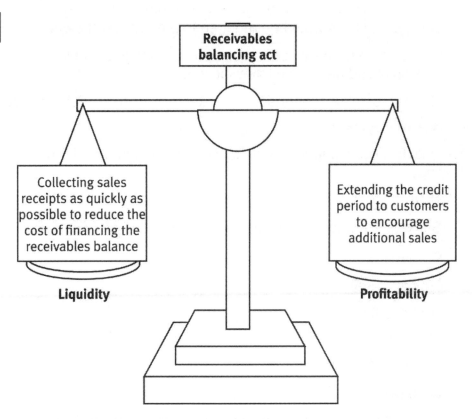

Remember this trade-off is a key factor in determining the entity's working capital investment.

## Different payment terms

The payment terms will need to consider the period of credit to be granted and how the payment will be made. The terms agreed will need to specify the price, the date of delivery, the payment date or dates, and any discounts to be allowed for early settlement.

Examples of payment terms may be

- Payment within a specified period. For example, customers must pay within 30 days.

- Payment within a specified period with discount. For example, a 2 per cent discount would be given to customers who pay within 10 days, and others would be required to pay within 30 days.

- Weekly credit. This would require all supplies in a week to be paid by a specified day in the following week.

- Related to delivery of goods. For example, cash on delivery (COD).

**Methods of payment**

Payments from customers may be accepted in a number of forms, including

- cash

- Bankers Automated Clearing Service (BACS)

- cheques

- banker's draft

- standing orders

- direct debit

- credit cards

- debit cards

- Clearing House Automated Payments System (CHAPS)

For accounts receivable, the entity's credit policy will be influenced by

- demand for products

- competitors' terms

- risk of irrecoverable debts

- financing costs

- costs of credit control

Receivables management has four key aspects:

1   Assessing creditworthiness of customers.

2   Setting credit limits.

3   Invoicing promptly and collecting overdue debts.

4   Monitoring the credit system.

This is a useful structure to adopt for examination questions that ask about the management of receivables.

## 3   Assessing creditworthiness

A firm should assess the creditworthiness of

- all new customers immediately, before offering credit terms
- existing customers periodically

Information may come from

- bank references
- trade references
- visit to the customer's premises
- competitors
- published information
- credit reference agencies
- legal sources of credit information
- entity's own sales records
- credit scoring
- credit rating (large corporate customers only)

**Assessing creditworthiness**

To minimise the risk of irrecoverable debts occurring, an entity should investigate the credit worthiness of all new customers (credit risk), and should review that of existing customers from time to time, especially if they request that their credit limit should be raised. Information about a customer's credit rating can be obtained from a variety of sources.

These include

- **Bank references** – A customer's permission must be sought. These tend to be fairly standardised in the UK, and so are not perhaps as helpful as they could be.

- **Trade references** – Suppliers already giving credit to the customer can give useful information about how good the customer is at paying bills on time. There is a danger that the customer will only nominate those suppliers that are being paid on time.

- **Visit to the customer's premises** – A sales representative might visit the business premises of the customer. A visit will provide information about the actual 'physical' operations and assets of the customer, and might provide some reassurance that the customer's business has substance.

- **Competitors** – in some industries such as insurance, competitors share information on customers, including creditworthiness.

- **Published information** – The customer's own annual accounts and reports will give some idea of the general financial position of the entity and its liquidity.

- **Credit reference agencies** – Agencies such as Dunn & Bradstreet publish general financial details of many entities, together with a credit rating. They will also produce a special report on an entity if requested. The information is provided for a fee.

- **Legal sources of credit information** – Instead of using a credit reference agency, an entity might check available legal records itself to find out whether the customer has a history of insolvency or non-payment. For example, in the UK information can be obtained from the Register of County Court Judgements and from the Individual Insolvency Register.

- **Entity's own sales records** – For an existing customer, the sales ledgers will show how prompt a payer the entity is, although they cannot show the ability of the customer to pay.

- **Credit scoring** – Indicators such as family circumstances, home ownership, occupation and age can be used to predict likely creditworthiness. This is useful when extending credit to the public where little other information is available. A variety of software packages is available which can assist with credit scoring.

- **Large corporate customers only: credit rating** – Very large entities might have a credit rating from one of the major credit rating agencies, Moody's and Standard & Poors. A supplier might use an entity's credit rating to decide how much credit to allow, without having to carry out a detailed credit check itself.

## 4 Setting credit limits

When setting credit limits there are two limits that need to be set

- the amount of credit available, and
- the length of time allowed before payment is due.

Both of these limits might be adjusted in accordance to the risk profile of the customer.

---

**Expandable Text**

The 'risk' associated with a customer's credit status should be based on

- the customer's payment record and history of prompt or late payments, and
- any new information that is obtained about the customer, for example from its most recent annual financial statements or recent press reports.

The level of credit available and the length of settlement period offered to a customer (if across-the-board standard terms are not used) should then be based on the assessment of this risk.

### Example

An entity might group its existing customers into six categories, as follows:

**Customer categories**

|  | Financially strong | Financially stable | Financially weak |
|---|---|---|---|
| Prompt payer | Category A | Category B | Category C |
| Late payer | Category D | Category E | Category F |

The amount of credit offered to the customer (and possibly also the length of the payment terms) would vary according to the category of the customer. If a customer moves from one category to a stronger category, a higher credit limit (or longer settlement period) would be allowed if required.

If the customer's credit status does not improve, a request for more credit from the customer should be refused.

The ledger account should be monitored to take account of orders in the pipeline as well as invoiced sales, before further credit is given.

## 5 Invoicing and collecting overdue debts

A credit period only begins once an invoice is received so prompt invoicing is essential. If debts go overdue, the risk of default increases, therefore a system of follow-up procedures is required

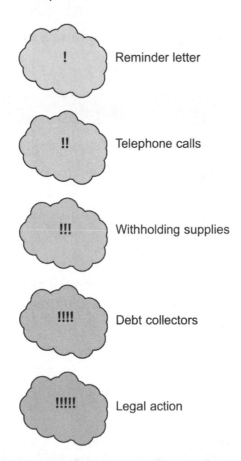

Reminder letter

Telephone calls

Withholding supplies

Debt collectors

Legal action

### Invoicing and collecting overdue debts

The longer a debt is allowed to run, the higher the probability of eventual default. A system of follow-up procedures is required, bearing in mind the risk of offending a valued customer to such an extent that their business is lost.

Techniques for 'chasing' overdue debts include the following

- **Reminder letters** – these are often regarded as being a relatively poor way of obtaining payment, as many customers simply ignore them. Sending reminders by email have proven to be more productive than using the postal system as it is harder for customers to claim that they have not received them.

- **Telephone calls** – these can be an efficient way of speeding up payment and identifying problems at an early stage.

- **Withholding supplies** – putting customers on the 'stop list' for further orders or spare parts can encourage rapid settlement of debts.

- **Debt collection agencies and trade associations** – these offer debt collection services on a fixed fee basis or on 'no collection no charge' terms. The quality of service provided varies considerably and care should be taken in selecting an agent.

- **Legal action** – this is often seen as a last resort. A solicitor's letter often prompts payment and many cases do not go to court. Court action is usually not cost effective but it can discourage other customers from delaying payment.

## Motivating credit control staff using collection targets

If employees in the payments collection team are to operate effectively, they need to be convinced of the value of their work and their contribution to the objectives of the organisation. One way of improving performance and increasing staff motivation might be to set collection targets. A collection target is a target for the amount of payments to collect for trade receivables within a given period of time.

Targets can be set for

- individual members of the collection team, and

- the credit control team as a whole.

Targets for collection will not be a motivator, however, unless performance is assessed and individuals are rewarded (with a bonus) on the basis of meeting or exceeding targets.

### Illustration on collection targets

Consider the following example of an entity aiming to set a collection target

At the end of March, the trade receivables of M were as follows:

|  |  | $ |
|---|---|---|
| From March sales | (100% of sales in the month) | 1,200,000 |
| From February sales | (70% of sales in the month) | 700,000 |
| From January sales | (30% of sales in the month) | 270,000 |
|  |  | 2,170,000 |

This represents an average of 60 days' sales outstanding, made up as follows

|  |  | Days |
|---|---|---|
| From March sales | (100% × 31 days) | 31 |
| From February sales | (70% × 28 days) | 20 |
| From January sales | (30% × 31 days) | 9 |
|  |  | 60 |

The entity wants to reduce its average day's sales outstanding from 60 days to 50 days by the end of April. Sales in April are expected to be $1,100,000, all on credit. It intends to do this by aiming to collect payments of the oldest outstanding receivables.

**Required**

Calculate the collection target that should be set for staff.

**Solution**

- If no money is collected at all during April, the days sales outstanding would increase from 60 days to 90 days (= 60 days + 30 days in April).

- If days sales outstanding is reduced to 50 days, representing the most recent sales, these will be the sales in April and 20 days of sales in March.

- To reach the target of 50 days by collecting the oldest unpaid receivables, the entity must collect 40 days of sales, representing.

|  | Days | $ |
|---|---|---|
| From March sales * | 11 | 425,806 |
| From February sales | 20 | 700,000 |
| From January sales | 9 | 270,000 |
|  |  | 1,395,806 |

\* March amount calculated as (11/31 × $1,200,000)

The collection target for April should therefore be $1,395,806.

**Note** in this example, the collection target focuses on the trade receivables that have been unpaid for the longest time. A different policy could be followed, such as chasing the customers who are most likely to pay early, or chasing customers who are overdue with their payment by only one or two weeks.

## 6  Monitoring the system

The position of receivables should be regularly reviewed as part of managing overall working capital and corrective action taken when needed. Methods include:

- age analysis
- ratios
- statistical data.

**Monitoring the system**

Management will require regular information to take corrective action and to measure the impact of giving credit on working capital investment. Typical management reports on the credit system will include the following points.

- Age analysis of outstanding debts.

  As an aid to effective credit control, an age analysis of outstanding debts may be produced. This is simply a list of the customers who currently owe money, showing the total amount owed and the period of time for which the money has been owed. The actual form of the age analysis report can vary widely, but a typical example is shown below for a sole trader called Robins.

| Account number | Name | Balance | Up to 30 days | 31–60 days | 61–90 days | Over 90 days |
|---|---|---|---|---|---|---|
| B002 | Brennan | 294.35 | 220.15 | 65.40 | 8.80 | 0.00 |
| G007 | Goodridge | 949.50 | 853.00 | 0.00 | 96.50 | 0.00 |
| T005 | Taylor | 371.26 | 340.66 | 30.60 | 0.00 | 0.00 |
| T010 | Thorpe | 1,438.93 | 0.00 | 0.00 | 567.98 | 870.95 |
| T011 | Tinnion | 423.48 | 312.71 | 110.77 | 0.00 | 0.00 |
| | | | | | | |
| Totals | | 3,477.52 | 1,726.52 | 206.77 | 673.28 | 870.95 |
| | | | | | | |
| Percentage | | 100% | 50% | 6% | 19% | 25% |

  To prepare the analysis, either use a computer programme or manually analyse each customer account. For each customer, every invoice is allocated to the month it was issued. Then when payment is received, the invoice is cancelled from the analysis, leaving the total of unpaid invoices for each month. Difficulties analysing the balance can occur if the customer pays lump sum on account, rather than specific invoices. Care must be taken to allocate all adjustments other than cash, such as credit notes, discounts given, etc.

  The age analysis of trade receivables can be used to help decide what action should be taken about debts that have been outstanding for longer than the specified credit period. It can be seen from the table above that 41 % of Robin's outstanding trade receivable balance is due by Thorpe. It may be that Thorpe is experiencing financial difficulties. There may already have been some correspondence between the two entities about the outstanding debts.

As well as providing information about individual customer balances, the age analysis of trade receivables provides additional information about the efficiency of cash collection. The table above shows that over 50 per cent of debts have been outstanding for more than 30 days. If the normal credit period is 30 days, there may be a suggestion of weaknesses in credit control. It may also be useful to show the credit limit for each customer on the report, to identify those customers who are close to, or have exceeded, their credit limit.

The age analysis can also provide information to assist in setting and monitoring collection targets for the credit control section. A collection target could be expressed as a percentage of credit sales collected within a specified period or it could be expressed in terms of the average number of trade receivable days outstanding. When trying to achieve a collection target, the age analysis can be very useful in identifying large balances that have been outstanding for long periods. These can be targeted for action to encourage payment.

– Ratios, compared with the previous period or target, to indicate trends in credit levels and the incidence of overdue and irrecoverable debts.

– Statistical data to identify causes of default and the incidence of irrecoverable debts among different classes of customer and types of trade.

### Test your understanding 1 – Credit limits

Explain the factors that might be considered when revising a credit limit for an existing customer, and list the tools that a credit controller can use to help in making a credit limit decision.

## 7 Accounts receivable – calculations

### Costs of financing receivables

 Key working:

Finance cost = Receivable balance × Interest (overdraft) rate

$$\text{Receivable balance} = \text{Sales} \times \frac{\text{Receivable days}}{365}$$

## Test your understanding 2 – Cost of financing receivables

Paisley has sales of $20 million for the previous year. Receivables at the year-end were $4 million, and the cost of financing receivables is covered by an overdraft at the interest rate of 12% p.a.

**Required**

(a)  Calculate the receivables days for Paisley

(b)  Calculate the annual cost of financing receivables.

## Early settlement discounts

Cash discounts are given to encourage early payment by customers. The cost of the discount is balanced against the savings the entity receives from having less capital tied up due to a lower receivables balance and a shorter average collection period. Discounts may also reduce the number of irrecoverable debts.

The calculation of the annual cost can be expressed as a formula:

$$\text{Annual cost of discount} = \left[1 + \frac{\text{discount}}{\text{amount left to pay}}\right]^{\text{no. of periods}} - 1$$

$$\text{where no of periods} = \frac{365/52/12}{\text{no. of days/weeks/months earlier the money is received}}$$

Notice that the annual cost calculation is always based on the amount left to pay, i.e. the amount net of discount.

If the cost of offering the discount exceeds the rate of overdraft interest, then the discount should not be offered.

## Test your understanding 3 – Early settlement discounts

Paisley has sales of $20 million for the previous year, receivables at the year end of $4 million and the cost of financing receivables is covered by an overdraft at the interest rate of 12% pa. It is now considering offering a cash discount of 2% for payment of debts within 10 days.

**Calculate whether the annualised cost of offering the discount and state whether you would advise the discount to be offered.**

## Evaluating a change in credit policy

In an examination, you may be required to evaluate whether a proposed change in credit policy is financially justified. The illustration below illustrates the approach required to carry out this evaluation.

## Evaluating a change in credit policy

An example is given below.

The table below gives information extracted from the annual accounts of Supergeordie.

|  | $ |
| --- | --- |
| Raw materials | 180,000 |
| Work in progress | 93,360 |
| Finished goods | 142,875 |
| Purchases | 720,000 |
| Cost of goods sold | 1,098,360 |
| Sales | 1,188,000 |
| Trade receivables | 297,000 |
| Trade payables | 126,000 |

The sales director of Supergeordie estimates that if the period of credit allowed to customers was reduced from its current level to 60 days, this would result in a 25 per cent reduction in sales but would probably eliminate about $30,000 per annum bad debts. It would be necessary to spend an additional $20,000 per annum on credit control. The entity at present relies heavily on overdraft finance costing 9 per cent per annum.

You are required to make calculations showing the effect of these changes, and to advise whether they would be financially justified. Assume that purchases and inventory holdings would be reduced proportionally to the reduction in sales value.

### Solution

The first stage is to identify the reduction in the level of working capital investment as a result of the change in policy. Inventory and trade payables are assumed to fall by 25 per cent in line with sales, but the new level of trade receivables will need to be calculated using the trade receivable collection formula.

### Reduction in working capital

|  | Existing level $ |  |  | New level $ | Change $ |
| --- | --- | --- | --- | --- | --- |
| Raw materials | 180,000 | × | 75% = | 135,000 | 45,000 |
| Work in progress | 93,360 | × | 75% = | 70,020 | 23,340 |
| Finished goods | 142,875 | × | 75% = | 107,156 | 35,719 |
| Trade receivables | 297,000 |  | (W1) | 146,466 | 150,534 |
| Trade payables | (126,000) | × | 75% = | (94,500) | (31,500) |
| Total | 587,235 |  |  | 364,142 | 223,093 |

**Working**

(W1)

$$\text{Receivable collection period} = \frac{\text{trade receivables}}{\text{sales}} \times 365$$

$$60 = \frac{\text{trade receivables}}{1,188,000 \times 75\%} \times 365$$

$$\text{Trade receivables} = \frac{891,000 \times 60}{865}$$

$$= \$146,466$$

The second stage is to consider the annual costs and benefits of changing the credit policy. A key element here is to recognise the saving in finance costs as a result of the reduction in the level of working capital investment recognised above.

**Annual costs and benefits**

|  |  | $ |
|---|---|---|
| Saving in finance costs (223,093 × 9%) | = | 20,078 |
| Reduction in gross profit (1,188,000 – 1,098,360) | = 89,640 × 25% | (22,410) |
| Reduction in bad debts | = | 30,000 |
| Credit control costs | = | (20,000) |
| | | ——— |
| Net saving per annum before tax | = | 7,668 |
| | | ——— |

The change in credit policy appears to be justified financially, but it should be remembered that there are a number of assumptions built in that could invalidate the calculations.

## 8 Accounts receivable – factoring

 Factoring is the 'sale of debts to a third party (the factor) at a discount in return for prompt cash' (CIMA Official Terminology).

The debts of the entity are effectively sold to a factor (normally owned by a bank). The factor takes on the responsibility of collecting the debt for a fee. The entity can choose one or both of the following services offered by the factor

1    debt collection and administration – recourse or non-recourse

2    credit insurance

These are of particular value to

- smaller firms

- fast growing firms

Make sure you can discuss the various services offered and remember that non-recourse factoring is more expensive as the factor bears the costs of any irrecoverable debts.

### More details

Debt collection and administration – the factor takes over the whole of the entity's sales ledger, issuing invoices and collecting debts.

Credit insurance – the factor agrees to insure the irrecoverable debts of the client. The factor would then determine to whom the entity was able to offer credit.

Some entities realise that, although it is necessary to extend trade credit to customers for competitive reasons, they need payment earlier than agreed in order to assist their own cash flow. Factors exist to help such entities.

Factoring is primarily designed to allow entities to accelerate cash flow, providing finance against outstanding trade receivables. This improves cash flow and liquidity. The factor will advance up to 80% of the value of a debt to the entity. The remainder (minus finance costs) being paid when the debts are collected. The factor becomes a source of finance. Finance costs are usually 1.5% to 3% above bank base rate and interest is charged on a daily basis.

Factoring is most suitable for

- small and medium-sized firms which often cannot afford sophisticated credit and sales accounting systems, and

- firms that are expanding rapidly. These often have a substantial and growing investment in receivables, which can be turned into cash by factoring the debts. Factoring debts can be a more flexible source of financing working capital than an overdraft or bank loan.

Factoring can be arranged on either a 'without recourse' basis or a 'with recourse' basis.

- When factoring is without recourse or 'non-recourse', the factor provides protection for the client against irrecoverable debts. The factor has no 'comeback' or recourse to the client if a customer defaults. When a customer of the client fails to pay a debt, the factor bears the loss and the client receives the money from the debt.

- When the service is with recourse ('recourse factoring'), the client must bear the loss from any irrecoverable debt, and so has to reimburse the factor for any money it has already received for the debt.

Credit protection is provided only when the service is non-recourse and this is obviously more costly.

## Typical factoring arrangements

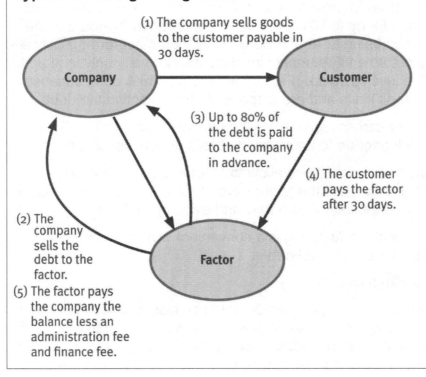

(1) The company sells goods to the customer payable in 30 days.

(3) Up to 80% of the debt is paid to the company in advance.

(4) The customer pays the factor after 30 days.

(2) The company sells the debt to the factor.

(5) The factor pays the company the balance less an administration fee and finance fee.

| Advantages | Disadvantages |
|---|---|
| 1 Saving in administration costs. | 1 Likely to be more costly than an efficiently run internal credit control department. |
| 2 Reduction in the need for management control. | |
| 3 Particularly useful for small and fast growing businesses where the credit control department may not be able to keep pace with volume growth. | 2 Factoring has a bad reputation associated with failing companies; using a factor may suggest your company has money worries. |
| | 3 Customers may not wish to deal with a factor. |
| | 4 Once you start factoring it is difficult to revert easily to an internal credit control system. |
| | 5 The company may give up the opportunity to decide to whom credit may be given (non-recourse factoring). |

## Benefits and problems with factoring

The benefits of factoring are as follows.

- A business improves its cash flow, because the factor provides finance for up to 80% or more of debts within 24 hours of the invoices being issued. A bank providing an overdraft facility secured against an entity's unpaid invoices will normally only lend up to 50% of the invoice value. (Factors will provide 80% or so because they set credit limits and are responsible for collecting the debts.)

- A factor can save the entity the administration costs of keeping the sales ledger up to date and the costs of debt collection.

- If the business were to allow the factor to administer the sales ledger, it can use the factor's credit control system to assess the creditworthiness of both new and existing customers.

- Non-recourse factoring is a convenient way of obtaining insurance against irrecoverable debts.

Problems with factoring

- Although factors provide valuable services, entities are sometimes wary about using them. A possible problem with factoring is that the intervention of the factor between the factor's client and the debtor entity could endanger trading relationships and damage goodwill. Customers might prefer to deal with the business, not a factor.

- When a non-recourse factoring service is used, the client loses control over decisions about granting credit to its customers.

- For this reason, some clients prefer to retain the risk of irrecoverable debts, and opt for a 'with recourse' factoring service. With this type of service, the client and not the factor decides whether extreme action (legal action) should be taken against a non-payer.

- On top of this, when suppliers and customers of the client find out that the client is using a factor to collect debts, it may arouse fears that the entity is beset by cash flow problems, raising fears about its viability. If so, its suppliers may impose more stringent payment terms, thus negating the benefits provided by the factor.

**Test your understanding 4 – Factoring arrangements**

Edden is a medium-sized entity producing a range of engineering products, which it sells to wholesale distributors. Recently, its sales have begun to rise rapidly due to economic recovery. However, it is concerned about its liquidity position and is looking at ways of improving cash flow.

Its sales are $16 million pa, and average receivables are $3.3 million (representing about 75 days of sales).

One way of speeding up collection from receivables is to use a factor. It has considered an agreement from an interested factoring entity.

The factor will pay 80% of the book value of invoices immediately, with finance costs charged on the advance at 10% pa.

The factor will charge 1% of sales as their fee for managing the sales ledger and there will be administrative savings of $100,000. It will be a non-recourse agreement – which means that the factor will bear the responsibility for any irrecoverable debts.

The entity is currently paying 8% interest on its overdraft.

**Required**

**Calculate the relative costs of using the factor and state whether it would be beneficial to the entity to use this facility.**

## 9 Accounts receivable – invoice discounting

Invoice discounting is a method of raising finance against the security of receivables without using the sales ledger administration services of a factor.

While specialist invoice discounting firms exist, this is a service also provided by a factoring entity. Selected invoices are used as security against which the entity may borrow funds. This is a temporary source of finance, repayable when the debt is cleared. The key advantage of invoice discounting is that it is a confidential service, and the customer need not know about it.

In some ways it is similar to the financing part of the factoring service without control of credit passing to the factor.

Ensure you can explain the difference between factoring and invoice discounting, and the situations where one may be more appropriate than the other.

**Invoice discounting**

## Typical arrangement

(1) The company sells goods to the customer payable in 30 days.

```
        Company  ──────────────▶  Customer

(2) The                    (3) The company
    company                    receives payment.
    borrows up
    to 80% of
    the value of
    the debt.
                    Invoice
                    discounter

(4) The company
    pays the invoice
    discounter the amount
    borrowed plus
    interest.
```

Invoice discounting is a method of raising finance against the security of receivables without using the sales ledger administration services of a factor. With invoice discounting, the business retains control over its sales ledger, and confidentiality in its dealings with customers. Firms of factors will also provide invoice discounting to clients.

### The method works as follows:

- The business sends out invoices, statements and reminders in the normal way, and collects the debts. With 'confidential invoice discounting', its customers are unaware that the business is using invoice discounting.

- The invoice discounter provides cash to the business for a proportion of the value of the invoice, as soon as it receives a copy of the invoice and agrees to discount it. The discounter will advance cash up to 80% of face value.

- When the business eventually collects the payment from its customer, the money must be paid into a bank account controlled by the invoice discounter. The invoice discounter then pays the business the remainder of the invoice, less interest and administration charges.

Invoice discounting can help a business that is trying to improve its cash flows, but does not want a factor to administer its sales ledger and collect its debts. It is therefore equivalent to the financing service provided by a factor.

Administration charges for this service are around 0.5–1 % of a client's turnover. It is more risky than factoring since the client retains control over its credit policy. Consequently, such facilities are usually confined to established entities with high sales revenue, and the business must be profitable. Finance costs are usually in the range 3–4% above base rate, although larger entities and those which arrange credit insurance may receive better terms.

The invoice discounter will check the sales ledger of the client regularly, perhaps every three months, to check that its debt collection procedures are adequate.

## Illustration of the invoice discounting process

At the beginning of August, Basildon sells goods for a total value of $300,000 to regular customers but decides that it requires payment earlier than the agreed 30-day credit period for these invoices.

A discounter agrees to finance 80% of their face value, i.e. $240,000, at an interest cost of 9% pa.

The invoices were due for payment in early September, but were subsequently settled in mid-September, exactly 45 days after the initial transactions. The invoice discounter's service charge is 1 % of invoice value. A special account is set up with a bank, into which all payments are made.

The sequence of cash flows is:

| | |
|---|---|
| **August** | Basildon receives cash advance of $240,000. |
| **Mid-September** | Customers pay $300,000. |
| | Invoice discounter receives the full $300,000 paid into the special bank account. |
| | Basildon receives the balance payable, less charges, i.e. |

|  |  |
|---|---|
| Service fee = 1% × $300,000 = | $3,000 |
| Finance cost = 9% × $240,000 × 45/365 = | $2,663 |
| | |
| Total charges | $5,663 |

| | Basildon receives: | |
|---|---|---|
| | Balance of payment from customer | $60,000 |
| | Less charges | $5,663 |
| | | $54,337 |
| **Summary $300,000 invoiced** | Total receipts by Basildon: $240,000 + $54,337 | $294,337 |
| | Invoice discounter's fee and interest charges | $5,663 |

## 2015 CIMA Professional Qualification Syllabus, Operational Level Case Study Exam, August 2018 v5 – Question (Modified)

You work in Herbaboil, a drinks manufacturer specialising in flavoured tea drinks. The entity runs a number of different lines of product, one of which is Butler Estates, a high end exotic tea product line.

Jack Ford, the Head of Finance, sends you the following email:

**From:** **Jack Ford,**

**To:** **Finance Officer**

**Subject** **Butler Estates: Receivables management**

Butler Estates seems to be going from strength to strength. Only two months ago, it was decided that we should target small, independent luxury delicatessens and food shops to start stocking Butler Estates tea. This has been very successful and we now have over 30 new customers as a result.

The new customers are great news for sales but potentially not so great for cash flow. Many of the customers that we took on two months ago are already behind on payments. I've suggested to the Finance Director, Christie Smith, that we think about factoring the receivable balances for these type of customers. She isn't against the idea, although has asked for a briefing paper on the benefits and drawbacks of factoring the receivable balances for these customers, that can be forwarded onto the other directors.

I need you to send me an email in which you:

- Prepare content for a briefing paper to the directors which explains the potential benefits and drawbacks to the business of factoring the receivables balances of the Butler Estates small independent customers.

Kind regards,

JF

## Case Study Suggested Answer

**2015 CIMA Professional Qualification Syllabus, Operational Level
Case Study Exam, August 2018 V5 – Suggested Answer**

**Note this is an extract from the suggested answer and focuses solely on the areas of the case study relevant to the F1 exam**

### FACTORING OF RECEIVABLES BALANCES OF BUTLER ESTATES SMALL INDEPENDENT BUSINESS CUSTOMERS

**Potential benefits:**

The main benefit of factoring the receivables balances of the small independent business customers is that we will receive the cash from sales to these customers more quickly than if we do not factor. Typically, factors advance around 80% of the invoice value on the raising of the invoice, with the remainder received a little later. This could be a huge benefit for us because, even after only two months, we know that this type of customer is slow at paying which is because they are small, probably owner-managed businesses where cash flow is very tight.

Another benefit is that if we use a non-recourse arrangement, we can transfer the risk of irrecoverable debts to the factor. The ability to do this is potentially very beneficial for this type of customer. Small independent retail businesses are far more likely to cease trading than larger more established businesses.

Another benefit is that a factor will be an expert in credit control and in dealing with customers like this. They will have set procedures and will promptly chase outstanding amounts. As mentioned above this is a different type of customer than either the Butler Estates finance departments are used to. Indeed, given the rapid growth in this customer base it is unlikely that we have the resource to manage the credit control function effectively without taking on and training new staff.

**Potential drawbacks:**

The main drawback of factoring is its cost. A factor will charge an administrative fee of a percentage of sales revenue. This is a cost against gross profit and will affect our margin. In addition, the factor will charge a finance fee on the monies advanced, which will affect our net profit. Given the nature of these customers and the relatively high risk of non-payment, it is likely that any factor willing to over us a service will expect a high level of fees in compensation.

Another drawback is that our customers might not be happy about the arrangement. With factoring, unlike invoice discounting, the customer will be fully aware of the arrangement because they will receive correspondence with the factor. Customers might feel that they have lost their link to Butler Estates and that we do not value their business, especially if the factor is aggressive in chasing for payment. The potential loss of business needs to be carefully considered.

## 10   Accounts payable – managing trade credit

Trade credit is the simplest and most important source of short-term finance for many entities.

 Again it is a balancing act between liquidity and profitability.

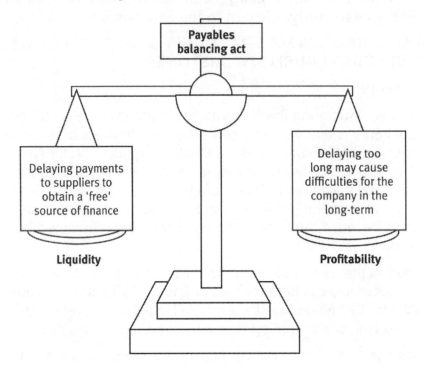

By delaying payment to suppliers, entities face possible problems such as:

*   suppliers may refuse to supply in future

*   suppliers may only supply on a cash basis

*   there may be loss of reputation

*   suppliers may increase price in future

Trade credit is normally seen as a 'free' source of finance. Whilst this is normally true, it may be that the supplier offers a discount for early payment. In this case, delaying payment is no longer free, since the cost will be the lost discount.

 In the examination, you need to be able to calculate the cost of this discount foregone.

## Trade payables

Using trade **credit** a firm is able to obtain goods (or services) from a supplier without immediate payment, the supplier accepting that the firm will pay at a later date.

Trade credit periods vary from industry to industry and each industry will have what is a generally accepted norm which would be from seven days upwards. A typical credit period might be 30 days, but it can range anywhere from 7 to 90 days, dependent on the relative power of the supplier and buyer. Normally considerable scope for flexibility exists and longer credit periods are sometimes offered, particularly where the type of business activity requires a long period to convert materials into saleable products, e.g. farming.

Some of the firm's suppliers may offer **settlement discounts**. However, if the firm is short of funds, it might wish to make maximum use of the credit period allowed by suppliers regardless of the settlement discounts offered. Favourable credit terms are one of several factors which influence the choice of a supplier. Furthermore, the act of accepting settlement discounts has an opportunity cost, i.e. the cost of finance obtained from another source to replace that not obtained from creditors.

Whilst trade credit may be seen as a source of free credit, there will be **costs** associated with extending credit taken beyond the norm – lost discounts, loss of supplier goodwill, more stringent terms for future sales.

In order to compare the cost of different sources of finance, all costs are usually converted to a rate per annum basis. The cost of extended trade credit is usually measured by loss of discount, but the calculation of its cost is complicated by such variables as the number of alternative sources of supply, and the general economic conditions.

Certain assumptions have to be made concerning (a) the maximum delay in payment which can be achieved before the supply of goods is withdrawn by the supplier, and (b) the availability of alternative sources of supply.

Also, it is a mistake to reduce working capital by holding on to creditors' money for a longer period than is allowed as, in the long-term, this will affect the **supplier's willingness to supply** goods and raw materials, and cause further embarrassment to the firm.

## Test your understanding 5 – Discounts for early payment

One supplier has offered a discount to Box of 2% on an invoice for $7,500, if payment is made within one month, rather than the three months normally taken to pay.

If Box's overdraft rate is 10% pa, calculate if it is financially worthwhile for them to accept the discount and pay early?

## Age analysis of payables

The value of an age analysis of trade payables is probably less obvious than the value of an age analysis of trade receivables. However, management needs to be aware of

- the total amount payable to suppliers

- when the money will be payable

- the amounts payable to each individual supplier, and how close this is to the credit limit available from the supplier

- whether the entity is failing to pay its trade suppliers on time

### Test your understanding 6 – Practice questions

1 **Which of the following will not influence an entity's overall credit policy.**

   A   Demand for products

   B   Costs of credit control

   C   Volume of purchases

   D   Risk of irrecoverable debts

2 An entity expects credit sales of $110,000 in July, rising by $10,000 each month for the next two months. Outstanding trade receivables at the beginning of July were $165,000, representing all of June sales and 22 days of May sales. Sales in June were $95,000.

   The entity wishes to reduce the average day's sales outstanding to 45 days by the end of July and 40 days by the end of August.

   **On the assumption that the target should be to collect first the receivables that have been unpaid for the longest time, calculate the collection targets for**

   (a)   July, and

   (b)   August.

3 **List five methods of carrying out a credit check on a potential new customer, before deciding whether to give credit and if so, what the credit limit should be.**

4   An entity is considering a change in its credit policy. It has estimated that if credit terms are extended from 30 days to 60 days, total annual sales will increase by 10% from the current level of $12 million. It has been estimated that as a consequence of the change in credit terms and the higher sales volume, irrecoverable debts would increase from 2% to 3% of sales. The entity's cost of capital is 8%.

The increase in sales would not affect annual fixed costs. The contribution to sales ratio is 40%.

**Required**

Calculate the effect of the change in credit policy on the annual profit before taxation. Assume a 360-day year of 30 days each month.

5   An entity is offering a cash discount of 2.5% to receivables if they agree to pay debts within one month. The usual credit period taken is three months.

**Calculate the effective annualised cost of offering the discount and should it be offered, if the bank would loan to the entity at 18% p.a?**

6   **Calculate the equivalent annual cost of the following credit terms: 1.75% discount for payment within three weeks.**

**Alternatively, full payment must be made within eight weeks of the invoice date.**

Assume there are 50 weeks in a year.

7   Marton produces a range of specialised components, supplying a wide range of customers, all on credit terms. 20% of revenue is sold to one firm. Having used generous credit policies to encourage past growth, Marton Co now has to finance a substantial overdraft and is concerned about its liquidity.

Marton borrows from its bank at 13% pa interest. No further sales growth in volume or value terms is planned for the next year.

In order to speed up collection from customers, Marton is considering two alternative policies:

**Option one**

Factoring on a non-recourse basis with the factor administering and collecting payment from Marton Co's customers. This is expected to generate administrative savings of $200,000 pa and to lower the average receivable collection period by 15 days. The factor will make a service charge of 1% of Marton Co's revenue and also provide credit insurance facilities for an annual premium of $80,000.

### Option two

Offering discounts to customers who settle their accounts early. The amount of the discount will depend on speed of payment as follows.

Payment within 10 days of despatch of invoices 3%

Payment within 20 days of despatch of invoices 1.5%

It is estimated that customers representing 20% and 30% of Marton Co's sales respectively will take up these offers, the remainder continuing to take their present credit period.

Extracts from Marton's most recent accounts are given below.

|  | ($000) |
|---|---|
| Sales (all on credit) | 20,000 |
| Cost of sales | (17,000) |
| Operating profit | 3,000 |
| Current assets | |
| Inventory | 2,500 |
| Receivables | 4,500 |
| Cash | Nil |

Calculate the costs and benefits of the entity using option one.

8   Using the information from question 7 calculate the costs and benefits of the entity using option two.

9   Using the information from questions 7 and 8 identify the most financially advantageous policy.

10  Fredrico has sales of $40 million for the previous year, receivables at the year end were $6 million, and the cost of financing receivables is covered by an overdraft at the interest rate of 10% p.a.

**Required:**

(a)   Calculate the receivables days for Paisley

(b)   Calculate the annual cost of financing receivables.

## 11 Summary Diagram

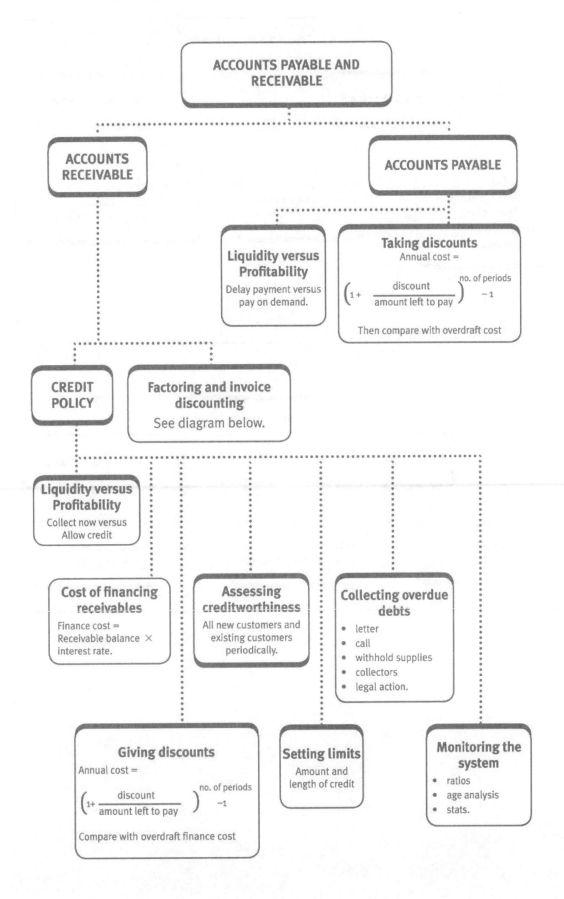

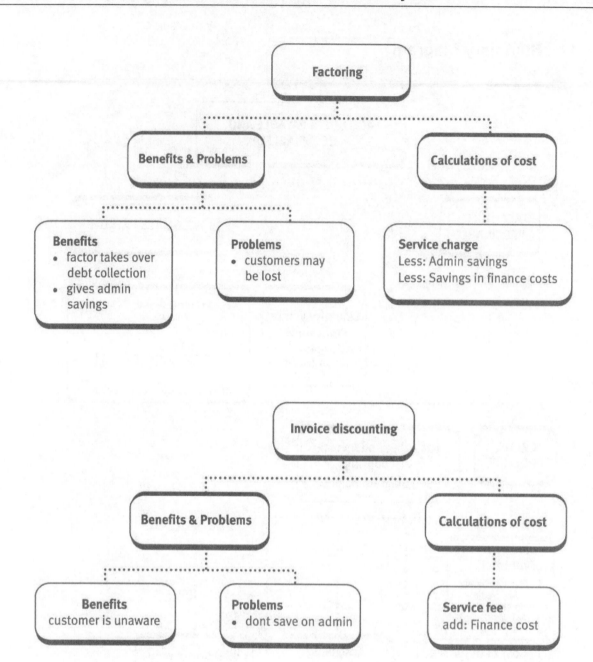

# Test your understanding answers

## Test your understanding 1 – Credit limits

There are a number of factors which a credit controller might consider, such as:

- the customers past payment history. If a customer has usually paid on time in the past then a higher credit limit might be approved.

- any new public information about the customer. For example, if recent press reports suggest that the customer might be in financial difficulty then it may be unwise to raise a customer's credit limit.

- a change in the customer's credit rating. For large customers especially, credit ratings are easily obtained and any change to a rating should have an impact on the amount of credit offered to the customer.

In making the decision the credit controller will be able to use a variety of tools, such as:

- past customer history

- an aged receivables report

- credit reference agencies

- ratio analysis

## Test your understanding 2 – Cost of financing receivables

(a)   Receivables days = \$4m ÷ \$20m × 365 = 73 days

(b)   Annual cost of financing receivables = \$4m × 12% = \$480,000.

## Test your understanding 3 – Early settlement discounts

Discount as a percentage of amount left to pay = 2 ÷ 98 = 2.04%

Receivables days are currently 73 (\$4m/\$20m × 365), so:

Saving is 63 days (dropping from 73 days to 10) and there are 365 ÷ 63 = 5.794 periods in a year

**Annualised cost of discount % is**

$(1 + 0.0204)^{5.794} - 1 = 0.1241 = 12.41\%$.

The overdraft rate is 12%.

**It would be marginally cheaper to borrow the money from the bank rather than offer the discount.**

**Test your understanding 4 – Factoring arrangements**

|  | Costs of factoring $ | Savings $ |
|---|---|---|
| Sales ledger administration | | |
| 1% × $16m | 160,000 | |
| Administration cost savings | | 100,000 |
| Cost of factor finance 10% × 80% | | |
| × $3.3m * | 264,000 | |
| Overdraft finance costs 8% × 80% | | |
| × $3.3m saved | | 211,200 |
| | ——— | ——— |
| Total | 424,000 | 311,200 |
| Net cost of factoring | 112,800 | |

The firm will have to balance this cost against the security offered by improved cash flows and greater liquidity.

* 80% of the average receivable balance is outstanding at any one time.

**Test your understanding 5 – Discounts for early payment**

Discount saves 2% of $7,500 = $150

Financed by overdraft for extra two months in order to pay early:

$7,500 – $150 = $7,350

$$10\% \times \frac{2}{12} \times 7,350 \qquad = (\$122.50)$$

Net saving                   = $27.50

It is worth accepting the discount.

**Alternatively:**

Discount as a percentage of amount to be paid $= \dfrac{150}{7,350} = 2.04\%$

Saving is 2 months and there are $\dfrac{12}{2} = 6$ periods in a year

Annualised cost of not taking the discount (and therefore borrowing from the supplier) is $(1 + 0.0204)^6 - 1 = 0.1288 = 12.88\%$

The overdraft rate is 10%.

It would be cheaper to borrow the money from the bank to pay early and accept the discount.

**Test your understanding 6 – Practice questions**

1    The correct answer is C.

Credit policies consist of the level of credit offered on sales to customers and are influenced by the levels of bad debt risk the entity is comfortable with. Purchases of good have nothing to do with an entity's credit risk policy.

2    **Target receivables**

| **End of July** | **Days** | | **$** |
|---|---|---|---|
| July sales | 31 | | 110,000 |
| June sales (balance) | 14 | (14/30 × $95,000) | 44,333 |
| | 45 | | 154,333 |

| **End of August** | **Days** | | **$** |
|---|---|---|---|
| August sales | 31 | | 120,000 |
| July sales (balance) | 9 | (9/31 × $110,000) | 31,935 |
| | 40 | | 151,935 |

**Target collections**

| | July $ | August $ |
|---|---|---|
| Receivables at the beginning of the month | 165,000 | 154,533 |
| Sales in the month | 110,000 | 120,000 |
| | 275,000 | 274,333 |
| Receivables at the end of the month | (154,333) | (151,935) |
| Target collections in the month | 120,667 | 122,398 |

3    Choose 5 from the following list:

-    bank references

-    trade references

-    visit to the customer's premises

-    competitors

-    published information

-    credit reference agencies

-    legal sources of credit information

-    entity sales records

-    credit scoring

-    credit rating (large corporate customers only).

4    The two options can be analysed as follows:

| | **Without the new credit policy** | **With the new credit policy** |
|---|---|---|
| Annual sales | $12,000,000 | $13,200,000 |
| Average trade receivables | $1,000,000 | $2,200,000 |
| | ($12m × 30/360) | ($13.2m × 60/360) |
| Increase in trade receivables | | $1,200,000 |
| Irrecoverable debts | $240,000 (= 2%) | $396,000 (= 3%) |
| Increase in Irrecoverable debts | | $156,000 |
| | | |
| Increase in annual sales | | $1,200,000 |

| | $ | $ |
|---|---|---|
| Increase in annual contribution (40%) | | 480,000 |
| Increase in Irrecoverable debts | 156,000 | |
| Increase in interest cost of receivables (8% × $1,200,000) | 96,000 | |
| | | (252,000) |
| Net increase in profit before tax | | 228,000 |

5   Discount as a percentage of amount to be paid = 2.5/97.5 = 2.56%

Saving is 2 months and there are 12/2 = 6 periods in a year.

Annualised cost of discount % is

$(1 + 0.0256)^6 - 1 = 0.1638 = 16.38\%$.

The loan rate is 18%.

It would therefore be worthwhile offering the discount.

6   The answer is 19.5%

**Step 1**

Work out the discount available and the amount due if the discount were taken.

Discount available on a $100 invoice = 1.75% × $100 = $1.75.

Amount due after discount = $100 × $1.75 = $98.25

**Step 2**

The effective interest cost of not taking the discount is:

1.75 ÷ 98.25 = 0.0178 (rounded to 0.018)

for an 8 – 3 = five-week period.

**Step 3**

Calculate the equivalent annual rate. There are ten five-week periods in a year.

The equivalent interest annual rate is $(1 + 0.018)^{10} - 1 = 0.195$ or 19.5%.

7   The relative costs and benefits are as follows:

**Option 1 – Factoring**

| | | |
|---|---|---|
| Reduction in receivables days | = 15 days | |
| Reduction in receivables | = 15 ÷ 365 × $20m | = $821,916 |
| Effect on profit before tax: | | |
| Finance cost saving | = (13% × $821,916) | = $106,849 |
| Administrative savings | | = $200,000 |
| Service charge | = (1% × $20m) | = ($200,000) |
| Insurance premium | | = ($80,000) |
| | | |
| Net profit benefit | | = $26,849 |

8    The relative costs and benefits are as follows

**Option 2 – The discount**

With year-end receivables at $4.5 million, the receivables collection period was: $4.5m ÷ $20m × 365 = 82 days.

The scheme of discounts would change this as follows:

10 days for 20% of customers

20 days for 30% of customers

82 days for 50% of customers

Average receivables days become:

$(20\% \times 10) + (30\% \times 20) + (50\% \times 82) = 49$ days

Hence, average receivables would reduce from the present $4.5 million to

$49 \times \$20m \div 365 = \$2,684,932$

Finance cost saving = $13\% \times (\$4,500,000 - \$2,684,932) = \$235,959$

The cost of the discount:

$(3\% \times 20\% \times \$20m) + (1.5\% \times 30\% \times \$20m) = (\$210,000)$

The net benefit to profit before tax: $25,959

9    The figures imply that **factoring is marginally the more attractive**, but this result relies on the predicted proportions of customers actually taking up the discount and paying on time. It also neglects the possibility that some customers will insist on taking the discount without bringing forward their payments. Marton would have to consider a suitable response to this problem.

Conversely, the assessment of the value of using the factor depends on the factor lowering Marton's receivables days. If the factor retains these benefits for itself, rather than passing them on to Marton, this will raise the cost of the factoring option. The two parties should clearly specify their mutual requirements from the factoring arrangement on a contractual basis.

10    The answer is

(a)    Receivables days = $6m ÷ $40m × 365 = 55 days

(b)    Cost of financing receivables = $6m × 10% = $600,000.

# Working Capital Management – Inventory Control

## Chapter learning objectives

| Lead outcome | Component outcome |
| --- | --- |
| D3. Apply different techniques used to manage working capital | a. Apply policies relating to elements of operating and cash cycle |
| | c. Explain risks relating to working capital |

## 1 Session content

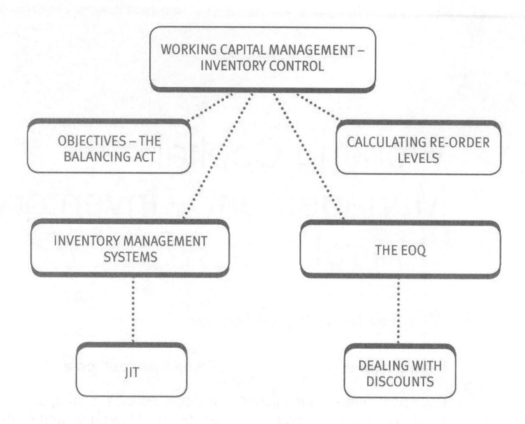

## 2 The objectives of inventory management

Inventory is a major investment for many entities. Manufacturing entities can potentially be carrying inventory equivalent to between 3 and 6 months' worth of sales depending on where they source their inventory from and the relative power of suppliers. It is therefore essential to reduce the levels of inventory held to the necessary minimum.

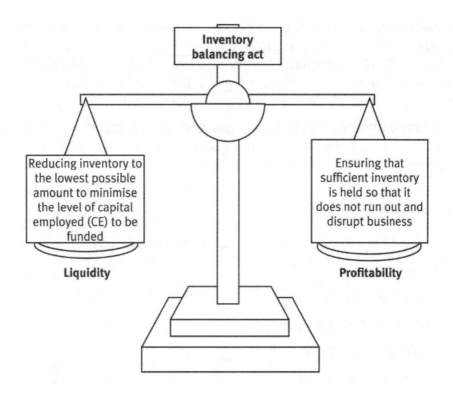

## Costs of high inventory levels

Keeping inventory levels high is expensive owing to:

- the foregone interest that is lost from tying up capital in inventory
- holding costs:
    - storage
    - stores administration
    - risk of theft/damage/obsolescence

### Costs of high inventory levels

Carrying inventory involves a major working capital investment and therefore levels need to be very tightly controlled. The cost is not just that of purchasing the goods, but also storing, insuring, and managing them once they are in inventory.

Interest costs: once goods are purchased, capital is tied up in them and until sold on (in their current state or converted into a finished product), the capital earns no return. This lost return is an opportunity cost of holding the inventory.

> **Other risks:** once stored, the goods will need to be insured. Specialist equipment may be needed to transport the inventory to where it is to be used. Staff will be required to manage the warehouse and protect against theft and if inventory levels are high, significant investment may be required in sophisticated inventory control systems.
>
> The longer inventory is held, the greater the risk that it will deteriorate or become out of date. This is true of perishable goods, fashion items and high-technology products, for example.

## Costs of low inventory levels

If inventory levels are kept too low, the business faces alternative problems:

- stockouts:
    - lost contribution
    - production stoppages
    - emergency orders
- high re-order/setup costs
- lost quantity discounts

### Costs of low inventory levels

> **Stockout:** if a business runs out of a particular product used in manufacturing it may cause interruptions to the production process – causing idle time, stockpiling of work-in-progress (WIP) or possibly missed orders. Alternatively, running out of finished goods or inventory can result in dissatisfied customers and perhaps future lost orders if custom is switched to alternative suppliers. If a stockout looms, the business may attempt to avoid it by acquiring the goods needed at short m, the amount of computerisation more expensive or poorer quality supplier.
>
> **Re-order/setup costs:** each time inventory runs out, new supplies must be acquired. If the goods are bought in, the costs that arise are associated with administration – completion of a purchase requisition, authorisation of the order, placing the order with the supplier, taking and checking the delivery and final settlement of the invoice. If the goods are to be manufactured, the costs of setting up the machinery will be incurred each time a new batch is produced.
>
> **Lost quantity discounts:** purchasing items in bulk will often attract a discount from the supplier. If only small amounts are bought at one time in order to keep inventory levels low, the quantity discounts will not be available.

## The challenge

 The objective of good inventory management is therefore to determine:

- the optimum re-order level – how many items should be left in inventory when the next order is placed, and

- the optimum re-order quantity – how many items should be ordered when the order is placed

In practice, this means striking a balance between holding costs on the one hand and stock-out and re-order costs on the other.

 The balancing act between liquidity and profitability, which might also be considered to be a trade-off between holding costs and stock-out/re-order costs, is key to any discussion on inventory management.

---

### Terminology

Other key terms associated with inventory management include:

- lead time – the lag between when an order is placed and the item is delivered

- buffer inventory – the basic level of inventory kept for emergencies. A buffer is required because both demand and lead time will fluctuate and predictions can only be based on best estimates.

Ensure you can distinguish between the various terms used: re-order level, re-order quantity, lead time and buffer inventory.

---

## 3 Economic order quantity (EOQ)

For businesses that do not use just in time (J IT) inventory management systems (discussed in more detail below), there is an optimum order quantity for inventory items, known as the EOQ.

## The challenge

The aim of the EOQ model is to minimise the total cost of holding and ordering inventory.

## The calculation

The EOQ can be found using a formula:

$$EOQ = \sqrt{\frac{2C_O D}{C_H}}$$

where:

$C_O$ = cost per order

D = annual demand

$C_H$ = cost of holding one unit for one year.

> ### Test your understanding 1 – EOQ
>
> An entity requires 1,000 units of material X per month. The cost per order is $30 regardless of the size of the order. The annual holding costs are $2.88 per unit.
>
> **Required:**
>
> Investigate the total cost of buying the material in quantities of 400, 500, or 600 units at one time. Identify the cheapest option.
>
> Apply the EOQ formula to prove your answer is correct.

## Assumptions

The following assumptions are made:

- demand and lead time are constant and known

- purchase price is constant

- no buffer inventory held as it is assumed that it is not needed since demand and lead times are known with certainty

 These assumptions are critical and should be discussed when considering the validity of the model and its conclusions, e.g. in practice, demand and/or lead time may vary.

## EOQ further information – explanation and derivation

To minimise the total cost of holding and ordering inventory, it is necessary to balance the relevant costs. These are:

- the variable costs of holding the inventory

- the fixed costs of placing the order

### Holding costs

The model assumes that it costs a certain amount to hold a unit of inventory for a year. Therefore, as the average level of inventory increases, so too will the total annual holding costs incurred.

Because of the assumption that demand per period is known and is constant (see below), conclusions can be drawn over the average inventory level in relationship to the order quantity.

When new batches or items of inventory are purchased or made at periodic intervals, the inventory levels are assumed to exhibit the following pattern over time.

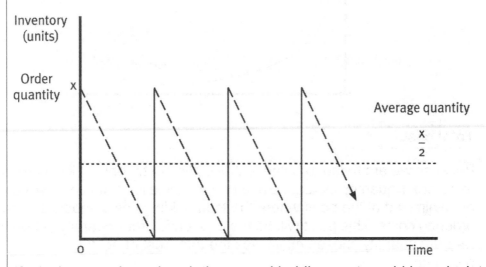

If x is the quantity ordered, the annual holding cost would be calculated as:

Holding cost per unit ($C_H$)× Average inventory:

$$C_H \times \frac{x}{2}$$

We therefore see an upward sloping, linear relationship between the re-order quantity and total annual holding costs.

## Ordering costs

The model assumes that a fixed cost is incurred every time an order is placed (referred to as $C_O$ in the formula). Therefore, as the order quantity increases, there is a fall in the number of orders required, which reduces the total ordering cost.

If D is the annual expected sales demand, the annual order cost is calculated as:

Order cost per order × no. of orders per annum.

$$C_O \times \frac{D}{X}$$

However, the fixed nature of the cost results in a downward sloping, curved relationship.

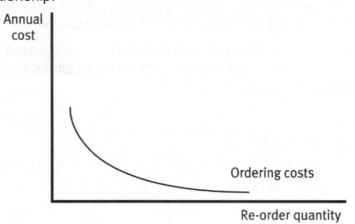

## Total costs

Because we are trying to balance these two costs (one which increases as re-order quantity increases and one which falls), total costs will always be minimised at the point where the total holding costs equals the total ordering costs. This point will be the economic order quantity (when the re-order quantity chosen minimises the total cost of holding and ordering).

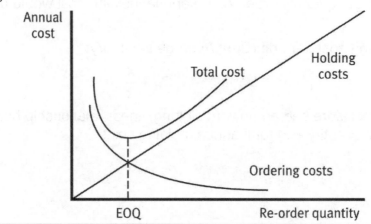

## Dealing with quantity discounts

Discounts may be offered for ordering in large quantities. If the EOQ is smaller than the order size needed for a discount, should the order size be increased above the EOQ?

To work out the answer you should carry out the following steps:

**Step 1:** Calculate EOQ, ignoring discounts.

**Step 2:** If the EOQ is below the quantity qualifying for a discount, calculate the total annual inventory cost arising from using the EOQ.

**Step 3:** Recalculate total annual inventory costs using the order size required to just obtain each discount.

**Step 4:** Compare the cost of Steps 2 and 3 with the saving from the discount, and select the minimum cost alternative.

**Step 5:** Repeat for all discount levels.

### Test your understanding 2 – EOQ and discounts

Wolvo is a retailer of barrels. The entity has an annual demand of 30,000 barrels. The barrels cost $12 each. Supplies can be obtained immediately, with ordering and transport costs amounting to $200 per order. The annual cost of holding one barrel in stock is estimated to be $1.20 per barrel.

A 2% discount is available on orders of at least 5,000 barrels and a 2.5% discount is available if the order quantity is 7,500 barrels or above.

**Required:**

Calculate the EOQ ignoring the discount and calculate if it would change once the discount is taken into account.

### Criticisms of EOQ

The EOQ model can be criticised in several ways:

- It is based on simplifying assumptions, such as constant and predictable material usage rates.
- It will not indicate the optimal purchase quantity when there are price discounts for buying in larger quantities.
- It ignores the problem of managing stock-outs.
- It is inconsistent with the philosophy of just-in-time management and total quality management.

### 2015 CIMA Professional Qualification Syllabus, Operational Level Case Study Exam, August 2018 v1 – Question (Modified)

You work in Herbaboil, a drinks manufacturer specialising in flavoured tea drinks.

Jack Ford, the Head of Finance, sends you the following email:

**From:    Jack Ford,**

**To:        Finance Officer**

**Subject: New range of infusions – inventory management**

I've been working with Steven Gomez, Head of Production, on some of the financial implications from expanding the infusions range of products to include Peppermint and Peach & Raspberry flavoured teas.

Steve has asked me whether the Economic Order Quantity (EOQ) model might be a useful tool for managing inventory levels. Inventory management is going to be particularly important for the new range because there are so many different raw material inputs that need to be held, which is going to increase our inventory holding costs. There are various bulk discounts available and I know that Steve is keen to take advantage of these as far as possible.

I would like you to prepare a briefing note that I can send to Steve which:

- Explains what information we would need to calculate the EOQ for infusion raw materials

- Explains the appropriateness of using the EOQ model to manage the level of inventory held

© Copyright CIMA – 2015 CIMA Professional Qualification Operational Level F1 Financial Reporting and Taxation Case Study Exam August 2018

**2015 CIMA Professional Qualification Syllabus, Operational Level Case Study Exam, August 2018 – Suggested Answer**

**Note this is an extract from the suggested answer and focuses solely on the areas of the case study relevant to the F1 exam**

## INVENTORY MANAGEMENT

### Information required to calculate EOQ

For each type of infusions raw material (for example, paper, packaging, dried fruit, fruit and herbal leaves) we will need to establish:

- Annual demand which will be driven by the level of anticipated production.

- The cost of an individual order which will include procurement staff time, internal administrative costs and any goods in delivery costs.

- The cost of holding one unit of inventory for one year. Holding costs will include insurance, storage costs (including energy used in the warehouse, staff training costs for safe handling, handling staff time) and the finance cost associated with the investment in working capital.

### The appropriateness of the EOQ model:

In principle, the EOQ model is useful because it would give us for each type of raw material inventory the order quantity which would minimise the overall cost of both ordering and holding that inventory. However, the EOQ model is based on assumptions which can make its practical application difficult.

The model assumes that demand for the raw material is constant throughout the year and can be determined with a reasonable level of certainty. There is still considerable uncertainty regarding how popular and successful the new range will be; there is also uncertainty over which flavours will be popular. Demand for the new infusions is likely to gradually grow through the year as more and more people hear about and try it.

It is assumed that the lead time is constant or zero, however for us it is possible that lead times will vary through the year, especially as a large portion of raw materials are plant-based and dependent upon harvests and crop yields. Both uncertainty in demand and variable lead times can be adjusted for in the EOQ model by setting a safety or buffer level of inventory. This increases overall holding costs but allows flexibility to schedule production where demand is higher than expected or where lead times are longer than expected. The downside though of holding safety inventory is that the risk of obsolescence increases (especially for the plant-based materials).

> The model also assumes that purchase costs are constant with no bulk discounts and that holding costs are variable with the level of inventory held. The former of these assumptions can be dealt with by expanding the analysis to consider the inventory level that minimises the total of holding, ordering and net of discount purchase costs. The latter assumption is more difficult to justify because in reality a significant portion of holding costs such as the costs of operating the warehouse are fixed in nature.
>
> In conclusion, the EOQ model is not going to be wholly appropriate to use on a practical level. This is because of the uncertainty of future demand and because of the nature of our inventory. However, it could be used as a guide with practical factors such as shelf life of the plant-based materials taken into account.

## 4 Inventory management systems

A number of systems have been developed to simplify the inventory management process:

- periodic review
- JIT.

### Periodic review system (constant order cycle system)

Inventory levels are reviewed at fixed intervals, e.g. every four weeks. The inventory in hand is then made up to a predetermined level, which takes account of:

- likely demand before the next review
- likely demand during the lead time.

Thus a four-weekly review in a system where the lead time was two weeks would demand that inventory be made up to the likely maximum demand for the next six weeks.

### Periodic review systems

A company has estimated that, for the coming season, weekly demand for components will be 80 units. At the most recent stock count, 250 units of inventory where counted.  Suppliers take three weeks on average to deliver goods once they have been ordered and a buffer inventory of 35 units is held.

**If the inventory levels are reviewed every six weeks, how many units will need to be ordered to ensure the buffer is maintained?**

**Solution**

Demand per week is 80 units. The next review will be in six weeks by which time 80 × 6 = 480 units will have been used.

An order would then be placed and during the lead time – three weeks – another 80 × 3 = 240 units will be used.

The business therefore needs to have 480 + 240 = 720 units in inventory to ensure a stock-out is avoided. Since buffer inventory of 35 units is required, the total number needed is 755 units.

Since the current inventory level is 250 units, an order must be placed for 755 – 250 = 505 units.

### Slow moving inventory

Certain items may have a high individual value, but be subject to infrequent demand.

In most organisations, about 20% of items held make up 80% of total usage (the 80/20 rule).

### Slow-moving inventory

Management need to review inventory usage to identify slow-moving inventory. An aged inventory analysis should be produced and reviewed regularly so that action can be taken. Actions could include:

- elimination of obsolete items

- slow-moving inventory items only ordered when actually needed (unless a minimum order quantity is imposed by the supplier)

- review of demand level estimates on which re-order decisions are based.

A regular report of slow-moving items is useful in that management is made aware of changes in demand and of possible obsolescence. Arrangements may then be made to reduce or eliminate inventory levels or, on confirmation of obsolescence, for disposal.

## Just in Time (JIT) systems

 JIT is a series of manufacturing and supply chain techniques that aim to minimise inventory levels and improve customer service by manufacturing not only at the exact time customers require, but also in the exact quantities they need and at competitive prices.

In JIT systems, the balancing act is dispensed with. Inventory is reduced to an absolute minimum or eliminated altogether.

Aims of JIT are:

- a smooth flow of work through the manufacturing plant

- a flexible production process which is responsive to the customer's requirements

- reduction in capital tied up in inventory.

This involves the elimination of all activities performed that do not add value = waste.

**Just in time systems**

JIT extends much further than a concentration on inventory levels. It centres around the elimination of waste. Waste is defined as any activity performed within a manufacturing company which does not add value to the product. Examples of waste are:

- raw material inventory
- WIP inventory
- finished goods inventory
- materials handling
- quality problems (rejects and reworks, etc.)
- queues and delays on the shop floor
- long raw material lead times
- long customer lead times
- unnecessary clerical and accounting procedures.

JIT attempts to eliminate waste at every stage of the manufacturing process, notably by the elimination of:

- WIP, by reducing batch sizes (often to one)
- raw materials inventory, by the suppliers delivering direct to the shop floor JIT for use
- scrap and rework, by an emphasis on total quality control of the design, of the process, and of the materials
- finished goods inventory, by reducing lead times so that all products are made to order
- material handling costs, by re-design of the shop floor so that goods move directly between adjacent work centres.

The combination of these concepts in JIT results in:

- a smooth flow of work through the manufacturing plant
- a flexible production process which is responsive to the customer's requirements
- reduction in capital tied up in inventory.

A JIT manufacturer looks for a single supplier who can provide **high quality,** frequent and **reliable** deliveries, rather than the lowest price. In return, the supplier can expect more business under long-term **purchase orders**, thus providing **greater certainty** in forecasting activity levels. Very often the suppliers will be located close to the company.

Long-term contracts and single sourcing strengthen buyer-supplier relationships and tend to result in a higher quality product. Inventory problems are shifted back onto suppliers, with deliveries being made as required.

The spread of JIT in the production process inevitably affects those in delivery and transportation. Smaller, more frequent loads are required at shorter notice. The haulier is regarded as almost a partner to the manufacturer, but tighter schedules are required of hauliers, with penalties for non-delivery.

Reduction in inventory levels reduces the time taken to count inventory and the clerical cost. However with JIT, although inventory holding costs are close to zero, inventory ordering costs are high

## 5 Inventory control systems

Three main systems are used to monitor and control inventory levels:

1 reorder level system (whereby inventory is ordered at a particular, set order level)

2 periodic review system (whereby inventory is checked and ordered at set periods in time)

3 mixed systems, incorporating elements of both of the above.

 **Control systems explained**

### Reorder level system

With this system, whenever the current inventory level falls below a pre-set 'reorder level' (ROL), a replenishment (replacement) order is made. Since there is normally a gap (lead time) between the placing of an order and receipt of supplies this has to be allowed for. Buffer inventory is usually held as insurance against variations in demand and lead time.

This system used to be known as the 'two-bin' system. Inventory is kept in two bins, one with an amount equal to the ROL quantity, and the rest in the other. Inventory is drawn from the latter until it runs out, whence a replenishment order is triggered.

A reorder level system is simple enough to implement if the variables (such as average usage, supplier lead time, etc.) are known with certainty. In practice, this is rarely the case.

### Periodic review system

This is also referred to as a 'constant cycle' system. Inventory levels are reviewed after a fixed interval, for example, on the first of the month. Replenishment orders are issued where necessary, to top up inventory levels to pre-set target levels. This means that order sizes are variable.

### Mixed systems

In practice, mixtures of both systems are sometimes used, depending on the nature of the problem, the amount of computerisation and so on.

## 6    Calculating the re-order level (ROL)

### Known demand and lead time

Having decided how much inventory to re-order, the next problem is when to re-order. The firm needs to identify a level of inventory which can be reached before an order needs to be placed.

 The **ROL** is the quantity of inventory on hand when an order is placed.

**When demand and lead time are known** with certainty the ROL may be calculated exactly, i.e. ROL = demand in the lead time.

### Test your understanding 3 – ROL

Using the data for Wolvo from TYU 2, assume that the entity adopts the EOQ as its order quantity and that it now takes two weeks for an order to be delivered.

**Calculate how frequently the entity will place an order? Calculate how much inventory it will have on hand when the order is placed?**

### ROL with variable demand or variable lead time

When there is uncertainty over demand or lead time are known then the **ROL will be calculated as maximum demand x maximum lead time**. This will lead to the creation of **buffer stock.**

### Buffer stock

Buffer stock is a quantity of inventory that should not usually be needed, but that might be needed if actual demand during the supply lead time exceeds the average demand or if lead times are longer than expected. Buffer stock has a cost. The annual cost of holding buffer stock is the amount of the buffer stock multiplied by the annual holding cost for one unit of the inventory item.

**Calculating buffer stock:**

|  | Units |
|---|---|
| Reorder level* <br> (Maximum demand per day, in units × maximum re-order lead time) | X |
| Average usage <br> (Average demand per day, in units × average re-order lead time) | Y |
| Buffer Stock | X – Y |

\* note that this is the ROL when demand or lead time are uncertain.

Where there is uncertainty, an optimum level of buffer stock (or inventory) must be found.

This depends on:

- variability of demand

- cost of holding inventory

- cost of stockouts

You will not be required to perform this calculation in the examination.

 **Inventory warning levels**

Two warning levels might also be used, to indicate when the quantity of an item in inventory is either:

- higher than should be expected, or

- below the buffer stock level.

If the quantity of inventory goes above the maximum level or below the minimum level, the inventory manager should monitor the position carefully, and where appropriate take control measures.

The **maximum inventory level** should be:

- Reorder level

- Plus reorder quantity

- Minus [Minimum demand per day/week, in units] × [Minimum re-order lead time].

The maximum inventory level will occur when a new order has just been delivered by the supplier, the order has been delivered within the minimum lead time, and demand has been at a minimum during the lead time.

The **minimum inventory level** should be the buffer stock level:

- Reorder level

- Minus [Average demand per day/week, in units] × [Average re-order lead time].

## Test your understanding 4 – Practice questions

1   Identify which of the following is not a required assumption for the basic EOQ model?

   A   The lead time is zero

   B   There are no stock-outs

   C   The demand is known and constant

   D   The purchase price is constant regardless of order quantity

2   Monthly demand for a product is 10,000 units. The purchase price is $10/unit and the entity's cost of finance is 15% pa. Warehouse storage costs per unit pa are $2/unit. The supplier charges $200 per order for delivery. Holding costs should include the 15% finance costs.

   **Calculate the EOQ.**

3   Doris uses component V22 in its construction process. The entity has a demand of 45,000 components pa. They cost $4.50 each. There is no lead time between order and delivery, and ordering costs amount to $100 per order. The annual cost of holding one component in inventory is estimated to be $0.65.

   A 0.5% discount is available on orders of at least 3,000 components and a 0.75% discount is available if the order quantity is 6,000 components or above.

   **Calculate the EOQ.**

4   **Using the information from question 3 calculate the total annual costs for the entity.**

5   **Using the information from questions 3 and 4 calculate the cost of ordering 6,000 units and identify any savings that could be made.**

6   Using the data in question 3 and ignoring discounts, assume that the entity adopts the EOQ as its order quantity and that it now takes three weeks for an order to be delivered.

   **Calculate how frequently will the entity place an order.**

7   **Using the data in question 6 calculate how much inventory it will have on hand when the order is placed.**

8    **Which ONE of the following would not normally be considered a cost of holding inventory?**

A    Inventory obsolescence

B    Insurance cost of inventory

C    Interest cost of cash invested in inventory

D    Loss of sales from a stock-out.

9    An entity uses the economic order quantity model (EOQ model). Demand for the entity's product is 36,000 units each year and is evenly distributed each day. The cost of placing an order is $10 and the cost of holding a unit of inventory for a year is $2.

**How many orders should the entity make in a year?**

A    60

B    120

C    300

D    600

## 7 Summary Diagram

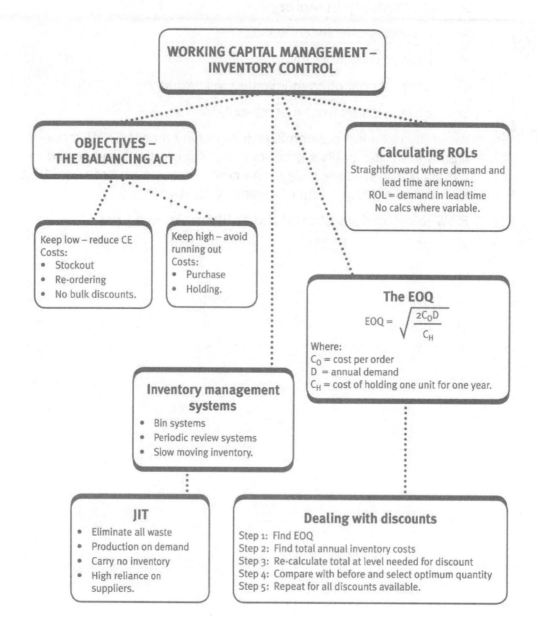

# Test your understanding answers

## Test your understanding 1 – EOQ

| | Order quantity | | |
| --- | --- | --- | --- |
| | **400 units** | **500 units** | **600 units** |
| Average inventory | 200 | 250 | 300 |
| No. of orders per annum | 30 | 24 | 20 |
| | $ | $ | $ |
| Holding cost – average inventory × $2.88 | 576 | 720 | 864 |

| | Order quantity | | |
| --- | --- | --- | --- |
| | **400 units** | **500 units** | **600 units** |
| Ordering cost – no. of orders × $30 | 900 | 720 | 600 |
| Total cost | 1,476 | 1,440 | 1,464 |

Therefore the best option is to order 500 units each time.

Note that this is the point at which total cost is minimised and the holding costs and order costs are equal.

**Solution using the formula:**

$$EOQ = \sqrt{\frac{2C_oD}{C_H}}$$

$C_O = 30$

$D = 1,000 \times 12 = 12,000$

$C_H = 2.88$

$$EOQ = \sqrt{\frac{EOQ = 2 \times 30 \times 12,000}{2.88}} = 500$$

## Test your understanding 2 – EOQ and discounts

**Step 1 Calculate EOQ, ignoring discounts.**

$$EOQ = \sqrt{\frac{2C_O D}{C_H}}$$

$C_O$ = $200

D = 30,000 units

$C_H$ = $1.20

$$EOQ = \sqrt{\frac{2 \times 200 \times 30,000}{1.2}} = 3,162$$

**Step 2 As this is below the level for discounts, calculate total annual inventory costs.**

Total annual costs for the entity will comprise holding costs plus re-ordering costs.

$$= \quad (\text{Average inventory} \times C_H) \quad + \quad (\text{Number of re-orders p.a.} \times C_O)$$

$$= \quad \frac{3,162}{2} \times \$1.20 \quad + \quad \frac{30,000}{3,162} \times \$200$$

= $1,897.20 + $1,897.53

= $3,794.73

**Step 3 Recalculate total annual inventory costs using the order size required to just obtain the discount.**

At order quantity 5,000, total costs are as follows.

$$= \quad (\text{Average inventory} \times C_H) \quad + \quad (\text{Number of re-orders p.a.} \times C_O)$$

$$= \quad \frac{5,000}{2} \times \$1.20 \quad + \quad \frac{30,000}{5,000} \times \$200$$

= $3,000 + $1,200

= $4,200

|  | $ |
|---|---|
| Extra costs of ordering in batches of 5,000 (4,200 – 3,795) | (405) |
| Saving on discount 2% × $12 × 30,000 | 7,200 |

**Step 4 Net saving** — 6,795

Hence batches of 5,000 are worthwhile.

## Step 3 (again)

At order quality 7,500, total costs are as follows:

$$= \quad (\text{Average inventory} \times C_H) \quad + \quad (\text{Number of re-orders p.a.} \times C_O)$$

$$= \quad \frac{7,500}{2} \times \$1.20 \quad + \quad \frac{30,000}{7,500} \times \$200$$

= $4,500 + $800

= $5,300

| | |
|---|---|
| Extra costs of ordering in batches of 7,500 (5,300 – 4,200) | (1,100) |
| Saving on extra discount (2.5% – 2%) × $12 × 30,000) | 1,800 |

**Step 4 Net saving (again)** — 700

So a further cost saving can be made on orders of 7,500 units.

**Note:** If Step 1 produces an EOQ at which a discount would have been available, and the holding cost would be reduced by taking the discount, i.e. where CH is based on the purchase price × the cost of finance, the EOQ must be recalculated using the new CH before the above steps are followed.

## Alternative approach

An alternative approach is to compare the total costs at each level and choose the lowest total cost as the best order level. The total cost will be made up of the total purchasing costs, the holding costs and the order costs as follows:

| Order size | 3,162 | 5,000 | 7,500 |
|---|---|---|---|
| | $ | $ | $ |
| Total purchase costs (30,000 barrels × $12 each) | 360,000 | 360,000 | 360,000 |
| Discount | nil | (7,200) | (9,000) |
| Holding and order costs | 3,795 | 4,200 | 5,300 |
| | 363,795 | 357,000 | 356,300 |

> **(Note that many of the same calculations would be needed in order to complete this table)**
>
> This confirms that the best order size would be 7,500 units.

**Test your understanding 3 - ROL**

- Annual demand is 30,000. The original EOQ is 3,162. The entity will therefore place an order once every

  3,162 ÷ 30,000 × 365 days = 38 days

- The entity must be sure that there is sufficient inventory on hand when it places an order to last the two weeks' lead time. It must therefore place an order when there is two weeks' worth of demand in inventory:

  i.e. ROL is 2 ÷ 52 × 30,000 = 1,154 units

**Test your understanding 4 – Practice questions**

1    The correct answer is A.

     The EOQ model assumes a known and constant order lead time. The lead time does not have to be zero.

2    The EOQ is 3,703 units

$$EOQ = \sqrt{\frac{2C_oD}{C_H}}$$

$C_O = 200$

$D = 10,000 \times 12 = 120,000$

$C_H = (10 \times 0.15) + 2 = 3.5$

$$EOQ = \sqrt{\frac{2 \times 200 \times 120,000}{3.5}} = 3,703$$

3    **EOQ = 3,721 units**

$$EOQ = \sqrt{\frac{2C_oD}{C_H}}$$

$C^O = 100$

$D = 45,000$

$C^H = 0.65$

$$EOQ = \sqrt{\frac{2 \times 100 \times 45,000}{0.65}} = 3,721,\text{ which would qualify for a 0.5\% discount}$$

4    Total annual costs for the entity will comprise holding costs plus re-ordering costs.

= (Average inventory × $C_H$) + (Number of re-orders pa × $C_O$)

$$= \left(\frac{3,721}{2} \times \$0.65\right) + \left(\frac{45,000}{3,721} \times \$100\right)$$

= \$2,419

5    At order quantity 6,000, total costs are as follows.

(6,000 × \$0.65/2) + (45,000 × \$100 ÷ 6,000) = \$2,700

A saving can be made on orders of 6,000 units as follows:

|  | $ |
|---|---:|
| Extra costs of ordering in batches of 6,000 (2,700 – 2,419) | (281) |
| Less: Saving on extra discount (0.75% – 0.5%) × \$4.5 × 45,000 | 506.25 |
| Net cost saving | 225.25 |

6    Annual demand is 45,000. The original EOQ is 3,721. The entity will therefore place an order once every

3,721 ÷ 45,000 × 365 days = 30 days

7    The entity must be sure that there is sufficient inventory on hand when it places its order to last the three weeks lead time. It must therefore place an order when there is three weeks work of demand in inventory, i.e. 3/52 × 45,000 = 2,596 units.

8    D

9    A

$$EOQ = \sqrt{\frac{2C_O D}{C_H}}$$

$C_O$ = 10

D = 36,000

$C_H$ = 2

$$EOQ = \sqrt{\frac{EOQ = 2 \times 10 \times 36,000}{2}} = 600$$

Therefore, EOQ = 600

If demand = 36,000 units per year and we order in quantities of 600 we will need to place 60 orders per year (36,000/600).

# Working Capital Management – Cash Control

## Chapter learning objectives

### Lead outcome

D3. Apply different techniques used to manage working capital

### Component outcome

a. Apply policies relating to elements of operating and cash cycle

b Prepare forecasts

c. Explain risks relating to working capital

## 1 Session content

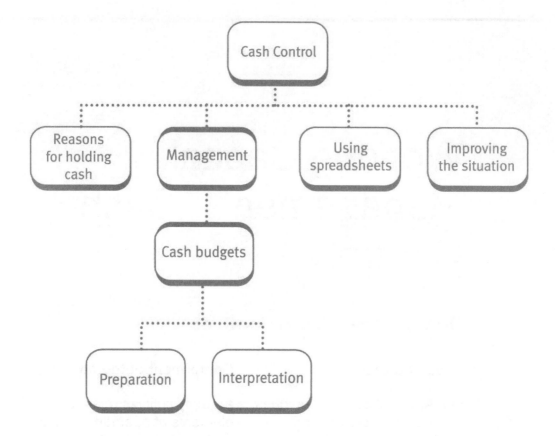

## 2 Reasons for holding cash

Although cash needs to be invested to earn returns, businesses need to keep a certain amount readily available. The reasons include:

- Transactions motive – cash required to meet day-to-day expenses, e.g. payroll, payment of suppliers, etc.

- Precautionary motive – cash held to give a cushion against unplanned expenditure (the cash equivalent of buffer inventory).

- Investment/speculative motive – cash kept available to take advantage of market investment opportunities.

Failure to carry sufficient cash levels can lead to:

- loss of settlement discounts

- loss of supplier goodwill – trade suppliers refuse to offer further credit, charge higher prices or downgrade the priority with which orders are processed

- poor industrial relations – if wages are not paid on time, industrial action may well result, damaging production in the short-term and relationships and motivation in the medium-term

- potential liquidation – a court may be petitioned to wind up the entity if it consistently fails to pay bills as they fall due.

## 3 Efficient cash management

The amount of cash available to an entity at any given time is largely dependent on the efficiency with which cash flows are managed.

The key principles of cash management are:

- collect debts as quickly as possible

- pay suppliers as late as possible

- bank cash takings promptly

Once again the firm faces a balancing act:

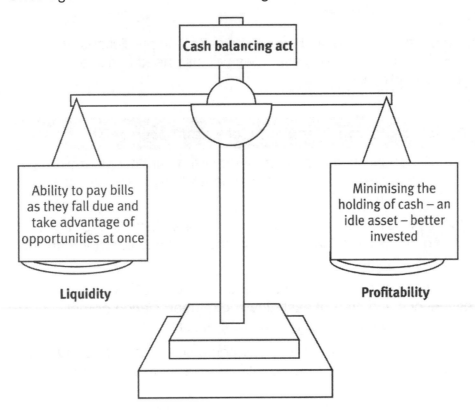

The main area associated with managing cash is the cash forecast and cash flow forecast.

## 4 Cash forecasts/budgets

 A **cash forecast** (sometimes referred to as a cash budget) is an estimate of cash receipts and payments for a future period under existing conditions.

Cash forecasts are used to:

- assess and integrate operating budgets

- plan for cash shortages and surpluses

- compare with actual spending.

There are two different techniques that can be used to create a cash budget:

- a receipts and payments forecast

- a statement of financial position forecast

## Receipts and payments forecast

This is a forecast of cash receipts and payments based on predictions of sales and cost of sales. The timings of the cash flows will also need consideration to produce a reasonable forecast.

### Preparing forecasts from planned receipts and payments

Every type of cash inflow and receipt, along with their timings, must be forecast. Note that cash receipts and payments differ from sales and cost of sales in the statement of profit or loss because:

- not all cash receipts or payments affect the statement of profit or loss, e.g. the issue of new shares or the purchase of a non-current asset

- some statement of profit or loss items are derived from accounting conventions and are not cash flows, e.g. depreciation or the profit/loss on the sale of a non-current asset

- the timing of cash receipts and payments does not coincide with the statement of profit or loss accounting period, e.g. a sale made on credit

- irrecoverable debts will never be received in cash and doubtful debts may not be received..

Approach to preparing a cash forecast:

### Step 1 – Prepare a pro-forma

There is no definitive format that should be used for a cash forecast. However, whichever format you decide to use, it should include the following:

(i)     A clear distinction between the cash receipts and cash payments for each control period. Your budget should not consist of a jumble of cash flows. It should be logically arranged with a subtotal for receipts and a subtotal for payments.

(ii)    A figure for the net cash flow for each period. Managers find that a figure for the net cash flow helps to draw attention to the cash flow implications of their actions during the period.

(iii)   The closing cash balance for each period. The closing balance for each period will be the opening balance for the following period.

The following is a typical format:

| Month: | 1 $ | 2 $ | 3 $ | 4 $ |
|---|---|---|---|---|
| Receipts (few lines) | | | | |
| Sub total | | | | |
| Payments (Many lines) | | | | |
| Sub total | | | | |
| Net cash flow | | | | |
| Opening balance | | | | |
| Closing balance | | | | |

## Step 2 – Fill in the simple figures

Some payments need only a small amount of work to identify the correct figure and timing and can be entered straight into the pro-forma. These would usually include:

- wages and salaries
- fixed overhead expenses
- dividend payments
- purchases of non-current assets.

## Step 3 – Work out the more complex figures

The information on sales and purchases can be more time consuming to deal with, e.g.:

- timings for both sales and purchases must be found from credit periods
- variable overheads may require information about production levels
- purchases may require calculations based on production schedules and inventory balances.

## Test your understanding 1 – Forecast cash receipts

The forecast sales for an entity are as follows:

|  | January $ | February $ | March $ | April $ |
|---|---|---|---|---|
| Sales | 6,000 | 8,000 | 4,000 | 5,000 |

All sales are on credit and receivables tend to pay in the following pattern:

|  | % |
|---|---|
| In month of sale | 10 |
| In month after sale | 40 |
| Two months after sale | 45 |

The entity expects the rate of irrecoverable debts to be 5%.

**Calculate the forecast cash receipts from receivables in April.**

## Test your understanding 2 – Forecast cash payments

A manufacturing business makes and sells widgets. Each widget requires two units of raw materials, which cost $3 each. Production and sales quantities of widgets each month are as follows:

| Month | Sales and production units |
|---|---|
| December (actual) | 50,000 |
| January (budget) | 55,000 |
| February (budget) | 60,000 |
| March (budget) | 65,000 |

In the past, the business has maintained its inventories of raw materials at 100,000 units. However, it plans to increase raw material inventories to 110,000 units at the end of January and 120,000 units at the end of February. The business takes one month's credit from its suppliers.

**Calculate the forecast payments to suppliers for January, February and March for raw material purchases.**

It is important to note candidates will **not** have to prepare a full cash flow forecast in your examination but may be asked to prepare any part of it. The following TYU enables practise of the entire forecast to improve understanding. Exam questions will focus on sections of the forecast.

## Test your understanding 3 – Full cash flow forecast

The following budgeted statement of profit or loss has been prepared for Quest entity for the four months January to April:

|  | January $000 | February $000 | March $000 | April $000 |
|---|---|---|---|---|
| Sales | 60.0 | 50.0 | 70.0 | 60.0 |
| Cost of production | 50.0 | 55.0 | 32.5 | 50.0 |
| (Increase)/decrease in inventory | (5.0) | (17.5) | 20.0 | (5.0) |
| Cost of sales | 45.0 | 37.5 | 52.5 | 45.0 |
| Gross profit | 15.0 | 12.5 | 17.5 | 15.0 |
| Administration and selling overhead | (8.0) | (7.5) | (8.5) | (8.0) |
| Profit before interest | 7.0 | 5.0 | 9.0 | 7.0 |

The working papers provide the following additional information:

- 40% of the production cost relates to direct materials. Materials are bought in the month prior to the month in which they are used. 50% of purchases are paid for in the month of purchase. The remainder are paid for one month later.

- 30% of the production cost relates to direct labour which is paid for when it is used.

- The remainder of the production cost is production overhead. $5,000 per month is a fixed cost which includes $3,000 depreciation. Fixed production overhead costs are paid monthly in arrears. The remaining overhead is variable. The variable production overhead is paid 40% in the month of usage and the balance one month later.

- The administration and selling costs are paid quarterly in advance on 1 January, 1 April, 1 July and 1 October. The amount payable is $15,000 per quarter.

- Trade payables on 1 January Year 5 are expected to be:
  - Direct materials: $10,000
  - Production overheads: $11,000

- All sales are on credit. 20% of receivables are expected to be paid in the month of sale and 80% in the following month. Unpaid trade receivables at the beginning of January were $44,000.

- The entity intends to purchase capital equipment costing $30,000 in February which will be payable in March.

- The bank balance on 1 January Year 5 is expected to be $5,000 overdrawn.

**Required:**

Prepare a cash forecast for each of the months January to March Year 5 for Quest.

## Preparing a cash forecast from a statement of financial position

This is a forecast derived from predictions of future statement of financial positions. Predictions are made of all items except cash, which is then derived as a balancing figure.

 **Illustration**

Used to predict the cash balance at the end of a given period, this method will typically require forecasts of:

- changes to non-current assets (acquisitions and disposals)

- future inventory levels

- future receivables levels

- future payables levels

- changes to share capital and other long-term funding (e.g. bank loans)

- changes to retained profits.

**Example**

CBA is a manufacturing entity in the furniture trade. Its sales have risen sharply over the past six months as a result of an improvement in the economy and a strong housing market. The entity is now showing signs of 'overtrading' and the financial manager, Ms Smith, is concerned about its liquidity. The entity is 1 month from its year-end. Estimated figures for the full 12 months of the current year and forecasts for next year, on present cash management policies, are shown below.

| | Next year $000 | Current year $000 |
|---|---|---|
| **Statement of profit or loss** | | |
| Turnover | 5,200 | 4,200 |
| Less: | | |
| Cost of sales (Note 1) | 3,224 | 2,520 |
| Operating expenses | 650 | 500 |
| | | |
| Operating profit | 1,326 | 1,180 |
| Interest paid | 54 | 48 |
| Tax payable | 305 | 283 |
| | | |
| Profit after tax | 967 | 849 |
| | | |
| Dividends declared | 387 | 339 |
| **Current assets and liabilities at year end:** | | |
| Inventory/work in progress | 625 | 350 |
| Trade receivables | 750 | 520 |
| Cash | 0 | 25 |
| Trade payables | (464) | (320) |
| Other payables (incl. dividends) | (692) | (622) |
| Overdraft | (11) | 0 |
| | | |
| Total equity and liabilities | 208 | (47) |

**Note 1:**

| | | |
|---|---|---|
| Cost of sales includes depreciation of | 225 | 175 |

Ms Smith is considering methods of improving the cash position. A number of actions are being discussed:

**Trade receivables**

Offer a 2 per cent discount to customers who pay within 10 days of despatch of invoices. It is estimated that 50 per cent of customers will take advantage of the new discount scheme. The other 50 per cent will continue to take the average credit period for next year.

**Trade payables and inventory**

Reduce the number of suppliers currently being used and negotiate better terms with respect to flexibility of delivery and lower purchase prices. The aim for next year will be to reduce the end-of-year forecast cost of sales (excluding depreciation) by 5 per cent and inventory/work in progress levels by 10 per cent. However, the number of days' credit taken by the entity will have to fall to 30 days to help persuade suppliers to improve their prices.

### Other information

- All sales are on credit. Official terms of sale at present require payment within 30 days. Interest is not charged on late payments.

- All purchases are made on credit.

- Operating expenses for next year will be $650,000 under either the existing or proposed policies.

- Tax and interest payments are paid in the year in which they arise.

- Dividends are paid in the year after they are declared.

- Capital expenditure of $550,000 is planned for next year.

### Required:

(a) Provide a cash flow forecast for next year, assuming:

(i) the entity does not change its policies and

(ii) the entity's proposals for managing trade receivables, trade payables and inventory are implemented.

In both cases, assume a full twelve-month period, i.e. the changes will be effective from day 1 of next year.

(b) As assistant to Ms Smith, write a short report to her evaluating the proposed actions. Include comments on the factors, financial and non-financial, that the entity should take into account before implementing the new policies.

### Solution

(a) All figures in $000s

|  | No change | With change |
|---|---|---|
| Profit from operations | 1,326 | 1,424 |
| + depreciation | 225 | 225 |
| +/– change in trade receivables | –230 | 72 |
| +/– change in trade payables | 144 | –86 |
| | | |
| Operating profit | 1,465 | 1,635 |
| Interest paid | –54 | –48 |
| Tax paid | –305 | –305 |
| Dividends declared | –339 | –339 |
| Investing activities | | |
| Non-current assets | –550 | –550 |
| Inventory | –275 | –212 |
| | | |
| Net cash flow | –58 | 181 |
| Opening balance | 25 | 25 |
| | | |
| Closing balance | –33 | 206 |

**Changes implemented**

1     **Profit from operations**

| | |
|---|---:|
| Turnover | 5200 |
| Less discounts | –52 |
| Cost of sales | –3,074 |
| (3,224 – 225) × 95% + 225) | |
| Operating expenses (unchanged) | –650 |
| Profit | 1,424 |

2     **Change in current assets**

Decrease in trade receivables

= 520 – [(2,600/365 × 53*) + (2,600/365 × 10*)] = 72

Decrease in trade payables

= [320 – (2,849**/365 × 30)] = 86

Change in inventory

= 350 – (625 × 90%) = 212

* Forecast receivables = 750/5,200 × 365 = 53, reduces to 10 days for 50% of turnover

** Forecast payables = 3,224 – 225 = 2,999, these reduce by 5% to 2,849.

(b)     **Report**

To: Ms Smith

From: Assistant

Subject: Proposed working capital policy changes

The answer should be set out in report format and include the following key points:

–     Comment that cash flow is improved by almost a quarter of a million pounds if the proposed changes are made.

–     Problems appear to have arisen because trade receivables and inventory control have not been adequate for increased levels of turnover.

–     Liquidity: current ratio was 0.95:1 (all current assets to trade and other payables), will be around 1.2:1 under both options. Perversely, ratio looks to improve even if the entity takes no action and causes an overdraft. This is because of high receivables and inventory levels. Moral: high current assets do not mean high cash. Cash ratio perhaps a better measure.

- Receivables' days last year was 45, forecast to rise to 53 on current policies despite 'official' terms being 30. Entity could perhaps look to improve its credit control before offering discounts.

- Trade payables' days were 46, forecast to rise to 52. Are discounts being ignored? Are relationships with suppliers being threatened?*

- Dramatic increase in inventory levels forecast: 50 days last year, 71 days forecast this year. If change implemented, inventory will still be 67 days.*

- Operating profit percentage forecast to fall to 25.5% from 28.1% if no changes made. Percentage will fall to 27.4% if changes implemented; a fall probably acceptable if cash flow improved and overdraft interest saved.

- Non-financial factors include relationships with customers and suppliers.

- Other financial factors, is increase in turnover sustainable?

*Using cost of sales figures including depreciation.

### Interpretation of a cash forecast

Examples of factors to consider when interpreting a cash forecast include:

- Is the balance at the end of the period acceptable/matching expectations?

- Does the cash balance become a deficit at any time in the period?

- Is there sufficient finance (e.g. an overdraft) to cover any cash deficits? Should new sources of finance be sought in advance?

- What are the key causes of cash deficits?

- Can/should discretionary expenditure (such as asset purchases) be made in another period in order to stabilise the pattern of cash flows?

- Is there a plan for dealing with cash surpluses (such as reinvesting them elsewhere)?

- When is the best time to make discretionary expenditure?

## Illustration

If we were to examine the cash forecast in TYU 3, the following issues might be brought to management's attention:

This cash forecast forewarns the management of the business that their plans will lead to a cash deficit of $16,650 at the end of March. They can also see that it will be a short-term deficit and can take appropriate action.

They may decide to delay the purchase of the capital equipment for one month in order to allow the cash position to move to a positive one before the investment is made. Alternatively, an extension of the overdraft facilities may be arranged for the appropriate period.

If it is decided that overdraft facilities are to be arranged, it is important that due account is taken of the timing of the receipts and payments within each month.

For example, all of the payments in January may be made at the beginning of the month but receipts may not be expected until nearer the end of the month. The cash deficit could then be considerably greater than it appears from looking only at the month-end balance.

If the worst possible situation arose, the overdrawn balance during January could become as large as $5,000 (Opening balance) minus $66,000 (January payments) = $71,000 before the receipts begin to arise. If management had used the month-end balances as a guide to the overdraft requirement during the period then they would not have arranged a large enough overdraft facility with the bank. It is important, therefore, that they look in detail at the information revealed by the cash forecast, and not simply at the closing cash balances.

## 5 Using spreadsheets in cash forecasting

Many businesses prepare cash forecasts and cash forecasts using a computer and spreadsheet software such as Excel®.

Spreadsheets are useful for cash forecasting for several important reasons:

- They **save time** in preparing forecasts. When the basic 'model' has been constructed, it is a relatively simple task to insert figures into the model, and leave it to the model to produce the completed forecast. The model, once established, can then be used whenever a new forecast is required.

- They are extremely useful for **sensitivity analysis**. When there is uncertainty in the forecast, the assumptions for the forecast can be changed and an alternative forecast produced. This allows management to consider a range of different possible outcomes, without needing much time or effort.

- Cash flow forecasts **can be consolidated**. For example, if the same spreadsheet model is used to prepare cash forecasts for each division or region in the entity, a spreadsheet model can also automatically produce a consolidated cash flow forecast for the entity as a whole.

### More details

#### Sensitivity analysis

When budgets are prepared, there are a very large number of assumptions and estimates, for example the estimated sales each month, the estimates of costs, assumptions about when receivables will pay and when suppliers will be paid, and so on. Any of these estimates and assumptions could turn out to be inaccurate.

One of the enormous benefits of using spreadsheets to prepare a cash forecast is that it is very easy to carry out sensitivity analysis.

Sensitivity analysis involves asking 'What if...?' questions, and finding out by how much the expected results will change if some of the forecasts or assumptions are altered.

For example, what if sales are 10% less than predicted, or what if capital expenditure is double the amount forecast? Depending on what the results of the analysis show, management might decide to take action to reduce the potential risks.

#### Consolidation

As well as being of assistance in preparing cash flow forecasts for individual business units, a computerised spreadsheet package may also be used to consolidate individual forecasts into one overall forecast for the organisation as a whole.

Individual forecasts may be prepared by:

- the various group entities
- individual operating units, e.g. branches of a retail store
- individual cost centres, e.g. stores, purchasing, production, service centres
- individual budget holders, e.g. marketing.

If all the individual forecasts are prepared using the same spreadsheet software, it will be possible for these to be uploaded to a central computer, programmed to produce a consolidated forecast.

## 6 Measures to improve a cash forecast situation

 **Introduction**

An initial cash forecast might predict an unsatisfactory cash flow situation. The forecast might indicate that the entity will have a cash deficit that cannot be met by existing short-term borrowing arrangements, such as a bank overdraft facility.

When this situation occurs, action will need to be taken to manage future cash flows in order to improve the forecast position. The nature of this management action will depend upon the answers to the following questions:

- Does the forecast indicate a continuing trend of an increasing surplus or an increasing cash deficit, or do net monthly balances move between surplus and deficit on a seasonal basis?

- What size of cash surpluses are forecast (if any) and for how long will they be available?

- Are the forecast cash deficits within the current overdraft facility?

- Which cash flows are to some extent discretionary, either in size or timing?

Cash deficits can arise from:

- Basic trading factors underlying the business, such as falling sales or increasing costs. To correct these, normal business measures need to be taken. Sales may be improved by increased marketing activity or revised pricing policies. Cost cutting exercises may also be necessary.

- Short-term deficiencies in the working capital cycle, such as an exceptionally long average holding period for inventory or a long average time to pay by credit customers.

Possible decisions that could be taken to deal with forecast short-term cash deficits include:

- additional short-term borrowing

- negotiating a higher overdraft limit with the bank

- the sale of short-term investments, if the entity has any

- using different forms of financing to reduce cash flows in the short term, such as leasing instead of buying outright

- changing the amount of discretionary cash flows, deferring expenditures or bringing forward revenues. For example:

    - reducing the dividend to shareholders

    - postponing non-essential capital expenditure

- bringing forward the planned disposal of non-current assets

- reducing inventory levels, perhaps incorporating 'just-in-time' techniques (although this will take time to implement)

- shortening the operating cycle by reducing the time taken to collect receivables, perhaps by offering a discount or using a factor or invoice discounting.

- shortening the operating cycle by delaying payment to payables.

## Cash surpluses

If the forecast shows cash surpluses, these will be dealt with according to their size and duration. Management should consider a policy for how surplus cash should be invested so as to achieve a return on the money, but without investing in items where the risk of a fall in value is considered too high. The interest or other return earned can be used to improve the overall cash position. Care must be taken to ensure these investments can be realised as needed, to fund forecast deficits.

Where long-term cash surpluses are forecast, management might consider other possible uses of the surpluses, such as paying a higher dividend or repaying loans and other debts.

## Test your understanding 4 – Practice questions

1   A business has estimated that 10% of its sales will be cash sales, and the remainder credit sales. It is also estimated that 50% of credit customers will pay in the month following sale, 30% two months after sale and 15% three months after sale and irrecoverable debts will be 5% of credit sales.

Total sales figures are as follows:

| Month | $ |
| --- | --- |
| October | 80,000 |
| November | 60,000 |
| December | 40,000 |
| January | 50,000 |
| February | 60,000 |
| March | 90,000 |

### Required:

Prepare a month-by-month budget of cash receipts from sales for the months January to March.

2   Winters expects 75% of sales to be collected in the month of sale, 20% in the month following and 5% to be irrecoverable debts. At 31 December 20X4, $50,000 of December's sales are still outstanding receivables.

**Identify receipts in January from sales in December:**

A   10,000

B   20,000

C   37,500

D   40,000

3   An entity sells a range of services, all on credit. Customers on average pay as follows:

|  | % |
|---|---|
| In month after sale | 30 |
| Two months after sale | 65 |

The organisation expects an irrecoverable debt rate of 5%.

At 1 January Year 2, opening trade receivables were $322,200, before deducting any allowance for doubtful debts. Sales in December Year 1 were $213,000.

**Required:**

Calculate the receipts from the opening trade receivables in January Year 2 and in February Year 2

4   You are given the following budgeted information about an entity:

|  | January | February | March |
|---|---|---|---|
| Opening inventory in units | 100 | 150 | 120 |
| Closing inventory in units | 150 | 120 | 180 |
| Sales in units | 400 | 450 | 420 |

The cost of materials is $2 per unit. 40% of purchases are paid for immediately in cash. 60% of purchases are on credit and are paid two months after the purchase.

**Required:**

Calculate the budgeted payments in March for purchases of materials.

5   Identify which of the following is unsuitable as a cash flow to be deferred to avoid a temporary cash shortage:

A   Replacement of office furniture

B   Investment in a short-term cash deposit

C   Investment in a long-term strategic expansion

D   Dividend payment (deferral agreed by the shareholders)

## 7 Summary Diagram

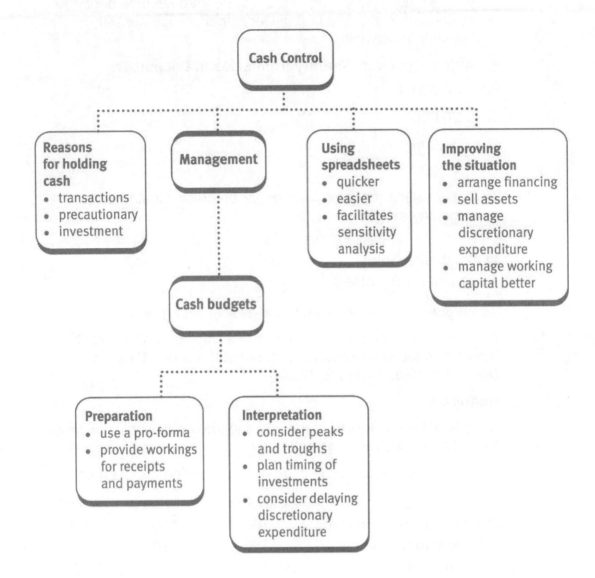

# Test your understanding answers

## Test your understanding 1 – Forecast cash receipts

| Cash from: | | $ |
|---|---|---|
| April sales: | 10% × $5,000 | 500 |
| March sales: | 40% × $4,000 | 1,600 |
| February sales: | 45% × $8,000 | 3,600 |
| | | ———— |
| | | 5,700 |

## Test your understanding 2 – Forecast cash payments

When inventories of raw materials are increased, the quantities purchased will exceed the quantities consumed in the period.

Figures for December are shown because December purchases will be paid for in January, which is in the budget period.

Quantity of raw material purchased in units:

| | Units of widgets produced | December | January | February | March |
|---|---|---|---|---|---|
| | Units | Units | Units | Units | Units |
| December | 50,000 | 100,000 | | | |
| January | 55,000 | | 110,000 | | |
| February | 60,000 | | | 120,000 | |
| March | 65,000 | | | | 130,000 |
| Increase in inventories | | – | 10,000 | 10,000 | – |
| Total purchase quantities | | 100,000 | 120,000 | 130,000 | 130,000 |
| At $3 per unit | | 300,000 | 360,000 | 390,000 | 390,000 |

Having established the purchases each month, we can go on to budget the amount of cash payments to suppliers each month. Here, the business will take one month's credit.

| | January | February | March |
|---|---|---|---|
| | $ | $ | $ |
| Payment to suppliers | 300,000 | 360,000 | 390,000 |

At the end of March, there will be payables of $390,000 for raw materials purchased, which will be paid in April.

**Test your understanding 3 – Full cash flow forecast**

We can take each item of cash flow in turn, and use workings tables to calculate what the monthly cash flows are.

**(W1) Cash from sales**

|  | Total sales | Cash receipts January | Cash receipts February | Cash receipts March |
|---|---|---|---|---|
|  | $ | $ | $ | $ |
| Opening receivables |  | 44,000 | – | – |
| January | 60,000 | 12,000 | 48,000 | – |
| February | 50,000 | – | 10,000 | 40,000 |
| March | 70,000 | – | – | 14,000 |
|  |  | 56,000 | 58,000 | 54,000 |

**(W2) Payments for materials purchases**

Material purchases are made in the month prior to the month in which they are used, so the starting point for working out materials purchases and payments for the purchases is the production costs in each month.

|  | January | February | March | April |
|---|---|---|---|---|
|  | $ | $ | $ | $ |
| Total cost of production | 50,000 | 55,000 | 32,500 | 50,000 |
| Material cost of production (40%) | 20,000 | 22,000 | 13,000 | 20,000 |
| Purchases in the month | 22,000 | 13,000 | 20,000 | unknown |

Payments are made 50% in the month of purchase and 50% in the following month. The trade payables at 1 January will all be paid in January, since these represent 50% of material purchases in December.

| | Purchases | January | February | March |
|---|---|---|---|---|
| | $ | $ | $ | $ |
| Opening payables for materials | | 10,000 | | |
| January | 22,000 | 11,000 | 11,000 | – |
| February | 13,000 | – | 6,500 | 6,500 |
| March | 20,000 | – | –10,000 | |
| | | | | |
| Total payments | | 21,000 | 17,500 | 16,500 |

## (W3) Payments for overheads

In this example, we have to separate fixed and variable overheads. Total overhead costs are 30% of production costs (100% – 40% direct materials – 30% direct labour).

| | January | February | March |
|---|---|---|---|
| | $ | $ | $ |
| Total cost of production | 50,000 | 55,000 | 32,500 |
| Overhead cost of production (30%) | 15,000 | 16,500 | 9,750 |
| Fixed costs | (5,000) | (5,000) | (5,000) |
| | | | |
| Variable overhead costs | 10,000 | 11,500 | 4,750 |

Of the monthly fixed overhead costs of $5,000, $3,000 is depreciation which is not a cash expenditure. Monthly fixed cost cash expenditure is therefore $2,000.

The opening balance of unpaid overhead costs at the beginning of January must consist of $2,000 fixed overheads and $9,000 (the balance) variable overheads. All these costs should be paid for in January. Variable overheads are paid 40% in the month of expenditure and 60% the following month.

| | Cost | January | February | March |
|---|---|---|---|---|
| Fixed overheads | $ | $ | $ | $ |
| Opening payables for fixed overheads | | 2,000 | | |
| January | 2,000 | – | 2,000 | – |
| February | 2,000 | – | – | 2,000 |
| March | 2,000 | – | | |
| | | | | |
| Total payments | | 2,000 | 2,000 | 2,000 |

| | Cost | January | February | March |
|---|---|---|---|---|
| Variable overheads | $ | $ | $ | $ |
| Opening payables for variable overheads | | 9,000 | | |
| January | 10,000 | 4,000 | 6,000 | – |
| February | 11,500 | – | 4,600 | 6,900 |
| March | 4,750 | – | – | 1,900 |
| | | ——— | ——— | ——— |
| Total payments | | 13,000 | 10,600 | 8,800 |

The other items of cash flow are straightforward, although it is important to notice that the payments for administration and selling overheads are paid quarterly, and the cash payment ($15,000) is not the same as the total overhead cost for the quarter. Presumably there are depreciation charges within the total costs given.

Payments for direct labour are 30% of direct labour costs (= 30% of production costs) in the month.

The cash forecast can be prepared as follows:

| | January | February | March |
|---|---|---|---|
| **Receipts** | $ | $ | $ |
| From sales | 56,000 | 58,000 | 54,000 |
| Payments | | | |
| Capital expenditure | – | – | 30,000 |
| For direct materials | 21,000 | 17,500 | 16,500 |
| For direct labour (30% × prod'n cost) | 15,000 | 16,500 | 9,750 |
| For fixed production overheads | 2,000 | 2,000 | 2,000 |
| For variable production overheads | 13,000 | 10,600 | 8,800 |
| For admin/selling overhead | 15,000 | – | – |
| | ——— | ——— | ——— |
| Total outflow | 66,000 | 46,600 | 67,050 |
| | ——— | ——— | ——— |
| Net cash flow for month | (10,000) | 11,400 | (13,050) |
| Opening balance | (5,000) | (15,000) | (3,600) |
| | ——— | ——— | ——— |
| Closing balance | (15,000) | (3,600) | (16,650) |

## Analysis

The entity will be overdrawn throughout the three-month period, therefore it is essential that it should have access to borrowings to cover the shortfall. The bank might already have agreed an overdraft facility, but this should be at least $16,650 and ideally higher, to allow for the possibility that the actual cash flows will be even worse than budgeted.

## Test your understanding 4 – Practice questions

1    The cash forecast is as follows:

| Sales month | Total sales | Cash receipts January | Cash receipts February | Cash receipts March |
|---|---|---|---|---|
| | $ | $ | $ | $ |
| October | 80,000 | 10,800 | – | – |
| November | 60,000 | 16,200 | 8,100 | – |
| December | 40,000 | 18,000 | 10,800 | 5,400 |
| January | 50,000 | 5,000 | 22,500 | 13,500 |
| February | 60,000 | – | 6,000 | 27,000 |
| March | 90,000 | – | – | 9,000 |
| | | | | |
| **Total receipts** | | 50,000 | 47,400 | 54,900 |

2    The correct answer is D.

$50,000 represents 25% of December sales (100% – 75%).

Total sales in December were therefore $5,000/25% = $200,000.

Expected amount to be received in January = 20% × $200,000 = $40,000.

3    The trade receivables at the beginning of January Year 2 represent 100% of sales in December Year 1 and the unpaid receivables for sales in November Year 1. They can be analysed as follows:

| | $ |
|---|---|
| Total trade receivables | 322,200 |
| Consisting of: | |
| 100% of sales for December Year 1 | (213,000) |
| | |
| Unpaid amounts for sales in November Year 1 | 109,200 |

The unpaid amounts from November Year 1 represent 70% of total sales in that month, because 30% pay in the month following sale (December Year 1).

It therefore follows that total sales in November Year 1 were $109,200/70% = $156,000.

| Sales month | Total sales | Cash receipts January | Cash receipts February |
|---|---|---|---|
| | $ | $ | $ |
| November | 156,000 65% | 101,400 | – |
| December | 213,000 30% | 63,900 65% | 138,450 |
| | | 165,300 | 138,450 |

4    The budget will be as follows:

| Purchases | January units | February units | March units |
|---|---|---|---|
| Sales quantity | 400 | 450 | 420 |
| Less: opening inventory | (100) | (150) | (120) |
| Add: closing inventory | 150 | 120 | 180 |
| Production in units = units purchased | 450 | 420 | 480 |
| Cost of purchase @ $2 per unit | $900 | $840 | $960 |

| Payments in March | | $ |
|---|---|---|
| For January purchases | (60% of $900) | 540 |
| For March purchases | (40% of $960) | 384 |
| Total payments for materials | | 924 |

5    The correct answer is B.

A short-term deposit is a cash equivalent. Deferring the transfer of cash to a short-term deposit will not deal with the problem of a temporary cash shortage, because it will usually be possible to withdraw the cash from deposit on demand, for the loss of some or all of the interest.

# References

## References

The Board (2016) *The Conceptual Framework for Financial Reporting*. London: IFRS Foundation

The Board (2016) IAS 1 *Presentation of Financial Reporting*. London: IFRS Foundation.

The Board (2016) IAS 2 *Inventories*. London: IFRS Foundation.

The Board (2016) IAS 7 *Statement of Cash Flows*. London: IFRS Foundation.

The Board (2016) IAS 10 *Events after the Reporting Period*. London: IFRS Foundation.

The Board (2016) IAS 16 *Property, Plant and Equipment*. London: IFRS Foundation.

The Board (2016) IAS 36 Impairment of Assets. London: IFRS Foundation.

The Board (2016) IFRS 5 *Non-current Assets Held for Sale and Discontinued Operations*. London: IFRS Foundation.

The Board (2016) IFRS 16 *Leases*. London: IFRS Foundation.

# Index

# Index